Microsoft

Visual Basic 6.0
Fundamentals

Microsoft

Mastering

PUBLISHED BY
Microsoft Press
A Division of Microsoft Corporation
One Microsoft Way
Redmond, Washington 98052-6399

Library of Congress Cataloging-in-Publication Data
Microsoft Mastering : Microsoft Visual Basic 6.0 Fundamentals /
    Microsoft Corporation.
        p. cm.
    ISBN 0-7356-0898-9
    1. Microsoft Visual BASIC.   2. BASIC (Computer program language)
    I. Microsoft Corporation.
    QA76.73.B3M5447   1999
    005.26'8--dc21   99-33884
                                                            CIP

Printed and bound in the United States of America.

1 2 3 4 5 6 7 8 9   WCWC   4 3 2 1 0 9

Distributed in Canada by Penguin Books Canada Limited.

A CIP catalogue record for this book is available from the British Library.

Microsoft Press books are available through booksellers and distributors worldwide. For further information about international editions, contact your local Microsoft Corporation office or contact Microsoft Press International directly at fax (425) 936-7329. Visit our Web site at mspress.microsoft.com.

Acquisitions Editor: Eric Stroo
Project Editor: Wendy Zucker

Acknowledgements

Authors:
Kamran Iqbal
Tony Jamieson

Developed with Training Associates, Inc.

Program Manager: Teresa Canady

Lead Subject Matter Expert: Kamran Iqbal

Lead Instructional Designer: Tony Jamieson

Production Manager: Miracle Davis

Production Coordinator: Susie Bayers (Online Training Solutions, Inc.)

Library: Leslie Eliel (Online Training Solutions, Inc.)

Media Production:
Staci Dinehart (S&T OnSite)
Stephanie Lewis (Training Associates, Inc.)

Editors:
Ed Harper (MacTemps)
Reid Bannecker (S&T OnSite)

Additional Content Design: Susie Parrent

Build and Testing Manager: Julie Challenger

Book Production Coordinator: Katharine Ford (ArtSource)

Book Design: Mary Rasmussen (Online Training Solutions, Inc.)

Book Layout:
R.J. Cadranell (Online Training Solutions, Inc.)
Jennifer Murphy (S&T OnSite)

Companion CD-ROM Design and Development: Jeff Brown

Companion CD-ROM Production: Eric Wagoner (Write Stuff)

About This Course

This course is designed to teach you how to write an application in Microsoft Visual Basic that has a graphical user interface; uses menus, forms, and controls; validates and checks for errors in user input; performs simple database access; implements drag-and-drop functionality; and has a Setup application.

Course Content

The course content is organized into the following 14 chapters.

Chapter 1: Introduction to Application Development Using Visual Basic

Chapter 1 introduces the Visual Basic development environment and shows how event-driven programming is different from programming with procedural languages.

Chapter 2: Visual Basic Fundamentals

Chapter 2 discusses the building blocks of Visual Basic programming—forms, controls, and code—and introduces objects, properties, methods, and events.

Chapter 3: Working with Code and Forms

Chapter 3 shows you how to write the code that ties the elements of your application together and demonstrates several Visual Basic tools that simplify the writing and editing of code.

Chapter 4: Variables and Procedures

Chapter 4 introduces the types of variables and constants that are supported by Visual Basic and shows you how to write and use procedures and functions.

Chapter 5: Controlling Program Execution

Chapter 5 explores the many conditional and looping structures that you can use in your programs and discusses functions that Visual Basic provides for tasks such as data conversion.

Chapter 6: Debugging

Chapter 6 discusses the different errors that can occur in a program and shows you how to use the Visual Basic debugging tools to find and correct those errors.

Chapter 7: Working with Controls

Chapter 7 shows you how to incorporate some of the more advanced standard controls in Visual Basic into your programs and demonstrates how you can expand the functionality of your application by incorporating ActiveX controls.

Chapter 8: Data Access Using the ADO Data Control

Chapter 8 discusses the types of databases that Visual Basic can access and shows how you can use the ActiveX Data Objects (ADO) data control to quickly add database features to your application.

Chapter 9: Input Validation

Chapter 9 explores the different methods that you can use in your applications to ensure that users enter valid data.

Chapter 10: Error Trapping

Chapter 10 demonstrates ways of trapping and handling errors in your application.

Chapter 11: Enhancing the User Interface

Chapter 11 shows how you can make your programs more usable by adding menus, status bars, and toolbars.

Chapter 12: Drag-and-Drop Operations

Chapter 12 discusses the two levels of drag-and-drop editing that Visual Basic supports and shows you how to enable the drag-and-drop feature in your applications.

Chapter 13: More About Controls

Chapter 13 builds on the understanding of controls that you've gained in earlier chapters and shows you how to use control arrays to implement option button groups and to write more efficient and error-free code.

Chapter 14: Finishing Touches

Chapter 14 discusses interface design principles and shows you how to use the Package & Deployment Wizard to package your applications for delivery and installation.

Labs

Each chapter in this course includes a lab that gives you hands-on experience with the skills that you learn in the chapter. A lab consists of one or more exercises that focus on how to use the information contained in the chapter. Lab hints, which provide code or other information that will help you complete an exercise, are included in Appendix B. You will see the following icon in the margin, indicating that a lab hint is given.

Lab Hint Icon

To complete the exercises and view the accompanying solution code, you will need to install the lab files that are found on the accompanying CD-ROM.

To complete the labs, you need:

◆ A PC with a Pentium-class processor, Pentium 133 or higher processor.

◆ Microsoft Visual Basic 6.0 Professional Edition.

Self-Check Questions

This course includes a number of self-check questions at the end of each chapter. You can use these multiple-choice questions to test your understanding of the information that has been covered in the course. Answers to self-check questions are provided in Appendix A. Each answer includes a reference to the associated chapter topic, so that you can easily review the content.

CD-ROM Contents

The *Mastering Microsoft Visual Basic 6 Fundamentals* CD-ROM that is included with this book contains multimedia, lab files, sample applications, and sample code that you may wish to view or install on your computer's hard drive. The content on the CD-ROM must be viewed by using an HTML browser that supports frames. A copy of Microsoft Internet Explorer has been included with this CD-ROM in case you do not have a browser or do not have one that supports frames, installed on your computer. Please refer to the ReadMe file on the CD-ROM for further instructions on installing Internet Explorer.

To begin browsing the content that is included on the CD-ROM, open the file, default.htm.

Lab Files

The files required to complete the lab exercises, as well as the lab solution files, are included on the accompanying CD-ROM.

Note Two megabytes (MB) of hard disk space is required to install the labs.

Multimedia

This course provides numerous audio/video demonstrations and animations that illustrate the concepts and techniques that are discussed in this course. The following icon will appear in the margin, indicating that a multimedia title can be found on the accompanying CD-ROM.

Multimedia Icon

In addition, at the beginning of each chapter is a list of the multimedia titles that are found in the chapter.

Note You can toggle the display of the text of a demonstration or animation on and off by choosing **Closed Caption** from the **View** menu.

Sample Code

This course contains numerous code samples.

Sample code has been provided on the accompanying CD-ROM for you to copy and paste into your own projects. The following icon appears in the margin, indicating that this piece of sample code is included on the CD-ROM.

Sample Code Icon

Internet Links

The following icon appears in the margin next to an Internet link, indicating that this link is included on the accompanying CD-ROM.

Internet Link Icon

Sample Applications

Visual Basic includes a large selection of sample applications. These applications demonstrate simple programming operations for beginners as well as more advanced topics for the experienced Visual Basic programmer. All of these sample applications can be found on the Microsoft Developer Network (MSDN) CD-ROM in the Samples\VB98 folder.

A number of sample applications are also included on the *Mastering Microsoft Visual Basic 6 Fundamentals* CD-ROM. The applications are organized in the following subfolders according to the primary topic that each demonstrates.

Note 500 kilobytes (KB) of hard disk space is required to install the sample applications.

Controls

CommDial   This program demonstrates what type of dialog windows the common dialog control is capable of opening.

FlagShow   This program displays a country's flag image based on a corresponding value chosen from a combo box.

FrameOpt   This example displays how to use a frame control to group controls.

ImgView   This program shows how to use the file, directory, and drive list boxes to open an image file.

Listboxs   This program demonstrates the various settings for a combo box and list box.

Data Types

Datatype   This example displays the minimum and maximum values for each Visual Basic data type.

Drag and Drop

DragDemo   This program demonstrates how a drag-and-drop feature works.

Flags   This program demonstrates how to code for a drag-and-drop event. A flag is dragged to an area, and a message is displayed based on its position.

Events

Clock   This program demonstrates how to use a timer control to build your own clock program.

MouseMv   This example demonstrates how to generate various color circles based on the **MouseMove** event.

Nameaddr   This example shows how to set focus to a control.

Functions and Subs

FuncSubs   This program explains the differences between subroutines and functions.

Input and Message Boxes

Inputmsg   This program demonstrates an input box and a message box by displaying their return values.

Looping

Looping   This program displays the advantages of using the various types of looping structures.

Modes

Modes   This program demonstrates the difference between modal and modeless forms.

String Functions

Reverse   This program shows how to reverse the order of a string value.

Conventions Used In This Course

The following table explains some of the typographic conventions used in this course.

Example of convention	Description
Sub, If, Case Else, Print, True, BackColor, Click, Debug, Long	In text, language-specific keywords appear in bold, with the initial letter capitalized.
File menu, **Add Project** dialog box	Most interface elements appear in bold, with the initial letter capitalized.
Setup	Words that you're instructed to type appear in bold.

table continued on next page

Example of convention	Description
Event-driven	In text, italic letters can indicate defined terms, usually the first time that they occur. Italic formatting is also used occasionally for emphasis.
Variable	In syntax and text, italic letters can indicate placeholders for information that you supply.
[expressionlist]	In syntax, items inside square brackets are optional.
{While	Until}	In syntax, braces and a vertical bar indicate a choice between two or more items. You must choose one of the items, unless all of the items are enclosed in square brackets.

`Sub HelloButton_Click()`
`Readout.Text = _`
`"Hello, world!"`
`End Sub`
	This font is used for code.

ENTER	Capital letters are used for the names of keys and key sequences, such as ENTER and CTRL+R.
ALT+F1	A plus sign (+) between key names indicates a combination of keys. For example, ALT+F1 means to hold down the ALT key while pressing the F1 key.
DOWN ARROW	Individual direction keys are referred to by the direction of the arrow on the key top (LEFT, RIGHT, UP, or DOWN). The phrase "arrow keys" is used when describing these keys collectively.
BACKSPACE, HOME	Other navigational keys are referred to by their specific names.
C:\Vb\Samples\Calldlls.vbp	Paths and file names are given in mixed case.

The following guidelines are used in writing code in this course:

◆ Keywords appear with initial letters capitalized:

```
' Sub, If, ChDir, Print, and True are keywords.
Print "Title Page"
```

◆ Line labels are used to mark position in code (instead of line numbers):

```
ErrorHandler:
Power = conFailure
End Function
```

◆ An apostrophe (') introduces comments:

```
' This is a comment; these two lines
' are ignored when the program is running.
```

◆ Control-flow blocks and statements in **Sub, Function,** and **Property** procedures are indented from the enclosing code:

```
Private Sub cmdRemove_Click ()
    Dim Ind As Integer
    ' Get index
    Ind = lstClient.ListIndex
    ' Make sure list item is selected
    If Ind >= 0 Then
        ' Remove it from list box
        lstClient.RemoveItem Ind
        ' Display number
        lblDisplay.Caption = lstClient.ListCount
    Else
        ' If nothing selected, beep
        Beep
    End If
End Sub
```

◆ Intrinsic constant names appear in a mixed-case format, with a two-character prefix indicating the object library that defines the constant. Constants from the Visual Basic and Visual Basic for Applications object libraries are prefaced with "vb"; constants from the ActiveX Data Objects (ADO) Library are prefaced with "ad"; constants from the Excel Object Library are prefaced with "xl". Examples are as follows:

```
vbTileHorizontal
adAddNew
xlDialogBorder
```

For more information about coding conventions, see "Programming Fundamentals" in the MSDN Visual Basic documentation.

Table of Contents

Chapter 1:
Introduction to Application Development Using Visual Basic

In this chapter, you will learn about the Microsoft Visual Basic development environment. Visual Basic is a powerful development tool that you can use to quickly and easily create feature-rich applications for Microsoft Windows and Windows NT operating systems. Although professional programmers use Visual Basic, it is easy for novices to program in Visual Basic with professional results.

Based on the Basic programming language, Visual Basic differs from previous versions of Basic because it is based on an event-driven programming model. Visual Basic provides a rapid application development (RAD) environment, a rich object-based language, and an easy-to-use set of debugging tools.

This chapter introduces you to the Visual Basic environment and explains some of the concepts that you need to understand to create programs for the Windows operating system.

Objectives

After completing this chapter, you will be able to:

◆ Identify the elements in the Visual Basic development environment.

◆ Explain the difference between design time and run time.

◆ Explain the concept of event-driven programming.

◆ Describe the purpose of a project file.

◆ List the file types that can be included in a project.

Features of Visual Basic

Using Visual Basic is the quickest and easiest way to create powerful, full-featured applications that take advantage of the graphical user interface in Windows. For companies developing custom applications, Visual Basic reduces development time and costs. Its intuitive interface makes Visual Basic an excellent tool for programmers.

New users benefit from mouse operations and a consistent look and feel; more advanced users benefit from easy-to-use features, such as drop-down list boxes and multiple-window applications.

Visual Basic provides the basis for the programming language that is used in all Microsoft Office applications, Visual Basic for Applications, and a variety of applications from other vendors.

Visual Basic supports a number of features that make it an excellent language for quickly creating full-featured solutions, including the following:

◆ Data access features

By using data access features, you can create databases, front-end applications, and scalable server-side components for most database formats, including Microsoft SQL Server and other enterprise-level databases.

◆ ActiveX technologies

With ActiveX technologies, you can use the functionality provided by other applications, such as the Word processor, the Microsoft Excel spreadsheet, and other Windows applications. You can even automate applications and objects that were created by using the Professional or Enterprise editions of Visual Basic.

◆ Internet capabilities

Internet capabilities make it easy to provide access to documents and applications across the Internet, or an intranet, from within your application, or to create Internet server applications.

◆ Rapid application development (RAD)

◆ Support for multilingual applications

◆ Interactive debugging support

Editions of Visual Basic

In this section, you will learn about the different editions of Visual Basic. The Visual Basic development system version 6.0 is available in the following three editions:

◆ Learning Edition

The Learning Edition allows programmers to easily create powerful applications for the Windows and Windows NT operating systems.

◆ Professional Edition

The Professional Edition adds to the capabilities of the Learning Edition by allowing you to create client/server or Internet-enabled applications.

◆ Enterprise Edition

Developers in a corporate environment benefit by using the advanced features in the Enterprise Edition to create robust distributed applications in a team setting.

This course is designed for programmers using the Professional or Enterprise Editions of Visual Basic.

Learning Edition

You can use the Learning Edition of Visual Basic to create 32-bit programs. The Learning Edition includes the following:

◆ The Visual Basic development environment

◆ Standard controls

◆ Samples

◆ Icons

◆ The Package & Deployment Wizard

◆ ActiveX Data Objects (ADO)

◆ **ADO Data** control

The **ADO Data** control is a new OLEDB-aware data source control that functions much like the intrinsic **Data** and **Remote Data** controls in that it allows you to create a database application with a minimum amount of code.

◆ The *Learn VB Now* multimedia course

◆ Microsoft Developer Network (MSDN) CDs containing full online documentation

Professional Edition

The Professional Edition of Visual Basic has all of the features that are found in the Learning Edition (except the *Learn VB Now* multimedia course), and also includes the following:

♦ Additional ActiveX controls

♦ Internet Information Server Application Designer

♦ Data Report Designer

♦ Dynamic HTML Page Designer

♦ Integrated Data Tools and Data Environment

♦ Visual Studio Professional Features book

Enterprise Edition

The Enterprise Edition includes all the features found in the Professional Edition, and also includes the following:

♦ Microsoft Visual SourceSafe

♦ Microsoft Internet Information Server

♦ Microsoft Transaction Server

♦ SQL Editor

   The SQL Editor allows you to create and edit stored procedures and triggers in both SQL Server and Oracle from within the Visual Basic development environment.

♦ Application Performance Explorer

♦ Visual Component Manager

Visual Basic Terminology

As with any programming language, using Visual Basic requires an understanding of some common terminology. The following table lists some key terms used in Visual Basic. You'll learn more about each term later in the course.

Term	Definition
Design time	Any time an application is being developed in the Visual Basic environment.
Run time	Any time an application is running. At run time, the programmer interacts with the application as the user would.
Forms	Windows that can be customized to serve as the interface for an application or as dialog boxes used to gather information from the user.
Controls	Graphic representations of objects, such as buttons, list boxes, and edit boxes, that users manipulate to provide information to the application.
Objects	A general term used to describe all the forms and controls that make up a program.
Properties	The characteristics of an object, such as size, caption, or color.
Methods	The actions that an object can perform or that can be performed on the object.
Events	Actions recognized by a form or control. Events occur as the user, operating system, or application interacts with the objects of a program.
Event-driven programming	When a program is event-driven, its code executes in response to events invoked by the user, operating system, or application. This differs from procedural programming, in which the program starts at the first line of code and follows a defined path, calling procedures as needed.

Working in the Development Environment

In this section, you will learn about the different elements of the Visual Basic development environment. When you start Visual Basic and select a project type, the graphical development environment appears. The following illustration shows some of the development environment's elements.

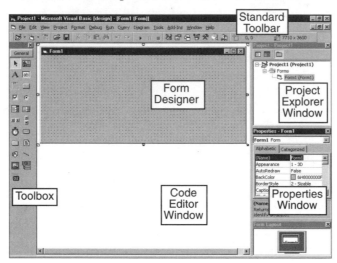

Visual Basic Project Types

Visual Basic offers several project templates that are designed to support the development of different kinds of applications and components. As you begin developing an application, you must first decide what kind of project template to use. A project template contains the basic project objects and environment settings that you need to create the type of application or component that you want to build.

This course discusses only the Standard EXE project. For more information on using the other projects in the following list, please see *Mastering Microsoft Visual Basic 6 Development*.

▶ **To create a new project**

1. On the **File** menu, click **New Project**.

   The **New Project** dialog box appears.

2. Select the project template that you want, and then click **OK**.

The following templates are available by default:

◆ Standard EXE

Standard EXE projects contain a form by default. Use this project template to develop a stand-alone application. This is the project type that you will be using in this course.

◆ Data Project

Use this project template to develop an application that reads or manipulates data from a data source.

◆ ActiveX EXE/ActiveX DLL

Use these project templates to develop COM components that expose functionality to other applications.

Use an ActiveX EXE project template if your component will both expose functionality programmatically and run as a stand-alone application. Use an ActiveX DLL project template if your component will only be used programmatically by another application.

◆ ActiveX Control

Use this project template to create a component that is designed to be a user interface element in a form or dialog box.

◆ ActiveX Document EXE/ActiveX Document DLL

Use these project templates to create components that are designed for use in a document object container, such as Microsoft Internet Explorer.

◆ DHTML Application

Use this project template to create a component that can be used on the client side of a Web application.

◆ IIS Application

Use this project template to create a component that can be used on the server side of a Web application.

Toolbox

The toolbox contains the objects and controls that you can add to forms to create the user interface of your applications. You can add additional controls to the toolbox by using the **Components** command on the **Project** menu. In addition, you can right-click anywhere in the toolbox and select **Components** from the pop-up menu.

The following illustration shows the toolbox.

Form Designer

In Visual Basic, a form is a window used in your application. For each form in your application, Visual Basic provides a Form Designer window at design time that contains the form and all of the controls that you place on the form.

The following illustration shows the Form Designer window and the default form. The default form contains the minimum elements used by most forms: a title bar, control box, and **Minimize**, **Maximize**, and **Close** buttons.

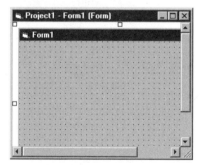

▶ **To open the Form Designer window**

1. In the Project Explorer window, click the form that you want to view.

2. Click the **View Object** button.

   –or–

   On the Visual Basic **View** menu, click **Object**.

Project Explorer Window

The Project Explorer window lists the collection of files used to build an application. The collection of files is called a project. You can switch between the Form and Code views by using the **View Form** and **View Code** buttons.

The following illustration shows the Project Explorer window.

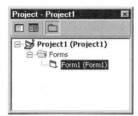

Properties Window

The Properties window lists the property settings for the selected form or control that can be modified while the program is being edited. (Other property settings can be modified only at run time.) A property describes a characteristic of an object, such as size, caption, or color.

You can view properties alphabetically or by category by clicking the **Alphabetic** or **Categorized** tabs in the Properties window. When you click a property, a short description of the property appears.

The following illustration shows the Properties window.

Code Editor Window

You write the code statements for a project in the Code Editor window (also known as the Code window). Visual Basic code can be either associated with a form in your project or contained in a separate code module. A separate Code Editor window is displayed for each form or module in your project, making it easy to organize, view, and navigate through the code.

The Code Editor contains two drop-down lists at the top of the window: the **Object** list and the **Procedure** list. The **Object** list contains a list of all the controls contained on the form. If you select a control name from the list, the **Procedure** list shows all of the events for that control (or actions that the control can perform and that can be interpreted by your application). By using the **Object** and **Procedure** lists together, you can quickly locate and edit the code in your application.

The following illustration shows the Code Editor window.

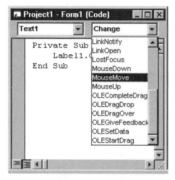

▶ **To open the Code Editor window**

1. In the Project Explorer window, click the form whose code you want to view.
2. Click the **View Code** button.

   –or–

   On the Visual Basic **View** menu, click **Code**.

Standard Toolbar

The **Standard** toolbar includes buttons for many of the most common commands used in Visual Basic, such as **Open Project, Save Project, Start, Break,** and **End**. This toolbar also contains buttons that display the Project Explorer, the Properties window, the toolbox, and other elements in the Visual Basic development environment.

The following illustration shows the **Standard** toolbar.

Toolbars can either be docked (attached) or floating. By default, most toolbars are docked; however, you can undock or dock a toolbar at any time. To undock a toolbar, click near the double bar along the left side of a toolbar, and drag the toolbar away from its docked position. To dock a toolbar, drag it to an edge of the main window.

Event-Driven Programming

Applications written in Visual Basic are event-driven. Event-driven programming can best be understood by contrasting it with procedural programming.

Procedural Programming vs. Event-Driven Programming

Applications written in procedural languages execute by proceeding logically through the program code, one line at a time. Logic flow can be temporarily transferred to other parts of the program through the **GoTo**, **GoSub**, and **Call** statements, directing the program from beginning to end.

In contrast, program statements in an event-driven application execute only when a specific event calls a section of code that is assigned to that event. Events can be triggered by keyboard input, mouse actions, the operating system, or code in the application. For example, consider what happens when the user clicks a command button named **Command1** on a form. The mouse click is an event. When the **Click** event occurs, Visual Basic executes the code in the **Sub** procedure named **Command1_Click**. When the code has finished running, Visual Basic waits for the next event.

The following illustration contrasts procedural and event-driven programming.

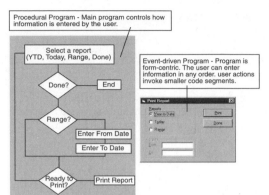

Event-Driven Programming in Visual Basic

To better understand how event-driven programming works in Visual Basic, consider the following example application. The application consists of a single form named **Simple Controls** that contains four objects: two command buttons, a label, and a text box. One button draws a border around the label. The other button resets the value in the text box to its initial value.

The following illustration shows the form that makes up the application's user interface.

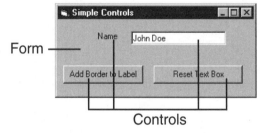

To see the demonstration "Understanding Event-Driven Programming," see the accompanying CD-ROM.

This application will also draw a border around the label when the user clicks a button. To add this functionality, you must write code to respond to the **Click** event for the **Add Border to Label** button.

```
Sub cmdBorder_Click()
    lblName.BorderStyle = vbFixedSingle
End Sub
```

To understand the code, you must know that the name of the **Add Border to Label** button is **cmdBorder**. The button's name is not the same as the text that appears on the button. (You'll learn more about this in "Setting Control Properties" on page 42 in Chapter 2, "Visual Basic Fundamentals.") The name of the procedure, **cmdBorder_Click**, denotes that the procedure responds to the **Click** event for the **cmdBorder** command button. Notice that the event is represented by adding an underscore and the name of the event to the name of the control.

The next statement adds the border to the **Label** control named **lblName**. **BorderStyle** is a property of the **Label** control. The statement changes the property from its initial setting, vbNormal, to a new setting, vbFixedSingle.

The final statement, **End Sub**, denotes the end of the procedure.

Note The purpose of this example application is to familiarize you with the basic approach used in event-driven programming. If the syntax being used seems unfamiliar, do not be concerned. It's explained in much more detail later in the course.

Now consider the code associated with the **Click** event for the **cmdReset** button. Clicking the button changes the **Text** property in the **txtName** text box back to its original value, "John Doe," as shown in the following example code:

```
Sub cmdReset_Click()
  txtName.Text = "John Doe"
End Sub
```

As in the previous procedure, the procedure name consists of the object name, an underscore, and the event to which the procedure responds.

The example application consists of two event procedures that contain a total of six lines of code. The event-driven nature of the application handles the logic required to direct program execution to the appropriate task in response to user actions. The programming logic required to implement the same type of application in a procedural language would be much more complicated and would involve many more lines of code.

Creating a Program in Visual Basic

Creating event-driven programs in Visual Basic requires a different approach than that used in procedural languages. If you are experienced with procedural programming, the approach may seem unusual at first. Both types of programming require logic and order, but Visual Basic requires a different type of logic and order. For example, to create an interface in Visual Basic, you draw the objects and controls on a blank form. Compared to the programming effort required to produce graphical objects in most procedural languages, the actual coding needed to provide functionality in Visual Basic is minimal.

Creating an application in Visual Basic involves eight basic steps:

1. Create a design plan.

   The design plan should be the road map that you use when creating an application. Before writing any code, take time to design the application that you will be building. Although Visual Basic provides tools to help you quickly develop a solution, having a clear understanding of the user needs and initial feature set will help you be more efficient in your development efforts. This will also help you save time by minimizing the potential for recoding because of a poor or nonexistent design plan.

2. Create the user interface.

   To create the interface for your application, first place controls and objects on a form by drawing or painting them in the Form Designer. You can look at other applications such as Excel or Word for ideas on how to design the interface. For information about interface design, see *The Windows Interface Guidelines for Software Design*, published by Microsoft Press.

3. Set the properties of interface objects.

   After you have added objects to a form, you can set their properties at design time, or you can use code statements to set properties at run time.

4. Write code for events.

   After you have set the initial properties for the form and its objects, you can add code that runs in response to events. Events occur when different actions are performed on a control or object. For example, a command button's **Click** event occurs when the user clicks it with the mouse.

5. Save the project.

   Next, save the project, giving it a unique and descriptive name. You should save the project frequently as you add code to it. Saving a project also saves its forms and code modules.

6. Test and debug the application.

As you add code to the project, you can run the application and view its behavior. Visual Basic offers numerous tools for debugging your application.

7. Make an executable file.

Upon completion of the project, you'll create an executable file. By doing this, you compile the various files that make up the program into a stand-alone executable file.

8. Create a Setup application.

To run your application, the user usually needs other files, such as any DLL files or custom control .ocx files that you used to create your application. Visual Basic provides the Package & Deployment Wizard, which automates the creation of the Setup program and ensures that the user has all of the necessary files.

Project and Executable Files

A Visual Basic project is made up of the forms, code modules, ActiveX controls, and environmental settings that an application requires. As you design an application, Visual Basic maintains a project file with the extension .vbp. The project file lists all the files that you need for your application, such as forms and code modules. In addition, the project file lists all the building blocks that you use, such as any ActiveX controls. The project file does not contain the files and building blocks themselves, so you can use the same file (for example, a form) in more than one project.

When you open a project file, the files listed in the project file are loaded.

In addition to the project file, a project can include the files listed in the following table.

File type	Extension	Description
Form files	.frm .frx	These files contain the form, the objects on the form, and the code that runs when an event occurs on that form.
Visual Basic standard modules	.bas	These modules contain **Sub** and **Function** procedures that can be called by any form or object on a form. Standard modules are optional.

table continued on next page

File type	Extension	Description
ActiveX controls	.ocx	These controls are available from Microsoft and third-party vendors. ActiveX controls are added by using the **Components** command on the **Project** menu. After they are added to a project, ActiveX controls appear in the toolbox.
Visual Basic class modules	.cls	These modules contain the class definition, methods, and properties. Class modules are optional and are not covered in this course.
Resource files	.res	These files contain binary information used by the application. Resource files are typically used when creating programs for multiple languages.
User controls	.ctl .ctx	These files contain source code and binary information for user controls. These files are compiled into ActiveX controls (.ocx files).
User documents	.dob .dox	These files contain base form and binary information for creating ActiveX documents.
ActiveX designers	.dsr	These files contain information about designers that are used in the project. For example, you can create a data environment for run-time data access.

Tip It's a good idea to organize projects by maintaining a separate directory for each project created.

Building an Executable (.Exe) File

When you're finished with your application and want to distribute it, you must first compile it into an executable file. Compiling your application creates a single executable file that contains all the forms and code modules specific to the project.

Users normally need additional files to be able to run the executable file. Before distributing your program, you typically use the Package & Deployment Wizard to bundle your program with these files. For more information, see "Using Package & Deployment Wizard" on page 359 in Chapter 14, "Finishing Touches."

Visual Basic Reference Materials

Visual Basic 6.0 includes the Microsoft Developer Network (MSDN) CDs to provide you with documentation, tutorials, and samples. All editions of Visual Basic include the following documentation within MSDN:

◆ *Programmer's Guide*

This guide teaches general programming concepts.

◆ *Component Tools Guide*

This suite of guides teaches you how to create and use components that operate through the Component Object Model (COM), which is the basis for ActiveX technology.

◆ *Enterprise Guide*

This guide includes a complete list of enterprise features included with the Visual Basic Enterprise Edition. It also includes Visual Studio's guide to distributed application development for business-critical data management.

◆ *Data Access Guide*

This guide covers tools and technology options and tutorials, and provides information on ADO. In addition, the guide discusses two older Visual Basic data access technologies, DAO and RDO.

◆ Samples

The Visual Basic sample applications are located on the MSDN CD. You can install them during MSDN Installation by selecting **Visual Basic 6.0 Product Samples** in the **Custom** dialog box. If you have installed the sample applications, the folders can be found in \Program Files\Microsoft Visual Studio\MSDN98\98VS\1033\samples\VB98\. If you have not installed the samples, you can copy the files from the MSDN Library CD.

Other good sources of information are Microsoft TechNet, the Microsoft Visual Basic Web, and newsgroups devoted to Visual Basic.

For information about Visual Basic, see the Microsoft Web site at http://www.microsoft.com/VBASIC/.

Lab 1: Creating a Simple Application

In this lab, you will learn how to create a simple application in Visual Basic. Subsequent labs in this course will explore each of the tasks here in more detail.

To see the demonstration "Lab 1 Solution," see the accompanying CD-ROM.

Estimated time to complete this lab: **45 minutes**

Objectives

After completing this lab, you will be able to:

- Identify the elements of the Visual Basic development environment.
- Add controls to forms.
- Use context-sensitive Help.
- Set control properties.
- Create an executable application.

To complete the exercises in this lab, you must have the required software. For detailed information about the labs and setup for the labs, see "Labs" in "About This Course."

The solution for this lab is located in the *<install folder>*\Labs\Lab01\Solution folder.

Prerequisites

There are no prerequisites for this lab.

Exercises

The following exercises provide practice in working with the concepts and techniques covered in this chapter:

- Exercise 1: Using Controls

  In this exercise, you will practice placing controls on a form to become more familiar with the Visual Basic development environment and controls.

- Exercise 2: Creating an Application with Code

  In this exercise, you will create an application that changes properties of controls while the application is running.

◆ Exercise 3: Using Code from the Help File

In this exercise, you will locate a code sample in MSDN Help and copy it into an application.

Exercise 1: Using Controls

In this exercise, you will practice placing controls on a form to become more familiar with the Visual Basic development environment and controls.

▶ **Start Visual Basic**

1. Click the **Start** button, point to **Programs**, then point to **Microsoft Visual Basic 6.0**, and then click **Microsoft Visual Basic 6.0**.

2. Click **Standard.exe**, and then click **Open** to start your new project.

   A new project with one form is created.

▶ **Add controls to a form**

1. Click a control in the toolbox.

2. Place the cross-hair pointer on the form at the desired position for the upper-left corner of the control.

3. Click and hold the left mouse button while dragging the pointer to the desired position for the lower-right corner of the control. Then, release the mouse button.

4. Repeat this process with a number of different controls in the toolbox.

▶ **Get Help on a control**

1. Click any control that you have placed on the form.

2. Press F1.

   MSDN Help should open to the topic of the selected control.

3. Examine the contents of the Help topic for the control, and then close the Help window.

▶ **Run the application**

1. On the **Run** menu, click **Start**.

   –or–

   On the **Visual Basic** toolbar, click the **Start** button.

   Visual Basic opens the form as a program.

2. Test the controls on the form.

Notice that the controls work as you would expect, even though you haven't written any code.

3. Close the running application and return to Design mode, by using one of these methods:

    a. On the **Toolbar**, click the **End** button.

    b. On the **Run** menu, click **End**.

    c. On the system menu, click **Close**.

    d. On the title bar, click the **Close** button.

▶ **Remove controls from a form**

1. Move the mouse pointer to the upper-left corner of the form.

2. Click and hold the left mouse button, and then drag the pointer to the lower-right corner of the form. Then, release the mouse button.

Grab handles will appear on all the controls on the form, indicating that all the controls have been selected.

3. On the **Edit** menu, click **Delete**, or press DELETE. All selected controls are removed from the form.

Exercise 2: Creating an Application with Code

In this exercise, you will use the same project used in Exercise 1 to create an application that changes properties of controls while the application is running.

▶ **Add a TextBox and a Label control to the form and align them horizontally**

1. Add a **TextBox** control to the form.

2. Add a **Label** control to the form, and position the **Label** control to the right side of the **TextBox** control.

3. Click on the form and drag a box around both controls to select them.

4. Click the control on the form with which you want the other controls to align. The control's grab handles should change to a solid color.

5. On the **Format** menu, click **Align**, and then click **Tops** to horizontally align the controls to the last selected control.

▶ **Set control properties at design time**

1. Click on the form to cancel the selection of the other controls, and then select the **Label** control on the form.

2. In the Properties window, change the **Caption** property to "My Label."

3. Select the **TextBox** control.

4. In the Properties window, change the **Text** property to "My TextBox."

▶ **Change control properties at run time**

1. Double-click the **TextBox** control on the form.

   The Code Editor window will open, showing the **Text1_Change** event procedure.

2. Add the following statement to the body of the procedure:

   ```
   Label1.Caption = Text1.Text
   ```

   This code statement changes the caption of the **Label** control to the text that the user types in the **TextBox** control.

3. Run the application and type some text in the text box. Note what happens.

4. Close the application and return to Design mode.

▶ **Save the project**

1. On the **File** menu, click **Save Project**.

2. When prompted to save the form, change the destination folder to *<install folder>*\Labs\Lab01, keep the default name of Form1, and click **Save**.

3. When prompted to save the project, change the destination folder to *<install folder>*\Labs\Lab01, keep the default name of Project1, and click **Save**.

▶ **Create an .exe file**

1. On the **File** menu, click **Make Project1.exe** to make the executable file. Make sure that the destination folder is *<install folder>*\Labs\Lab01.

2. In the **File name** text box, type **Firstapp** and then click **OK**. Visual Basic compiles the current project and creates an executable file that can be run directly from Windows.

3. Exit Visual Basic and save changes if prompted.

▶ **Run the .exe file**

1. Click the **Start** button, point to **Programs,** and then click **Windows Explorer.**

2. In Windows Explorer, navigate to the *<install folder>*\Labs\Lab01 folder.

3. Run the application that you just created by double-clicking on the Firstapp executable file.

4. Test the application by typing some text in the text box.

5. Close the application.

Exercise 3: Using Code from the Help File

In this exercise, you will locate a code sample in MSDN Help and copy it into an application.

▶ **Open Project1**

1. Start Visual Basic.

2. Click the **Recent** tab, select Project1, and then click **Open.**

3. If the form is not visible, select it in the Project Explorer window and click **View Object.**

▶ **Use context-sensitive Help**

1. Double-click anywhere on the form, outside of the **TextBox** or **Label** controls.

   The following lines of code will appear in the Code Editor window:

   ```
   Private Sub Form_Load()
   End Sub
   ```

2. In the Code Editor window, from the **Procedure** list, select **MouseMove.**

   The contents of the Code Editor window will change to the following:

   ```
   Private Sub Form_MouseMove(Button As Integer, Shift As _
       Integer, X As Single, Y As Single)
   End Sub
   ```

3. Type **FillColor** between the **Sub** and **End Sub** lines.

4. Highlight the word **FillColor,** and press F1.

   MSDN Help will display the "FillColor Property" Help topic.

▶ **Copy example code from MSDN Help and paste it into a Visual Basic application**

1. Click the **Example** jump topic at the top of the Help window.

   A Help window should open with an example of how to use the **FillColor** property.

2. Select the three lines of code between the **Sub** and **End Sub** statements.

3. Right-click anywhere on the selected text and click **Copy** to copy the selected lines to the Clipboard.

4. Close the MSDN Help window.

   You should now be back in the Code Editor window, which should be displaying the **Form_MouseMove** event procedure. If it is not, in the Code Editor window, from the **Object** list, click **Form,** and from the **Procedure** list, click **MouseMove** to move to the **Form_MouseMove** event procedure.

5. Highlight the **FillColor** command in the procedure.

6. On the **Edit** menu, click **Paste** to paste the copied code into the **Form_MouseMove** event procedure. The resulting event procedure should look similar to the following code:

```
Private Sub Form_MouseMove(Button As Integer, Shift As Integer, _
    X As Single, Y As Single)
    '    Choose random FillColor
    FillColor = QBColor(Int(Rnd * 15))
    '    Choose random FillStyle
    FillStyle = Int(Rnd * 8)
    '    Draw a circle
    Circle (X, Y), 250
End Sub
```

▶ **Save and test your application**

1. On the **File** menu, click **Save Project** to save the changes to the project and the form in *<install folder>*\Labs\Lab01.

2. Run the application and move the mouse pointer around on the form. What happens?

3. Close the application.

To see the answer to the question in Step 2, see Hint 1.1 in Appendix B.

Self-Check Questions

See page 373 for answers.

1. **Visual Basic is the basis for a common programming language known as:**
   A. C++.
   B. QuickBasic.
   C. PC Basic.
   D. Visual Basic for Applications.

2. **A small business plans to create applications that share an Access database and create custom data reports. The business owners do not require any remote database access tools. Which edition of Visual Basic is best suited for their purposes?**
   A. Learning
   B. Professional
   C. Enterprise
   D. None of the above

3. **The actions an object can perform are called _____, while those recognized by an object are _____ .**
   A. events, methods
   B. methods, events
   C. properties, methods
   D. procedures, events

4. **To distribute an application, you first create a single executable file containing all the forms and code modules for a project. To do this, you:**
   A. Create a test project.
   B. Zip the project.
   C. Compile the project.
   D. Assemble the project.

Chapter 2:
Visual Basic Fundamentals

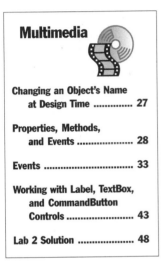
In this chapter, you will learn the basics of using Microsoft Visual Basic forms, controls, and code to create an application. You will learn about objects, properties, methods, and events, and you will see how they are implemented in Visual Basic.

Objectives

After completing this chapter, you will be able to:

◆ Create a simple application in Visual Basic.

◆ Define and provide examples of each of the following: object, property, method, and event.

◆ Describe some of the properties and events associated with a form.

◆ Set properties for command buttons, text boxes, and labels.

◆ Use the **With...End With** statement to set multiple property values for a single object.

◆ Assign code to a control to respond to the **Click** event.

Introduction to Objects

In Visual Basic, an object is a combination of code and data that can be treated and controlled as a unit. Command buttons and other controls on a form are objects. Each form in a Visual Basic project is a separate object.

Objects can contain other objects; for example, a form can contain command buttons. The following illustration shows a form that contains four objects: two command buttons, a label, and a text box.

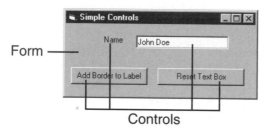

Form ⎯

Controls

A Microsoft Excel spreadsheet is an example of an object containing other objects such as workbooks, sheets, and charts.

Because an object contains both data and code, inserting an existing object into a program also inserts the object's code. For example, when a command button is inserted into a program, the command button already contains the code to react to certain events, such as a mouse click. When the **Click** event occurs, the button responds by changing appearance.

A more elaborate example of an object is the **CommonDialog** control in Visual Basic. This object contains all of the code required to implement **File Open** and **File Save** dialog boxes in your applications.

Naming Objects

When an object is created, it is assigned a default name based on its object type, such as **Form1, Command2,** or **Text3.** You should immediately change the **Name** property of each control to a name that describes the purpose of the control. Changing the **Name** property makes the code in your application easier to read and debug. In addition, the code associated with an object is based on its name. If you change the object's name after code is written, the code loses its association to the control.

To see the demonstration "Changing an Object's Name at Design Time," see the accompanying CD-ROM.

Standard Naming Conventions

Although you can assign any name to an object, it is a good idea to adopt a naming convention and use it consistently throughout your programs.

The following table lists the standard naming conventions used in Visual Basic. Adopting these conventions makes it easier for others who are familiar with the standard naming conventions to understand your code.

Object	Prefix	Example
Check box	chk	chkReadOnly
Combo box	cbo	cboEnglish
Command button	cmd	cmdCancel
Data	dat	datBiblio
Directory list box	dir	dirSource
Drive list box	drv	drvTarget
File list box	fil	filSource
Form	frm	frmFileOpen
Frame	fra	fraLanguage
Grid	grd	grdPrices
Horizontal scroll bar	hsb	hsbVolume
Image	img	imgIcon
Label	lbl	lblHelpMessage
Line	lin	linVertical
List box	lst	lstPolicyCodes
Menu	mnu	mnuFileOpen
OLE	ole	oleObject1

table continued on next page

Object	Prefix	Example
Option button	opt	optFrench
Picture box	pic	picDiskSpace
Shape	shp	shpCircle
Text box	txt	txtGetText
Timer	tmr	tmrAlarm
Vertical scroll bar	vsb	vsbRate

For more information about standard Visual Basic naming conventions, search for "Object Naming Conventions" in MSDN Help.

Controlling Objects

To control an object, you use its properties, methods, and events. Properties are an object's data, settings, and attributes. Methods are procedures that operate on the object or that the object performs on data. Events are triggered when some aspect of the object is changed.

To understand the relationship between objects, properties, and methods, consider a stereo radio. The radio is an object and has a number of properties, such as volume, bass, and treble. The radio's volume is a property that you can change. You can also change the radio station, another property, by using the radio's "tune" method.

Each of these properties and methods performs a specific purpose and is used to attain a given goal or objective, such as tuning the radio. As a radio owner, you learn how to use these objects; but for the most part, you do not learn how to install, maintain, or repair them. You need to know only how to operate them and what to expect.

In the same way, Visual Basic lets you use objects—forms and controls—to build applications. For the most part, you can use objects without having a detailed understanding of how they work.

To see the animation "Properties, Methods and Events," see the accompanying CD-ROM.

Properties, Methods, and Events

Properties define the appearance and behavior of objects. **Text, Caption,** and **Name** are common examples of properties.

You can set most properties at both design time and run time. Some properties can be set at design time by using the Properties window. Other properties are not available at design time; you use code to set these properties at run time.

Setting Properties at Design Time

To set object properties at design time, use the Properties window. Any property settings that you establish at design time are used as the initial settings each time your application runs. The following list shows some common properties that you typically set at design time:

BackStyle	FillColor
BorderStyle	FillStyle
Caption	Name
Enabled	Visible

▶ **To set the value of a property at design time**

1. In the Form Designer window, select the form or control for which you want to set a property.

   Visual Basic activates the form or control and displays the properties for that object in the Properties window.

2. In the Properties window, select the property that you want to set.

3. Type or select the property setting that you want.

Tip To quickly access a property, press the key representing the first letter of the property's name while holding down the CTRL+SHIFT. Continue to press the key to view all the properties that start with that letter.

To view the possible values for a property, double-click the property's name in the Properties window.

Setting Properties at Run Time

To set an object property at run time, use the following syntax:

Object.Property = Expression

The following example code, for instance, displays "Hello, World!" in a text box named **txtMessage**:

```
txtMessage.Text = "Hello, World!"
```

Note In Visual Basic, literal strings (such as "Hello, World!" in the previous example) are surrounded by double quotes to distinguish them from values or constants.

Visual Basic Constants

Some properties must be set to a specific value in order to have the intended meaning in your application. For example, a **CheckBox** control can appear in one of three states: checked, unchecked, or unavailable (dimmed). You set the **Value** property of the **CheckBox** control to 0, 1, or 2 to establish its state.

Visual Basic supplies many defined constants that you can use in your code in place of values. Constants use descriptive names that are identified by their "vb" prefix, such as vbNormal. Using constants in place of values will make your code easier to read.

For example, the **Value** property for the **CheckBox** control can accept the constants listed in the following table.

Constant	Value	Description
vbUnchecked	0	Cleared (unchecked)
vbChecked	1	Selected (checked)
vbGrayed	2	Unavailable (grayed)

The following example code causes the check box, **chkMuteOn**, to appear selected. Because each line does the same thing, you would use either one line of code or the other, but not both.

```
chkMuteOn.Value = 1
chkMuteOn.Value = vbChecked
```

Returning Property Values

Sometimes you need the value of an object's property in order to perform a calculation or some other task in an application. For example, you can get, or "return," the **Text** property of a text box control if you need to know the contents of the text box before running code that might change the value.

To return the value of an object's property, use the following syntax to set the value of a variable equal to the value of the property:

Variable = Object.Property

The following example code places the contents of a text box named **txtName** (the contents are stored in its **Text** property) in a variable named strUserName:

```
strUserName = txtName.Text
```

Tip If you're going to use the value of a property more than once, your code will run faster if you store the value in a variable.

In the following example code, the value of the **Text** property of the **txtCustomerName** text box is set to a string:

```
txtCustomerName.Text = "Nancy Davolio"
```

Methods

Besides having characteristics (properties), objects can also perform actions through methods. To use methods, you must know the definition of a method and understand the syntax for using a method.

Definition

Methods cause an object to perform an action or task. **Move** and **SetFocus** are common examples of methods. Like properties, methods are a part of objects. Generally, methods are actions that you want to perform, whereas properties are the attributes that you set or retrieve.

Methods can affect the values of properties. For example, list boxes have a **List** property; you can change the **List** property with the **Clear** method to remove all of the items from a list, or you can use the **AddItem** method to add a new item to a list.

Syntax

You can call methods in several different ways. The syntax used to call a method depends on whether the method returns a value and if that value will be used by your application.

To call a method that does not return a value, or if you don't want to use the value returned by the method, use the following syntax:

Object.Method [arg1, arg2, ..]

Optionally, you can place parentheses around the arguments when you want to use the value returned by the method. Generally, use parentheses any time the method appears to the right of an equal sign. To use the value returned by the method, use the following syntax:

Variable = Object.Method ([arg1, arg2, ..])

The **SetFocus** method, common to many Visual Basic objects, is an example of a method that does not have arguments. The following example code sets the text box **txtName** as the active control on the form:

```
txtName.SetFocus
```

In contrast, the **Move** method, which repositions an object, has four arguments: **left, top, width,** and **height.** If a method takes more than one argument, you must separate the arguments with a comma. The following example code moves the form frmStartUp to the upper-left corner of the program window:

```
frmStartUp.Move 0, 0
```

Note Although the **Move** method accepts up to four arguments, some are optional. For more information about arguments, see "Named Arguments" on page 77 in Chapter 3, "Working with Code and Forms" and "Using General Procedures" on page 115 in Chapter 4, "Variables and Procedures."

Events

An event is an action that is recognized by a form or control. Clicking a mouse or pressing a key is an example of an event. You can write code in an event procedure that runs whenever the event occurs. Any action can be associated with a Visual Basic event, giving you complete control over how an application responds to each action.

Events are triggered when some aspect of an object is changed. For example, moving the scroll box in a vertical scroll bar triggers the **Scroll** event.

Every object in Visual Basic has a set of events that it recognizes. For example, a **Form** object recognizes the **Load, Unload,** and **Activate** events.

The following is a list of some of the events that you use in Visual Basic:

Activate	**DragOver**	**Load**
Change	**GotFocus**	**LostFocus**
Click	**KeyDown**	**MouseDown**
DblClick	**KeyPress**	**MouseMove**
DragDrop	**KeyUp**	**MouseUp**

Note Each object has its own set of events that it recognizes. The events listed do not apply to all objects. For example, a form can recognize either a **Click** or **DblClick** event, while a button recognizes only a **Click** event.

To see the demonstration "Events," see the accompanying CD-ROM.

Working with Forms

Form objects are the basic building blocks of applications written in Visual Basic. The user interacts with an application primarily through form objects and the controls placed on them. Forms have their own properties, events, and methods, which you can use to control their appearance and behavior.

Tip When Visual Basic opens a new Standard EXE project, a default form, **Form1**, is added to the development environment. Visual Basic applies a default set of properties to this form and any new forms that you add to your project. You can use these properties to change the form's appearance and behavior.

A good way to become familiar with the many form properties is to experiment. Try changing some of the properties of the default form in the Properties window, and then run the application to see the effect. Context-sensitive Help is available for each property by selecting the property and pressing F1. To run an application in Visual Basic, press F5. To end an application, close all of the application's forms, or click **End** on the **Run** menu.

Design-Time and Run-Time Settable Properties

As with any other objects, you can set form properties at design time in the Properties window, or you can set them at run time by writing code.

Caption

The **Caption** property determines the text value that appears in the form's title bar. This text also appears below the form's icon when the form is minimized.

Note Don't confuse a form's name with its caption. The form name is used in code to refer to the form. The caption is the text that appears in the title bar.

Use the Properties window to set the **Caption** property at design time. To change the **Caption** property at run time, use the following syntax:

object.*Caption [*= string*]*

The following example code sets the **Caption** property at run time:

```
frmCalculator.Caption = "Calculator Display"
```

Name

The default name for a new form is Form, plus a unique integer. For example, the first new Form object is **Form1**, the second is **Form2**, and so on.

Because a form's name is used to reference it in code, it is important to set the **Name** property early in the development process, preferably when you create the form. A form's **Name** property must start with a letter; the name can include numbers and underline (_) characters, but it cannot include punctuation or spaces.

Note Forms cannot have the same name as another public object, such as Clipboard, Screen, or App. Although the **Name** property setting can be a keyword, property name, or the name of another object, this can create conflicts in your code.

Font

Use the **Font** property to set the font on the form. By default, other controls placed on the form will use the font that is set for the form.

This setting does not affect the form's caption in the title bar.

Left, Top, Width, and Height

To set the size and location of a form, you use its **Left**, **Top**, **Width**, and **Height** properties. The default units for these properties are twips. A twip is 1/1,440 of an inch.

You can set a form's size and location at design time or at run time. The following example code resizes a form at run time:

```
'Sets the left side of the form one inch from the left border
frmCalculator.Left = 1440
```

At design time, you can set form size and location by using either the Properties window or the mouse. To set the **Height** and **Width** properties, drag the form's bottom and right borders. To set the **Left** and **Top** properties, drag the form representation in the Form Layout window to the correct location.

Note While making changes to the form's size and location, you can view the location and size coordinates on the toolbar.

BackColor and ForeColor

A form has two color properties:

◆ BackColor

Returns or sets the background color of an object.

◆ ForeColor

Returns or sets the foreground color used to display text and graphics in an object.

Setting the **BackColor** property on a **Form** object at run time erases all text and graphics, including the persistent graphics. Setting the **ForeColor** property does not affect graphics or print output that has already been drawn.

Note To display text, both the text and background colors must be solid. If you select a dithered color (a color that is produced by combining different-colored pixels), the nearest solid color will be substituted.

Icon

The **Icon** property specifies the icon that appears when a form is minimized. In Windows, the icon also appears in the title bar.

You set the **Icon** property at design time. Visual Basic supplies a large library of icons for your applications, but you can use any file with the extension .ico.

MousePointer

The **MousePointer** property returns or sets a value that indicates the type of mouse pointer displayed when the mouse pointer appears over a particular area of an object at run time. You can use the **MousePointer** property to indicate changes in functionality that occur as the mouse pointer passes over controls on a form or dialog box. For example, you can set Mouse Pointer to 11 (vbHourglass) to indicate that the user should wait for a process or operation to finish.

To set the **MousePointer** property, use the following syntax:

object.*MousePointer [= value]*

The following example code sets the default mouse pointer for the form, frmCalculator, to the hourglass:

```
frmCalculator.MousePointer = vbHourglass
```

If other objects contained within frmCalculator use the default **MousePointer** property setting (vbDefault), this example sets the mouse pointer for these objects as well.

WindowState

The **WindowState** property determines how the form will appear (normal, minimized, or maximized). You set the **WindowState** property at run time. Before a form is displayed, the **WindowState** property is always set to vbNormal, regardless of its initial setting.

To set the **WindowState** property, use the following syntax:

object.*WindowState* = value

The following table lists possible values for the **WindowState** property.

Constant	Setting	Description
VbNormal	0	Set to normal size (default)
VbMinimized	1	Minimized to an icon
VbMaximized	2	Enlarged to maximum size

The following example code maximizes frmCalculator:

```
frmCalculator.WindowState = vbMaximized
```

For more information about displaying and hiding forms, see "Form Methods and Events" on page 39 in this chapter.

Design-Time-Only Settable Properties

Several form properties can be set only at design time, through the Properties window. Writing code to change settings for those properties has no effect at run time.

BorderStyle

The **BorderStyle** property controls the appearance of the form's border. This property also determines whether the user can resize, minimize, or maximize the form.

The following table lists the **BorderStyle** property settings for a **Form** object.

Constant	Setting	Description
vbBSNone	0	None (no border or border-related elements).
vbFixedSingle	1	Can include **Control** menu box, title bar, **Maximize** button, and **Minimize** button. Resizable only by using **Maximize** and **Minimize** buttons.
vbSizable	2	(Default) Resizable by using any of the optional border elements listed for setting 1.
vbFixedDialog	3	Can include **Control** menu box and title bar; cannot include **Maximize** or **Minimize** buttons. Not resizable.
vbFixedToolWindow	4	Displays a nonsizable window with a **Close** button and title bar text in a reduced font size. The form does not appear in the Microsoft Windows 98 taskbar.
vbSizableToolWindow	5	Displays a sizable tool window with a **Close** button and title bar text in a reduced font size. The form does not appear in the Windows 98 taskbar.

MaxButton and MinButton

The **MaxButton** and **MinButton** properties determine whether standard Windows **Maximize** and **Minimize** buttons. Setting these properties has no effect, unless the **BorderStyle** property is set to **1, 2,** or **3** (vbFixedSingle, vbSizable, or vbFixedDialog).

ControlBox

The **ControlBox** property determines whether a standard Windows control box appears on a form. When you set the **ControlBox** property to **True,** you must also set the **BorderStyle** property to **1, 2,** or **3** (vbFixedSingle, vbSizable, or vbFixedDouble) to display the control box.

Form Methods and Events

Like any other object, a form exposes methods and responds to events.

Form Methods

Methods of the **Form** object include the following:

Hide	PrintForm	Show
Move	Refresh	
Print	SetFocus	

Two of the most important form methods are the **Show** and the **Hide** methods. Invoking the **Show** method has the same effect as setting a form's **Visible** property to **True**. The following example code makes a form visible by invoking the **Show** method:

```
frmCalculator.Show
```

Many of a form's other methods involve text or graphics. For example, you use the **Print, Line, Circle,** and **Refresh** methods for printing or drawing directly on a form.

Form Events

Events of the **Form** object include the following:

Activate	DragOver	MouseMove
Click	GotFocus	MouseUp
DblClick	Load	Unload
Deactivate	LostFocus	
DragDrop	MouseDown	

The **Resize** event of a form is triggered whenever a form is resized, either by user interaction or through code. This allows you to write code that responds to changes in the form's dimensions. For example, you can write code that moves or resizes controls when the size of a form changes.

The **Activate** event occurs whenever a form becomes the active form; the **Deactivate** event occurs when another form or application becomes active. These events are useful for initializing or finalizing the form's behavior. For example, the **Activate** event can respond by running code that highlights the text in a particular text box, and the **Load** event can be used to retrieve data from a file or database.

For more information about the methods and events of the **Form** object, search for "Form Object" in MSDN Help.

Introduction to Controls

Almost every application that you write in Visual Basic uses controls placed on a form. Controls are objects that are contained within form objects. Command buttons, list boxes, and scroll bars are examples of controls. Each type of control has its own set of properties, methods, and events that make it suitable for a particular purpose.

In this section, you will learn about a few of the standard controls in the toolbox. You will also learn about other controls in more detail as you use them.

Adding Controls to a Form

The toolbox contains the following standard controls:

PictureBox	Label	TextBox
Frame	CommandButton	CheckBox
OptionButton	ComboBox	ListBox
HScrollBar	VScrollBar	Timer
DriveListBox	DirListBox	FileListBox
Shape	Line	Image
Data	OLE	

You can add control objects to a form in two ways. One way is to double-click the toolbox icon of the control you want to add, which places an instance of the control with the default size in the center of the active form. When you add multiple controls in this manner, they are placed on top of each other in the center of the form. After you add the controls, you can reposition them one at a time.

The second way to add control objects to a form, described as follows, gives you more control over the size and position of the control.

▶ **To add controls to a form**

1. Click the toolbox icon for the control that you want to add.
2. Move the mouse pointer over the form.

   The pointer changes to a cross hair.

3. Position the cross hair where you want the upper-left corner of the control.
4. Drag (click and hold the left mouse button) to the lower-right corner.

   A rectangle is drawn on the screen, indicating the size and location of the control.

5. When the control is correctly sized, release the mouse button.

   The control snaps into place on the form.

After the control has been added to the form, it can be positioned and resized. To reposition the control, click the control to select it, then drag the control to the correct position. To resize the control, drag one of the eight sizing handles until the control is properly sized, and then release the mouse button.

Tip When placing several controls on a form, use the commands on the **Format** menu to place and size the controls. First, drag the mouse around the controls to select them. By using the commands on the **Format** menu, you can then align or size the controls as necessary.

Setting Control Properties

Each type of control has properties that are related to the control's functions. Like form properties, control properties can generally be set at either design time or run time, as discussed in "Properties, Methods, and Events" on page 29 in this chapter.

Setting the Name Property

The **Name** property is always set at design time. When a control is created, Visual Basic gives it a default name, indicating the type of control, plus a unique integer. For example, the first new **CommandButton** object is Command1, the second is Command2, and so on. It's important to change the **Name** property early in the application development, because a control's name is used to reference the control in code. If you change the control's name, any code in its events, or code that references the name, it will no longer run.

Note A control's **Name** property must start with a letter and can include numbers and underline (_) characters but not punctuation or spaces.

Using the With...End With Statement to Set Object Properties

When setting properties and calling methods for objects, you often write a number of code statements that act on the same object. In these cases, you can make your code more efficient and easier to read by using the **With...End With** statement. By using the **With** statement, you can set multiple properties and call multiple methods quickly and easily. Because the object is evaluated only once, your code executes more quickly. The **With...End With** statement can be nested to multiple levels.

The **With...End With** statement uses the following syntax:

> *With* Object
>   [Statements]
> *End With*

The name of the object is placed on the With line. All subsequent lines of code are written without the object qualifier and automatically apply to that object.

> **Note** The period (.) that separates the object from its property or method must still be included in the statement.

The following example code sets some properties of a text box:

```
txtName.Font.Bold = True
txtName.Font.Size = 24
txtName.Text = "Hello, World!"
```

The following example code sets properties of a text box by using the **With...End With** statement:

```
With txtName
  .Font.Bold = True
  .Font.Size = 24
  .Text = "Hello, World!"
End With
```

In this instance, using the **With...End With** statement results in two additional lines of code; Visual Basic is able to execute the code in the **With** statement more quickly though, because it evaluates the **txtName** object once, rather than three times.

Basic Controls

Three of the most commonly used controls are **Label**, **TextBox**, and **CommandButton**. Almost every application written in Visual Basic uses these controls.

To see the demonstration "Working with Label, TextBox, and CommandButton Controls," see the accompanying CD-ROM.

Label

A label is a graphical control used to display text. Because a label is a graphical control, the user cannot edit the text. The most common use for a **Label** control is to identify controls that do not have a **Caption** property, such as the **TextBox** control.

The following illustration shows a label that is used to identify the purpose of a text box.

Label Control

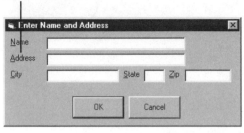

Frequently used properties for the **Label** control include the following:

Alignment	**Caption**	**Name**
AutoSize	**Font**	**WordWrap**
ToolTipText		

Setting the Caption

You use the **Caption** property to change the text displayed in the **Label** control. At design time, you set this property by selecting it from the Properties window of the control.

At run time, you can set the **Caption** property of a label to provide instructions or additional help to the user. The following example code provides instructions for entering data into a text box:

```
lblGetName.Caption = "Enter your full name, last name first."
```

Aligning Label Text

The **Alignment** property sets the alignment of the text within a **Label** control to either left-justified (0—vbLeftJustify), right-justified (1—vbRightJustify), or centered (2—vbCenter). By default, text is left-justified.

The following illustration shows each of the alignment options for labels.

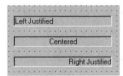

Using AutoSize and WordWrap

By default, when the amount of text entered in the **Caption** property exceeds the width of the **Label** control, the text wraps to the next line. If the control's height is exceeded, the text is clipped. Setting the **AutoSize** property to **True** causes the control to horizontally expand and adjust to the size of its contents. To cause the contents to wrap to the next line and expand vertically, you can set the **WordWrap** property to **True**.

The following illustration shows the effect of using the **AutoSize** and **WordWrap** properties.

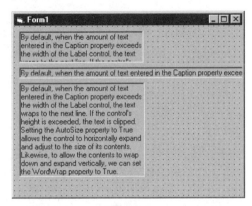

Note Consider setting the **BackStyle** property of the label to **Transparent**. If the color of the form changes, the label will automatically show this new color as its own background.

TextBox

You use a **TextBox** control to obtain information from the user or to display information provided by the application. Unlike information that appears in a label, information displayed in a text box can be changed by the user. Text boxes can be used in conjunction with a **Data** control to display information from a database. You can also use text boxes to set up database queries or to edit records in a database.

The following illustration shows several **TextBox** controls that are used to collect information from the user.

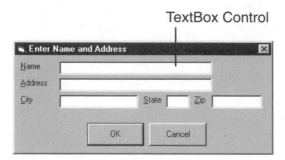

TextBox Control

Creating a Multiple-Line Text Box

The **MultiLine** property of the **TextBox** control, when used in conjunction with the **ScrollBars** property, allows multiple lines of text to be displayed. The **MultiLine** property can be set to **True** or **False**, and the **ScrollBars** property can be set to none (0—vbSBNone), horizontal (1—vbHorizontal), vertical (2—vbVertical), or both (3—vbBoth).

If the **MultiLine** property is set to **True**, the **Alignment** property can be used to set the alignment of text within the text box. The text is left-justified by default. If the **MultiLine** property is **False**, setting the **Alignment** property has no effect.

CommandButton

A command button performs a task when the user clicks the button. You use a **CommandButton** control to begin, interrupt, or end a process. Because a command button appears to be pushed in when clicked, it is sometimes called a push button. The most common event for a **CommandButton** control is the **Click** event.

The following illustration shows two command buttons; one accepts information that the user enters on the form and the other disregards that information.

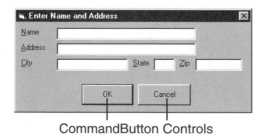

CommandButton Controls

You display text on a **CommandButton** control by using its **Caption** property. A user can always choose a **CommandButton** control by clicking it. To allow the user to choose the button by pressing ENTER, set the **Default** property to **True**. To allow the user to choose the button by pressing ESC, set the **Cancel** property of the **CommandButton** control to **True**.

Note When you design a form, it's usually a good idea to place buttons horizontally along the bottom of the form or vertically along the right side of the form.

Following are some of the properties, methods, and events that you commonly use with the **CommandButton** control:

♦ **Cancel, Caption, Default, Font, Name, ToolTipText**, and **Visible** properties

♦ **SetFocus** method

♦ **Click, MouseDown, MouseMove**, and **MouseUp** events

For more information about the properties, methods, and events of the **CommandButton** control, search for "CommandButton Control" in MSDN Help.

Lab 2: Creating a Visual Basic Application

In Labs 2, 3, 4, 5, 7, 9, 10, 11, and 14, you will create a loan-payment-estimate application. You will create the full application in stages, each stage building on the code created in the previous lab. At the beginning of each lab, you can either continue with your own files or start with the files provided for you.

In this lab, you will begin the loan-payment-estimate application by creating a logon screen.

To see the demonstration "Lab 2 Solution," see the accompanying CD-ROM.

Estimated time to complete this lab: **30 minutes**

Objectives

After completing this lab, you will be able to:

◆ Create a simple application in Visual Basic.

◆ Create an event procedure.

◆ Retrieve object properties at run time.

To complete the exercises in this lab, you must have the required software. For detailed information about the labs and setup for the labs, see "Labs" in "About This Course."

The solution for this lab is located in the *<install folder>*\Labs\Lab02\Solution folder.

Prerequisites

There are no prerequisites for this lab.

Exercises

The following exercises provide practice in working with the concepts covered in this chapter:

◆ Exercise 1: Creating a Logon Screen

In this exercise, you will create a logon screen for the loan-payment-estimate application. You will start a new project, rename the form, place controls on the form, and set properties for the controls.

◆ Exercise 2: Adding Code to Enable and Disable a Button

In this exercise, you will add code that will enable the **OK** button only when both a user name and a password have been entered.

◆ Exercise 3 (Optional): Adding an Icon

In this exercise, you will add an icon to a form by using the **Image** control.

Exercise 1: Creating a Logon Screen

In this exercise, you will create a logon screen for the loan-payment-estimate application. You will start a new project, rename the form, place controls on the form, and set properties for the controls.

▶ **Start a new project**

1. Start Visual Basic from the **Start** menu (if Visual Basic isn't already running). Otherwise, on the **File** menu, click **New Project** to start Visual Basic.

2. Choose **Standard EXE**, and then click **OK**.

▶ **Add controls to the default form**

1. Add three **Label** controls to the form.

2. Add two **TextBox** controls to the form.

3. Add two **CommandButton** controls to the form.

4. Move and size the controls so they look like the following illustration.

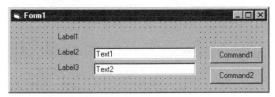

▶ **Set properties for the controls**

1. Select any control on the form.

2. In the Properties window, select the property for the control as listed in the following table.

3. Enter the new value for the property as specified in the following table.

Current name	Property	New value
Label1	Name	lblInstruction
	Caption	Type your name and password to log on.
Label2	Name	lblUserName
	Caption	&User Name
Label3	Name	lblPassword
	Caption	&Password
Text1	Name	txtUserName
	Text	<blank>
Text2	Name	txtPassword
	Text	<blank>
	PasswordChar	*
Command1	Name	cmdOK
	Caption	OK
	Default	True
Command2	Name	cmdCancel
	Caption	Cancel
	Cancel	True
Form1	Name	frmLogon
	Caption	Enter Program Password
	BorderStyle	1 - Fixed Single

Note At the top of the Properties window is a drop-down list of all of the controls on the current form. When setting properties on many different controls, it is often easier to use the drop-down list to switch between controls.

The resulting form should look something like the following illustration.

▶ **Add code to the cmdOK Click event**

1. Double-click the **cmdOK** command button. This opens the Code Editor window with the following code already inserted:

```
Private Sub cmdOK_Click()

End Sub
```

2. Add code to the **Click** event procedure to display a message box with the current values of the **User Name** and **Password** text boxes:

```
MsgBox "User Name = " & txtUserName.Text & _
    ", Password = " & txtPassword.Text
```

Note The space and underscore in the previous code is used to break a single statement across multiple lines. The ampersand is used to force the combining of two expressions.

3. Run the application. Type in a user name and a password, and then click **OK**. What happens?

4. Type in a different user name and password, and then press ENTER. What happens? Why?

5. Close the running application and return to Design mode.

To see answers to the previous questions, see Hint 2.1 in Appendix B.

▶ **Add code to the cmdCancel Click event**

1. Double-click the **cmdCancel** command button. This opens the Code Editor window with the following code already inserted:

```
Private Sub cmdCancel_Click()

End Sub
```

2. Add code to the **Click** event procedure to display a message box:

```
MsgBox "This is the Cancel button."
```

3. Run the application. Type in a user name and a password, and then click **Cancel**. What happens?

4. Type in a different user name and password, and then press ESC. What happens? Why?

5. Close the running application and return to Design mode.

To see answers to the previous questions, see Lab Hint 2.2 in Appendix B.

▶ **Name the project**

1. On the **Project** menu, click **Project1 Properties**.

2. In the **Project Name** box, type **LoanProject**, and click **OK**.

▶ **Save the project**

1. On the **File** menu, click **Save Project**.

2. When prompted to save the form, change the destination folder to *<install folder>*\Labs\Lab02, type **frmLogon** for the file name, and click **Save**.

3. When prompted to save the project, change the destination folder to *<install folder>*\Labs\Lab02, type **Loan** for the file name, and click **Save**.

Exercise 2: Adding Code to Enable and Disable a Button

In this exercise, you will add code that will enable the **OK** button only when both a user name and a password have been entered.

When you write an application, you should minimize the possibility of users making mistakes. One way to do this is to disable controls that, when selected would cause errors. For example, users shouldn't be able to click the **OK** button on the logon form until they enter a user name and a password.

▶ **Enable the OK button**

1. In the Properties window, set the **Enabled** property of the **cmdOK** command button to **False**.

2. Double-click the **txtUserName** text box.

   The Code Editor window opens to the **txtUserName_Change** event procedure.

3. Add the following lines of code to the **txtUserName Change** event:

```
If txtUserName.Text <> "" And txtPassword.Text <> "" Then
    cmdOK.Enabled = True
Else
    cmdOK.Enabled = False
End If
```

> **Note** There should be no spaces between quotes. By placing a space between the quotes, the condition in the **If** statement checks for the space character in the **Textbox** instead of a zero-length string.

4. Copy the code from the **txtUserName_Change** event to the **Change** event of the **txtPassword** text box.

5. Save and test your application. Is the **OK** button enabled?

6. Type a user name. Is the **OK** button enabled? Why?

7. Now, type a password. Is the **OK** button enabled? Why?

To see answers to the questions in steps 5 through 7, see Hint 2.3 in Appendix B.

Exercise 3 (Optional): Adding an Icon

In this exercise, you will add an icon to a form by using the **Image** control.

▶ **Add a graphic to the logon form**

1. Add an **Image** control to the upper-left side of the form.

2. Set the **Name** property of the **Image** control to **imgLogo**.

3. Set the **BorderStyle** property of the **Image** control to **1 - Fixed Single**.

4. Set the **Picture** property of the **Image** control to an icon by clicking the button (...) in the Properties window. The **Load Picture** dialog box will appear.

5. Select the Pc04.ico file from the *<install folder>*\Labs\Lab02\Solution folder and click **Open**.

6. Use the **LoadPicture** function to change the **Picture** property of the **Image** control in the **Click** event of the **Image** control.

```
imgLogo.Picture = LoadPicture("\Path\filename")
```

Use the Face03.ico file in the *<install folder>*\Labs\Lab02\Solution folder as the new filename.

7. Save and test your application. Which picture is displayed when the application starts?

8. Click the image. What happens?

To see answers to the questions in steps 7 and 8, see Hint 2.4 in Appendix B.

Self-Check Questions

See page 376 for answers.

1. In the following line of code, frmEdit is the _____, Caption is the _____, and Edit is the _____.

   ```
   frmEdit.Caption = "Edit"
   ```

   A. object, property, value
   B. object, method, value
   C. method, event, property
   D. method, object, value

2. You are writing a program and need to place the contents of the txtFirstName text box into a variable called CustomerName. Which of the following lines of code does this correctly?

   A. txtFirstName.Value = CustomerName
   B. CustomerName = txtFirstName.Value
   C. CustomerName = txtFirstName.Text
   D. CustomerName = txtFirstName.Caption

3. An error occurs when you enter the following code segment. What is causing the error?

   ```
   With txtName
       FontBold = True
       FontSize = 24
       Text = "Hello, World!"
   End With
   ```

   A. Only two properties can be set by using a **With** statement.
   B. The equal sign (=) is missing after txtName.
   C. Both "True" and "24" need to be enclosed in quotations.
   D. A period (.) is missing before each of the properties.

Chapter 3:
Working with Code and Forms

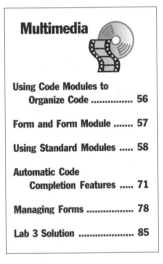
After your forms and controls are in place, you can write the code that ties the elements of your application together.

In this chapter, you will learn how code is stored in a Microsoft Visual Basic project. You will also learn how to simplify writing and editing code by using the editing tools available in Visual Basic. Finally, you will learn some code statements to manage forms and provide simple user interactions.

Objectives

After completing this chapter, you will be able to:

◆ Use the editing tools in the Visual Basic Code Editor window to write organized and well-documented code.

◆ Control the Visual Basic environment and customize it to your needs.

◆ Create message boxes.

◆ Use Visual Basic constants and named arguments.

◆ Differentiate between the **Load** and **Unload** statements.

◆ Use the **Show** and **Hide** methods.

◆ Control a program's closing routine.

Understanding Modules

One of the most important and overlooked processes in creating a Visual Basic application is designing code structure. Visual Basic stores code in containers called modules, which allow you to organize your code for increased performance and make it easier to maintain your code.

In this section, you will learn about the different types of code modules provided by Visual Basic.

To see the animation "Using Code Modules to Organize Code," see the accompanying CD-ROM.

Form Modules

Each form in an application has an associated form module (.frm file extension) that can contain:

◆ Property settings for the form and its controls.

Settings for a form are stored in text format within the .frm file. If you open the .frm file in a text editor, you can modify property settings for the form.

◆ Form-level variable declarations.

You can place variable, constant, type, and dynamic-link library (DLL) procedure declarations at the module level of form, class, or standard modules.

◆ Event procedures and form-level general procedures.

A **Sub, Function,** or **Event** procedure contains pieces of code that can be executed as a unit.

Note For information about form-level variable declarations and general procedures, see "Scope of Variables" on page 99 in Chapter 4, "Variables and Procedures."

In addition, you can set properties for the form and its controls through the Properties window.

The following illustration shows a form module for the form RedTop.

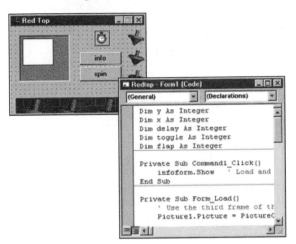

To see the demonstration "Form and Form Module," see the accompanying CD-ROM.

Standard Modules

When an application contains code that is shared by several forms, you should store it in a standard module. Code in a standard module can be public, making it available to all modules in the application. Procedures stored in a standard module are called general procedures.

Standard modules (.bas file extension) can contain public (available to the entire application) or private (module-level) declarations of variables, constants, types, external procedures, and global procedures. The code that is written in a standard module is not necessarily limited to a particular application; you can reuse code from a standard module in many different applications. For information about form-level variable declarations and general procedures, see "Scope of Variables" on page 99 in Chapter 4, "Variables and Procedures."

Note Procedures that you create in standard modules are public by default. Other code modules can then use these procedures. In contrast, procedures and functions specified as private are visible only in the module in which they are declared. Event procedures are private by default.

To see the demonstration "Using Standard Modules," see the accompanying CD-ROM.

Note Earlier versions of Visual Basic referred to a standard module as a code module.

▶ **To create a standard module**

♦ Click the **Add Form** button (down-arrow) on the toolbar, and then click **Module**.
 −or−

♦ Right-click in the Project Explorer window, click **Add,** and then click **Module** from the pop-up menu that appears.

Class Modules

The third type of code module is the class module. Class modules contain the definition of classes (property and method definitions) used to create new objects. These new objects can include customized properties and methods.

Examination of class modules is beyond the scope of this course, but class modules are covered in *Mastering Microsoft Visual Basic 6 Development.*

Using the Code Editor Window

The Visual Basic Code Editor window (also known as the Code window) is where you write Visual Basic code for your application. The Code Editor is like a highly specialized word processor with a number of features that make writing Visual Basic code easier.

In this section, you will learn about the features of the Visual Basic Code Editor window.

Code Editor Window Layout

The Code Editor window enables you to select, view, and work with procedures from form, standard, and code modules.

The following illustration shows the Code Editor window.

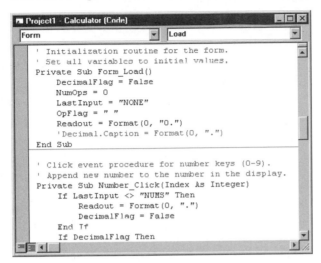

By default, all of the procedures for the module appear in the Code Editor window, with each separated by an optional procedure separator line. This is called Full Module view. Another option, the Procedure view, displays only one procedure at a time in the Code Editor window. You can choose the default view for the Code Editor window, depending on your preference.

▶ **To switch between Full Module view and Procedure view**

◆ On the lower-left corner of the Code Editor window, click the **Procedure View** button or the **Full Module View** button.

▶ **To set the default view for the Code Editor window**

1. On the **Tools** menu, click **Options**.

2. Click the **Editor** tab.

3. Set or clear the **Default to Full Module View** option.

▶ **To view event procedures for an object on a form**

◆ Double-click the object.

▶ **To view code for a module**

1. Right-click a form or standard module in the Project window.

2. Click **View Code**.

Viewing Multiple Code Modules

Because you write Visual Basic code in modules, Visual Basic lets you open a separate Code Editor window for each module that you select from the Project Explorer. By using this technique, you can view code in form, standard, and class modules simultaneously, and you can copy and paste code between modules.

Tip To move code from one Code Editor window to another Code Editor window, highlight the code and drag it into the other window. To copy code from one Code Editor window into another, press and hold CTRL while dragging the code between the windows. Release CTRL after releasing the mouse button.

The following illustration shows the code for two form modules displayed at the same time.

Using the Object List Box

The **Object** list box in the Code Editor window makes it easier to navigate to a specific object by displaying a list of all objects associated with the module.

The following illustration shows the **Object** list box in a form module.

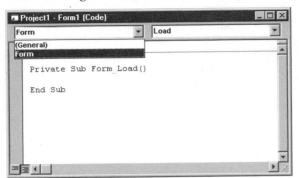

The code within each module is subdivided into separate sections for each object in the module. In a form module, the list includes a general section, a section for the form itself, and a section for each object contained on the form. For a class module, the list includes a general section and a class section. A standard module shows only a general section. You can switch between the sections by using the **Object** list box.

▶ **To open the Object list box**

◆ Click the arrow to the right of the **Object** list box.

Using the Procedure List Box

A module can contain several different procedures. You view the procedures by using the **Procedure** list box. The **Procedure** list box contains event names recognized by Visual Basic for the form or control that is selected in the **Object** list box. If an event procedure contains code, the event name appears in bold within the **Procedure** list box. When an event name is selected from the **Procedure** list box, the event procedure appears in the Code Editor window.

The following illustration shows the **Procedure** list box.

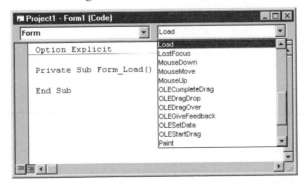

▶ **To open the Procedure list box**

♦ Click the arrow to the right of the **Procedure** list box.

Note All procedures in a module are displayed in the same Code Editor window.

Using the Split Bar

The split bar is located at the top of the vertical scroll bar. Dragging the split bar downward will split the Code Editor window into two horizontal panes. You can use the scroll bars within each pane to browse through each event procedure within the Code editor window. If you click an area within a pane, that pane will receive focus. The information that appears in the **Object** and **Procedure** list boxes will correspond to the event procedure within the pane that has focus. Dragging the split bar to the top of the window closes a pane.

The following illustration shows the Code Editor window separated into two panes by the split bar.

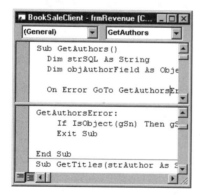

Other Code Navigation Features

It is difficult to navigate through an application that contains a lot of code. The **Object** and **Procedure** list boxes help you to locate procedures within your application. Visual Basic also assists you by providing the functionality to find text, browse to procedures in any active or referenced project or library, jump to a called procedure, or place bookmarks in code.

Finding Text

The **Find** command on the **Edit** menu is useful when searching for specific text. The following illustration shows how you can use the **Find** command to search for text in specific sections of code, such as the current selection, procedure, or module, or the entire project.

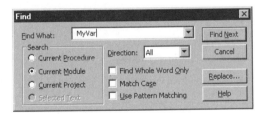

▶ **To find text**

1. On the **Edit** menu, click **Find**.

2. In the **Find What** box, type the text for which you want to search.

3. In the **Search** box, choose the section of code that you want to search.

4. Set the desired search options.

5. Click the **Find Next** button to find the next occurrence (if any) of the text.

Displaying Procedures by Using the Object Browser

The Object Browser displays the procedures that are available in any active or referenced project or library.

The following illustration shows the Object Browser.

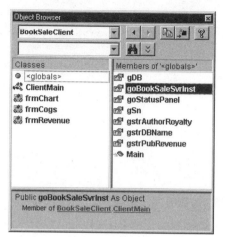

▶ To display a procedure in a project or library

1. On the **Standard** toolbar, click the **Object Browser** button, or press F2. The following illustration shows the **Object Browser** button.

2. In the **Project/Library** box, click the project or library containing the procedures that you want to view.

3. In the **Classes** list box, click the class or module name that contains the desired procedure.

4. From the **Members** list box, click the procedure name. On the **Object Browser** tollbar, click the **View Definition** button.

Viewing a Called Procedure

You can quickly view a procedure that is called by your code.

▶ To view a procedure that is called by your code

1. Position the insertion point within the called procedure.

2. Press SHIFT+F2.

3. Press CTRL+SHIFT+F2 to return to the previous location.

Note Visual Basic keeps track of the last eight lines that were accessed or edited. You can also access the **Last Position** command on the **View** menu to quickly navigate to a previous location in your code.

Using Bookmarks

Bookmarks are placeholders in the Code Editor window. You can set bookmarks to mark points in the code that you want to access quickly.

▶ **To set a bookmark**

1. Position the cursor at the desired line of code.

2. On the **Edit** menu, select **Bookmarks,** then click **Toggle.**

▶ **To clear a bookmark**

1. Position the cursor at the line of code that is marked.

2. On the **Edit** menu, select **Bookmarks,** then click **Toggle.**

▶ **To jump to a bookmark**

♦ On the **Edit** menu, select **Bookmarks,** then click **Next Bookmark** or **Previous Bookmark.**

▶ **To clear all bookmarks**

♦ On the **Edit** menu, select **Bookmarks,** then click **Clear All Bookmarks.**

The following illustration shows a bookmark placed in a code window.

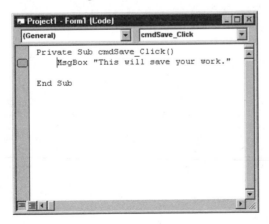

Code Documentation and Formatting

In this section, you will learn about editing features in Visual Basic that make your code easier to read. These features include breaking and combining lines of code, adding comments to code, and following naming conventions in Visual Basic.

Indenting

Indenting is used to differentiate parts of code, such as loops and conditional branches. To indent a selection of code statements, press TAB or click the **Indent** command on the **Edit** menu. Similarly, pressing SHIFT+TAB or clicking the **Outdent** command repositions the lines one tab stop to the left. The following example shows indented code:

```
Private Sub ChangeSignal()
    If imgGreen.Visible = True Then
        imgGreen.Visible = False
        imgYellow.Visible = True
    ElseIf imgYellow.Visible = True Then
        imgYellow.Visible = False
        imgRed.Visible = True
    Else
        imgRed.Visible = False
        imgGreen.Visible = True
    End If
End Sub
```

Note The **Editor** tab in the **Options** dialog box contains settings for indenting, such as turning automatic indenting on or off and changing the width of a tab from the default of four spaces.

Using the Line-Continuation Character

You can use the line-continuation character, the underscore (_), to break up a single code statement into multiple lines. This makes the code statement easier to read because it's fully contained within the Code Editor window.

The line-continuation character is placed after a space in the statement, as shown in the following example code:

```
MsgBox "User Name = " & txtUserName.Text & _
   ", Password = " & txtPassword.Text
```

Note The line-continuation character cannot be used within a text string. Comments cannot follow a line-continuation character on the same line.

Adding Comments

Adding comments to code makes it easier for someone else to determine what the code does. It also helps you to understand the code at some later date. Visual Basic offers two methods for adding comments to code. Because Visual Basic ignores anything following a single quote ('), comments can be placed on their own line or at the end of a line of code. Also, preceding any line of code with Rem (an abbreviation of "Remark") instructs Visual Basic to ignore that code.

The following illustration demonstrates both types of comments, which appear in green text by default in the Code Editor window.

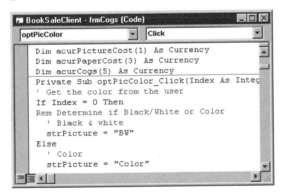

You can turn entire sections of text or code into comments, or you can turn commented code blocks back into executable code.

▶ **To comment on a section**

1. Select the lines of text or code on which to comment.

2. On the **Edit** toolbar, click **Comment Block**.

▶ **To restore code**

1. Select the comment block in the Code Editor window.
2. On the **Edit** toolbar, click **Uncomment Block**.

Note You may want to add comments on a separate line—either before or after the line(s) of code that performs an action. This keeps individual lines shorter and enables them to fit within the Code Editor window. You can then view the entire line of code without scrolling outside the window.

Using Visual Basic Naming Conventions

As you write code in Visual Basic, you name many elements, such as **Sub** and **Function** procedures, variables, and constants. The names of the declared procedures, variables, and constants must adhere to the following guidelines:

◆ They must begin with a letter.

◆ They can't contain embedded periods or type-declaration characters (special characters that specify a data type).

◆ They can't be the same as restricted keywords.

For more information about naming procedures, variables, and constants, search for "Visual Basic (Coding Conventions)" in MSDN Help.

Note A restricted keyword is a word that Visual Basic uses as part of its language. This includes predefined statements (such as **If** and **Loop**), functions (such as **Len** and **Abs**), and operators (such as **Or** and **Mod**).

Setting Environment Options

The environment options of Visual Basic give you a great deal of control over how Visual Basic looks and operates. When you make changes to the options, your changes are saved in the registry file and are loaded every time Visual Basic starts.

▶ **To change environment options**

1. On the **Tools** menu, click **Options**.

   The **Options** dialog box appears.

2. Click the **Environment** tab.

   The following illustration shows the **Environment** tab in the **Options** dialog box.

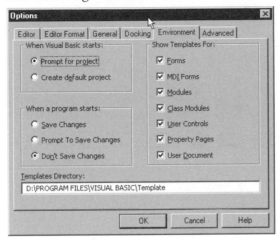

3. Change the desired settings and click **OK**.

Options on the **Environment** tab enable you to choose the behavior of Visual Basic at startup as well as determining how program changes are saved when a program is run. In addition, you can control what templates are available in Visual Basic.

For more information about the options on the **Environment** tab, search for "Environment Tab (Options Dialog Box)" in MSDN Help.

Setting Code Formatting Options

The **Editor Format** tab includes a list of the types of text found in code and list boxes to specify attributes for selected text types. These attributes include the ability to specify code and code-window color, font and font size, and whether the Margin Indicator Bar appears. Changes made to the setting for the Code Editor apply to all projects.

The following illustration shows the **Editor Format** tab on the **Options** dialog box.

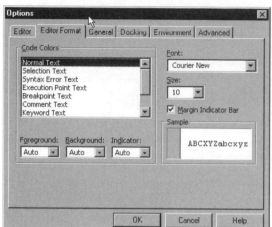

Tip	
Option	**Purpose**
Code Colors	Determines the foreground and background colors used for the type of text selected in the list box.
Text List	Lists the text items that have customizable colors.
Foreground	Specifies the foreground color for the text selected in the Color Text List.
Background	Specifies the background color for text selected in the Color Text List.
Indicator	Specifies the margin indicator color.
Font	Specifies the font used for all code.
Size	Specifies the size of the font used for code.
Margin Indicator Bar	Hides or displays the margin indicator bar.
Sample	Displays sample text for the font, size, and color settings.

For more information about code formatting options, search for "Editor Format Tab (Options Dialog Box)" in MSDN Help.

Automatic Code Completion Features

Visual Basic makes writing code much easier with features that can automatically fill in statements, properties, and arguments. As code is entered, the editor displays lists of appropriate choices, statement or function prototypes, or values. The editor even displays the syntax for statements and functions.

To see the demonstration "Automatic Code Completion Features," see the accompanying CD-ROM.

Options for enabling or disabling these and other code settings are available on the **Editor** tab of the **Options** dialog box, which you can access through the **Options** command on the **Tools** menu.

The following illustration shows the **Editor** tab on the **Options** dialog box.

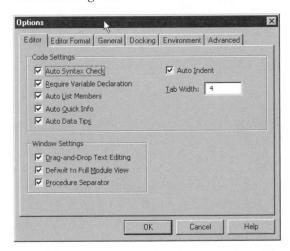

For more information about automatic code completion features, search for "Editor Tab (Options Dialog Box)" in MSDN Help.

Interacting with the User

In Windows-based applications, dialog boxes are used to prompt the user for data that the application needs before continuing or to give information to the user. Dialog boxes are a special type of form object that you can create in one of three ways:

◆ Predefined dialog boxes can be created from code by using the **MsgBox** or **InputBox** functions.

- Customized dialog boxes can be created by using a standard form or by customizing an existing dialog box. For more information, see "Working with Forms" on page 34 in Chapter 2, "Visual Basic Fundamentals."

- Standard dialog boxes, such as **Print** and **File Open**, can be created by using the **CommonDialog** control.

One of the simplest ways to get information to and from the user is to include a message box using the **MsgBox** function, and to query the user with the **InputBox** function.

Note Multiple forms are often used for gathering more sophisticated information. When necessary, these forms are called to obtain user input or display information, in much the same way dialog boxes are used in Microsoft Office applications.

Using the MsgBox Function

Message boxes are a simple, fast way to query the user for simple information or to allow the user to make decisions about the program's course. Message boxes display text and provide buttons with which the user can respond.

In this section, you will learn how to use the **MsgBox** function to create a message box. You will learn how to set the appearance of the message box and how to get input from the user.

MsgBox Arguments

To set the appearance of a message box, you pass information, in the form of arguments, to the **MsgBox** function. Examples include the message text, a constant (numeric value) to determine the style of the dialog box, and a title. Styles are available with various combinations of buttons and icons to make creating dialog boxes easy.

The **MsgBox** function uses the following syntax:

    MsgBox(prompt [, buttons] [, title] [, helpFilc, context])

The arguments for the **MsgBox** function are described in the following table.

Argument	Description
prompt	Text that contains a message to the user.
buttons	Determines the number of and type of message box buttons as well as the type of symbol that appears on the message box. For more information about using **MsgBox** function constants, search for "MsgBox arguments" in MSDN Help.
title	The text that appears in the title bar of the message box.
helpFile	A string that identifies the Help file to use to provide context-sensitive Help for the dialog box. If **helpfile** is provided, **context** must also be provided.
context	Numeric expression that identifies the specific topic in the Help file that appears. If **context** is provided, **helpfile** must also be provided.

Note Any arguments that are not enclosed in square brackets are required. You must supply a value for these arguments. Arguments that are enclosed in brackets are optional. If values are not supplied for these arguments, Visual Basic will use the default value. For more information on arguments, see "Named Arguments" on page 77 in this chapter and "Passing Arguments to Procedures" on page 121 in Chapter 4, "Variables and Procedures."

The following illustration shows a simple message box that is generated by the **MsgBox** function.

The following example code displays the previous message box:

```
MsgBox "There no are users with that I.D.," _
    & vbCrLf & "please retry.", _
    vbExclamation, "Signon Error"
```

Note The **vbCrLf** string constant is the same as **Chr(13)** & **Chr(10)**; this forces a carriage return–linefeed combination, which places any text that follows on the next line.

Note For user input that requires more than clicking a button, use the **InputBox** function.

Using Returned Values

Often the **MsgBox** function is used to get a simple response from the user. You can assign the value returned by the **MsgBox** function to a variable and then write code to handle the response.

The following illustration shows a simple message box.

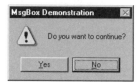

The following sample code displays a message box and then conditionally performs one of two tasks, based upon the button clicked. To copy this code for use in your own projects, see "Using Message Boxes" on the accompanying CD-ROM.

```
Dim strMsg As String
Dim strTitle As String
Dim lngStyle As Long
Dim intResponse As Integer

strMsg = "Do you want to continue?"
lngStyle = vbYesNo + vbExclamation + vbDefaultButton2
strTitle = "MsgBox Demonstration"

intResponse = MsgBox(strMsg, lngStyle, strTitle)

If intResponse = vbYes Then
    'User chose Yes button
Else
    'User chose No button
End If
```

In the previous code sample, the lngStyle variable combines Visual Basic constants to determine the style of the message box being displayed. A Visual Basic constant was also used to evaluate the user's response to the message box.

For information about using constants in Visual Basic, see "Predefined Visual Basic Constants" on page 76 in this chapter.

Using the InputBox Function

Input boxes are an easy way for you to ask the user for input that can't be answered by clicking a button.

The following illustration shows a simple input box that prompts the user for a name.

```
RetValue = _
  InputBox(prompt:=Please enter your name.", _
  title:="InputBox Demo", default="Bob")
```

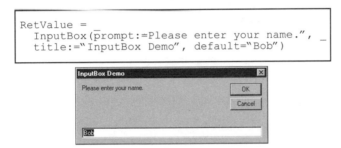

The **InputBox** function generates a dialog box that allows the user to enter text. To use the **InputBox** function, use the following syntax:

InputBox(prompt[, title][, default][, xPos][, yPos][, helpFile, context])

The following example code displays a simple input box:

```
strFileName = InputBox("Enter file to open:", "File Open")
```

The following illustration shows the input box that is generated by the previous code.

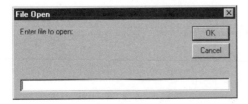

Note For user input that requires no more than clicking a button, use the **MsgBox** function. When using the **InputBox** function, there is little control over the components of the dialog box. Only the following can be changed: the text in the title bar, the command prompt displayed to the user, the position of the dialog box on the screen, and whether or not the dialog box displays a **Help** button. The **MsgBox** function provides more control over the appearance of the dialog box.

Working with Code Statements

The predefined constants in Visual Basic simplify your code by acting as aliases for numeric constants. Named arguments make your code easier to read and offer other advantages as well. In this section, you will learn how to make your code easier to read through the use of these coding features.

Predefined Visual Basic Constants

Visual Basic recognizes a number of predefined constants that you can use anywhere in code in place of the actual numeric values. These constants make the code easier to read and write. When you use constants, your code will be compatible with later versions of Visual Basic, which may use different values for the constants.

The following example code sets the window state of a form to maximized:

```
frmLogOn.WindowState = 2
```

The same task can be performed by using a Visual Basic constant, as shown in the following example code:

```
frmLogOn.WindowState = vbMaximized
```

The result is a statement that's easier to read and understand.

Combining Visual Basic Constants

Visual Basic constants can be combined in cases in which a function accepts a single argument. For example, to use the **MsgBox** function, use the following syntax:

MsgBox(prompt[, buttons][, title][, helpfile, context])

To provide an argument to the function that will create a message box containing **OK** and **Cancel** buttons and an exclamation point icon, you can combine the corresponding Visual Basic constants, as shown in the following example code:

```
MsgBox "Invalid Password", _
    buttons:=vbOKCancel + vbExclamation
```

> **Note** Because each Visual Basic constant represents a value, combining these constants can specify more than one option.

Named Arguments

Arguments can be passed to methods, functions, and procedures either by position or by name.

Named arguments have several advantages over positional arguments. As implied by their name, positional arguments are specified by passing arguments in a predefined order. When a function accepts multiple arguments, you must provide the associated values in the correct order, using comma placeholders for any arguments that you skip. With the multiple arguments, the possibility of error is increased, and the resulting code is difficult to read. The following example code shows the **MsgBox** function, using positional arguments:

```
MsgBox "The password is invalid!", vbOKCancel + vbExclamation + _
    vbMsgBoxHelpButton, "Sign In", "SignIn.hlp", 3
```

In contrast, named arguments, which are predefined in the object library, can be specified in any order. The argument's name is indicative of its function. Using named arguments reduces errors and makes code easier to read and understand. The following example code uses named constants to provide the same functionality as the previous code example:

```
MsgBox prompt:="The password is invalid!", _
    buttons:=vbOKCancel + vbExclamation + _
    vbMsgBoxHelpButton, _
    title:="Sign In", _
    helpfile:="SignIn.hlp", _
    context:=3
```

Note Named arguments are not supported by all functions and methods in Visual Basic. To see whether a Visual Basic function or method supports named arguments, search for the individual function or method name in MSDN Help.

Managing Forms

In most applications, the user interface is composed of multiple windows or dialog boxes. Visual Basic provides a variety of methods and statements for showing, hiding, loading, and unloading forms.

In this section, you will learn how to manage the forms in a Visual Basic application so that the user can navigate between, and respond logically to, multiple windows and dialog boxes.

To see the demonstration "Managing Forms," see the accompanying CD-ROM.

Displaying Forms

You can use both the **Show** method and the **Load** statement to load a form into memory; however, the **Show** method displays the form, while the **Load** statement does not.

Using the Show Method

The **Show** method displays a **Form** object. If the form is not already loaded, the **Show** method will automatically load it for you. To use the **Show** method, use the following syntax:

> **object.***Show* style, ownerform

The style parameter is an integer value that determines if the form being shown is modal or modeless. A modal form requires the user to take some action before the focus can switch to another form within an application. A modeless form does not require a response from the user before the focus can be switched to another form within an application. The ownerform parameter specifies the component that "owns" the form being shown. Both the style and ownerform parameters are optional.

The following example code uses the **Show** method:

```
frmCustomerInfo.Show
```

Using the Load Statement

The **Load** statement loads a form into memory but does not display it. To use the **Load** statement, use the following syntax:

Load object

The following example code uses the **Load** statement:

```
Load frmCustomerInfo
```

Note You don't need to use the **Load** statement with forms unless you want to load a form without displaying it. Any reference to a form automatically loads the form, if the form is not already loaded. After the form is loaded, its properties and controls can be altered by the application, whether or not the form is actually visible.

Using the Load Event

The **Load** event occurs when a form is loaded into memory, either through the use of the **Load** statement or the **Show** method.

Typically, you use a **Load** event procedure to initialize the form. For example, the **Form_Load** event can run code that specifies default settings for controls, indicates contents to be loaded into **ComboBox** or **ListBox** controls, and initializes form-level variables.

Modal and Modeless Forms

The **Show** method enables a form to appear as either modal or modeless. Like a message box, a modal form doesn't allow the user to interact with other forms in the application until the modal form has been unloaded. A modeless form allows the user to switch to another form or dialog box.

The **style** argument for the **Show** method determines if the form is modal or modeless. If the style is **vbModeless**, the form is modeless; if the style is **vbModal**, the form is modal, as shown in the following example code:

```
'Form is modeless
frmCustomerInfo.Show vbModeless

'Form is modal
frmCustomerInfo.Show vbModal
```

Hiding and Unloading Forms

If you need to remove a form from the screen, you can either hide or unload the form. The **Hide** method will make the form invisible on the screen, but the form will still be loaded in memory. The **Unload** statement will remove the form from memory, and the form will no longer be displayed.

Using the Hide Method

The **Hide** method will cause the form to be invisible, athough the form remains in memory.

To use the **Hide** method, use the following syntax:

object.*Hide*

The following example code invokes the **Hide** method:

```
frmMain.Hide
```

Note If the form isn't loaded when the **Hide** method is invoked, the **Hide** method loads the form but doesn't display it.

Using the Unload Statement

Unloading a form removes the form from the display and releases its memory. You can also unload a form, and load it again to reset its properties to their original values. The **Unload** statement:

◆ Unloads a form or control from memory.
◆ Releases the display component of the form from memory.

- Resets the form and control properties to their original values. If any changes were made to the form, either by the program or by the user, these changes are lost.
- Invokes the **Unload** event.
- Terminates execution of the application if the unloaded form is the only form in the application.

To use the **Unload** statement, use the following syntax:

Unload object

The following example code invokes the **Unload** statement:

```
Unload frmMain
```

Note You can use the Me keyword to reference the current form. For example, Unload Me unloads the current form from memory.

Note An application does not end until all forms are unloaded from memory. The **End** statement removes all forms from memory and ends the application.

Using the Unload Event

Use an **Unload** event procedure to verify that the form should be unloaded or to specify actions that you want to take place when the form is unloaded. Any form-level validation code needed for closing the form or saving its data to a file can also be included. The **Unload** event occurs when:

- The form is unloaded by using the **Unload** statement.
- The form is closed by the user either clicking the **Close** command on the application menu or clicking the **Close** button on the application title bar.

Note The Unload event does not occur if the form is removed from memory by the **End** statement.

Note If you plan to use a form repeatedly, it's faster to hide and show the form, rather than load and unload it.

Example of Form Display Capabilities

The following example code controls the startup of a program. It loads and displays a splash screen, loads the first form, hides the splash screen, and then displays the first form.

```
Sub Main()
  frmSplashScreen.Show
  Load frmFirstForm
  frmSplashScreen.Hide
  frmFirstForm.Show
End Sub
```

Ending an Application

You can end execution of your program by unloading the last form in your application or by using the **End** statement. The **End** statement terminates execution of your application and unloads all forms from memory.

Ensuring an Orderly Shutdown with the Unload Event

In Windows, the user can close forms by clicking the **Close** command on the application menu or by clicking the **Close** button on the application title bar. If the user unloads the last open form, the application terminates. This can be undesirable if the user hasn't entered all required information or if any required finish-up code hasn't been executed. To ensure that everything is unloaded, you should place the **End** statement in the **Unload** event of the main form, after a procedure for the **Unload** event that runs any "cleanup" code, as shown in the following example code:

```
Sub Form_Unload()
  [Final code statements]
  End
End Sub
```

Understanding Form Events

Forms support a number of events that fire at various times throughout the life of the form and the life of the application. These events include the following:

Initialize	Activate	LostFocus	QueryUnload	Terminate
Load	GotFocus	Deactivate	Unload	

Initialize

The **Initialize** event occurs when an application creates an instance of a form before the form is loaded or displayed. The code that you place in the **Form_Initialize** event procedure is therefore the first code that is executed when a form is created. In the initialization state, the form exists as an object, but it has no window. The **Initialize** event occurs only the first time a form is loaded, unless the form is set to **Nothing**, as shown in the following example code:

```
Set frmCustomerInfo = Nothing
```

Load

The **Load** event fires each time a form loads—when the **Load** method is used, the **Show** method is used, or a control is referenced on a form that has not yet been loaded.

Activate

The **Activate** event occurs when the form receives focus. As a user moves from one form to another in a modeless environment, the **Activate** event fires.

GotFocus

A form receives a **GotFocus** event only if no controls on the form are capable of receiving the focus. Typically, you use a **GotFocus** event procedure to specify the actions that occur when a control or form first receives focus.

> **Note** If you add code to the form's **Activate** event, the **GotFocus** event will not fire.

LostFocus

Like the **GotFocus** event, the **LostFocus** event will only fire if no controls on the form are capable of losing focus.

Deactivate

The **Deactivate** event occurs when the form loses focus.

> **Note** If you add code to the **LostFocus** event, the **Deactivate** event will not fire.

QueryUnload

The **QueryUnload** event fires when the form receives a command to unload. This event provides developers with the ability to evaluate how the form received the request to unload and cancel the unload process. The **QueryUnload** event will fire before the **Unload** event. If the **QueryUnload** event cancels the unload request, the **Unload** event will not fire.

Unload

The **Unload** event fires each time a form is unloaded from memory—when an application ends, by using the **End** statement, or when the form is explicitly unloaded with the **Unload** method.

Terminate

The only way to release all memory and resources is to unload the form and then set all references to **Nothing**. Your form receives its **Terminate** event just before it is destroyed (set to **Nothing**) or the application ends. If the **End** statement is used, however, the **Terminate** event will not fire.

Order of Execution

The events listed previously execute in a specific order. It is important to understand this order when deciding where to place code that initializes controls, prompts the user to save changes, or closes database connections. The following list describes the general flow of event execution:

1. **Initialize** (fires once when the form is first referenced)
2. **Load** (fires every time the form loads)
3. **Activate** (fires whenever the form is activated from within the program)
4. **GotFocus** (fires only if no controls on the form can receive focus)
5. **LostFocus** (fires when focus changes to another form)
6. **Deactivate** (fires when the form in no longer active within the program)
7. **QueryUnload** (fires when the form receives an unload command)
8. **Unload** (fires after the **QueryUnload** event)
9. **Terminate** (fires when the form is set to **Nothing** or the program ends)

Lab 3: Working with Forms

In this lab, you will add functionality to the loan project that you started in Lab 2. You will create a shell for the main application form. From that shell, you will load the logon form and then show the main form of the application. You can continue to work with the files that you created in Lab 2, or you can use the files provided for you in the *<install folder>*\Labs\Lab03 folder.

To see the demonstration of "Lab 3 Solution," see the accompanying CD-ROM.

Estimated time to complete this lab: **30 minutes**

Objectives

After completing this lab, you will be able to:

◆ Add a new form to an existing project.

◆ Change the startup form of a project.

◆ Load and display a form from another form.

To complete the exercises in this lab, you must have the required software. For detailed information about the labs and setup for the labs, see "Labs" in "About This Course."

The solution for this lab is located in the *<install folder>*\Labs\Lab03\Solution folder.

Prerequisites

There are no prerequisites for this lab.

Exercises

The following exercises provide practice in working with the concepts covered in this chapter:

◆ Exercise 1: Adding the Main Form

In this exercise, you will add a form, frmMain, to the project. This form will eventually become the main form of the application. For now, frmMain will be used to load frmLogon.

◆ Exercise 2: Closing Forms and Ending an Application

In this exercise, you will add code to close the logon form when **OK** or **Cancel** is clicked, and to end the application when **Done** is clicked.

◆ Exercise 3: Adding a Message Box

In this exercise, you will add code to the main form that verifies that the user wants to exit the application. You'll also set a property on the logon form to center the form when it is shown.

Exercise 1: Adding the Main Form

In this exercise, you will add a form, frmMain, to the project. This form will eventually become the main form of the application. For now, frmMain will be used to load frmLogon.

▶ **Open the loan application project**

◆ Open either the loan application project on which you have been working or the loan application project located in the *<install folder>*\Labs\Lab03 folder.

▶ **Add a new form to the project**

1. On the **Project** menu, click **Add Form**.

2. In the **Add Form** dialog box, click **Form**, and then click **Open**.

A new form should be added to the project and displayed in the Visual Basic environment.

3. Set the form properties as shown in the following table.

Property	Setting
(Name)	frmMain
Caption	Loan Payment Estimate
BorderStyle	1 - Fixed Single
MinButton	True

▶ **Add controls to frmMain**

1. Add a command button to frmMain that will close the form.

Your form should look similar to the following illustration:

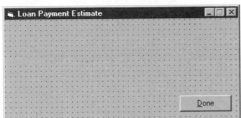

2. Set the properties for the command button as shown in the following table.

Property	Setting
(Name)	cmdDone
Caption	&Done
Cancel	True

▶ **Show the logon form**

1. Double-click anywhere on the frmMain form.

   The Code Editor window appears with the following code segment:

   ```
   Private Sub Form_Load()

   End Sub
   ```

2. Within this procedure, add a line of code to display the logon form modally.

   To see an example of how your code should look, see Hint 3.1 in Appendix B.

▶ **Change the startup form**

1. On the **Project** menu, click **LoanProject Properties**.

2. In the **Startup Object** drop-down list box, select **frmMain,** and then click **OK**.

▶ **Save and test the application**

1. Save the project.

2. Run the application. Type a user name and password, and click **OK**. What happens? Why doesn't the logon form disappear?

   To see the answers to the questions in Step 2, see Hint 3.2 in Appendix B.

3. Close the running application and return to Design mode.

Exercise 2: Closing Forms and Ending an Application

In this exercise, you will add code to close the logon form when **OK** or **Cancel** is clicked, and to end the application when the **Done** button of the Main form is clicked.

▶ **Unload the logon form when the user clicks OK on frmLogon**

- ◆ Add the following code to the **Click** event procedure of the **cmdOK** button on **frmLogon** to close the form after displaying the message box:

  ```
  Unload frmLogon
  ```

▶ **End the application when the user clicks Cancel on frmLogon, or Done on frmMain**

1. Add the following code to the **Click** event procedure of the **cmdCancel** button on **frmLogon** to end the application:

   ```
   End
   ```

2. Add the following code to the **Click** event procedure of the **cmdDone** button on **frmMain** to unload the form:

   ```
   Unload frmMain
   ```

3. Add the following code to the **Unload** event procedure of **frmMain** to end the application:

   ```
   End
   ```

▶ **Save and test the application**

1. Save the project to the *<install folder>*\Labs\Lab03 folder.

2. Run the application. Type a user name and password. Click **OK**. What happens?

3. Now click **Done**. What happens?

   To see the answers to the questions in Steps 2 and 3, see Hint 3.3 in Appendix B.

4. Close the running application and return to Design mode.

Exercise 3: Adding a Message Box

In this exercise, you will add code to the main form that verifies that the user wants to exit the application. You'll also set a property on the logon form to center the form when it is shown.

Instead of ending the application in the **Unload** event of the main form, you can enable the user to choose between closing the application or continuing to use it.

▶ **Query the user before exiting the application**

◆ Edit the code in the **Form_Unload** event procedure of **frmMain** to appear as follows:

```
Dim iAnswer As Integer

iAnswer = MsgBox ("Are you sure you're done?", vbYesNo)
If iAnswer = vbNo Then
    Cancel = True
Else
    End
End If
```

▶ **Center the forms**

1. Set the **frmLogon** and **frmMain StartUpPosition** properties to the center of the screen (**2 – CenterScreen**).

2. Save and test the application.

Self-Check Questions

See page 378 for answers.

1. You are writing several Sub procedures that will be accessed from several forms. What type of module should be used?

A. Form

B. Standard

C. Class

D. Project

2. Which of the following lines of code displays a message box titled "Invalid File Name" and a message indicating that the chosen filename was not valid?

A. intReturnValue = MsgBox ("The selected file name was not valid", vbOKOnly, "Invalid File Name")

B. intReturnValue = MsgBox (vbOKOnly, "The selected file name was not valid", "Invalid File Name")

C. intReturnValue = MsgBox ("The selected file name was not valid", "Invalid File Name", vbOKOnly)

D. intReturnValue = MsgBox ("Invalid File Name", "The selected file name was not valid", vbOKOnly)

3. A form's Load event occurs:

A. As the result of the use of a **Load** statement.

B. The first time that a form's **Show** method is used.

C. The first time that the form is referenced, if it isn't loaded.

D. When each of the above occurs.

4. The End statement terminates:

A. Only the form that contains it.

B. All of the forms in a module.

C. The last form opened.

D. All forms and modules.

Chapter 4:
Variables and Procedures

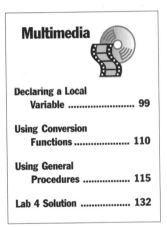

Multimedia

In this chapter, you will learn how to write code in Microsoft Visual Basic. The code that you write adds functionality to the forms and controls. You place code into procedures in order to perform various tasks, and you use variables both inside and outside of procedures to store data.

Objectives

After completing this chapter, you will be able to:

◆ Explain the various data types used when declaring variables.

◆ Declare private and public variables.

◆ Convert values to specific data types.

◆ Use public variables to enable use of data in multiple forms.

◆ Describe the difference between a variable and a constant.

◆ Differentiate between a **Sub** procedure and a **Function** procedure.

◆ Create a **Function** procedure that accepts arguments and returns a value.

◆ Describe how a Standard module differs from a Form module.

◆ Add a Standard module to a project to store general procedures and variables.

◆ Use Visual Basic functions to manipulate text strings and return the current date and time.

Overview of Variables

In this section, you will learn about variables, data types in Visual Basic, and conventions for naming variables. Variables store values that can change during the execution of your application. When you use a variable in Visual Basic, memory is reserved for the variable so that your application can access and manipulate its value. You will use various kinds of variables to store different data types. For example, some variables can hold numbers, text, or the Boolean values **True** or **False**.

Constants are similar to variables in Visual Basic, except that their values cannot be changed at run time. The value of a constant is always set at design time.

Introduction to Variables

In Visual Basic, you use variables to temporarily store values during the execution of an application. Variables have a name (the word you use to refer to the value that the variable contains) and a data type (which determines the kind of data that the variable can store).

Variables can be used in many ways, including:

◆ As a counter that stores the number of times a procedure or code block executes.

◆ As a temporary storage for property values.

◆ As a place to hold a value returned from a function.

◆ As a place to store directory or file names.

You can use variables to store data that originated from:

◆ An expression, as shown in the following example code:

```
strNewMessage = "You have new Mail!"
intCalcValue = intTotal - intReadMail
```

◆ Input from the user, as shown in the following example code:

```
strUserName = txtName.Text
```

◆ An object, as shown in the following example code:

```
Set x = frmMainForm
```

◆ A property value, as shown in the following example code:

```
strColor = frmMainForm.BackColor
```

◆ A value returned by a method or function, as shown in the following example code:

```
varMyDate = CDate(txtDate.Text)
```

Understanding Visual Basic Data Types

Visual Basic variables can store strings of text, numbers, objects, or unknown data types. For efficiency, Visual Basic provides variables that store specific data types.

There are two data types that store text:

◆ **String (variable length)**
◆ **String (fixed length)**

There are four data types that store numbers:

◆ **Integer**
◆ **Long**
◆ **Single**
◆ **Double**

There is one data type that stores the values **True** or **False**:

◆ **Boolean**

Other data types include:

◆ **Variant**
◆ **Object**
◆ **Currency**
◆ **Date**

For more information about Visual Basic data types, search for "Declaring Variables with Data Types" in MSDN Help.

Selecting a Data Type

Visual Basic does not require that you explicitly select a data type when you declare a variable. Nevertheless, it's a good idea to do so; it will make your applications more reliable, and they will require less memory.

By default, Visual Basic variables are **Variant** data types. A **Variant** data type can store any kind of value, including text, numbers, objects, and null. Although you can utilize **Variants** in some instances, they can also have drawbacks. For example, the **Variant** data type requires a large amount of memory (22 or more bytes when storing characters) compared to other data types. Also, you sacrifice speed because Visual Basic must determine and convert **Variant** values. For information about automatic data type conversion, see "Converting Data Types" on page 109 in this chapter.

By using the appropriate data type for a variable, you make your code more efficient and help to avoid data-conversion errors. For example, Visual Basic can process integers faster than variants, so it would be better to use an **Integer** data type to store a value of 10.

Another consideration is numeric accuracy. Because computers store values in binary format (Base2), there are some inherent inaccuracies when a computer makes calculations, especially those involving decimals. Calculations based on currency values are more accurate than either of the floating-point data types (**Single** and **Double**), and calculations based on double precision are more accurate than single precision.

Note When you store whole numbers in **Variant** variables, Visual Basic uses the most compact representation possible. For example, if you store a small number without a decimal fraction, the **Variant** uses an **Integer** representation for the value. If the number is very large or has a fractional component, a **Double** value will be used.

For more information about the amount of memory a **Variant** uses, see "Advanced Variant Topics" in MSDN Help.

Naming Variables

When you declare a variable, it's important to develop a naming strategy. Both clarity and consistency are important, especially when others will need to read or maintain your code.

Naming Rules

Variables follow the same naming rules as forms and controls. In large programs especially, it's a good idea to give variables meaningful, descriptive names.

Variable names:

◆ Must begin with an alphabetic character.

◆ May not contain spaces.

◆ Cannot contain an embedded period or type-declaration character (%, &, !, #, @, or $).

◆ Must be unique within the same scope.

Tip Try to use names that are indicative of the variable's purpose without being cumbersome. Capitalizing the first letter of a word within a variable (for example, naming a variable strUserInput rather than struserinput) makes it easier to interpret a variable's purpose. Another key point is that although typing in a long variable name can be tedious when coding, it will make your code more readable and easier to maintain, which is worthwhile in most cases.

Naming Conventions

Like naming conventions for controls and forms, you should use proper naming conventions for variables; this makes your code easier to read and maintain. It is common to add a prefix, which is an abbreviation of the data type.

The following table lists suggested variable name prefixes.

Data type	Prefix
Boolean	bln
Byte	byt
Currency	cur
Date	dt
Double	dbl
Integer	int
Long	lng
Object	[Use the prefix of the object—frm, txt, and so on.]
Single	sng
String	str
Variant	var

Another common practice is to prefix the variable name with an abbreviation representing the scope of the variable. For example, use g for Global, m for Module/Form, and l for Local. For more information about scope, see "Scope of Variables" on page 99 in this chapter.

Declaring Variables

In this section, you will learn about statements necessary to declare variables in your application. You will also learn about the benefits of using the **Option Explicit** statement.

Using the Dim Statement

Visual Basic reserves space in memory for variables that you declare. However, Visual Basic does not require that you declare a variable before you use it. When Visual Basic encounters an undeclared variable, it assigns it the default variable type (**Variant**) and the value empty (""). This is called implicit declaration.

Implicit declaration is convenient, but it limits control over variables. It is better coding practice to explicitly declare your variables. To declare a variable explicitly, you use the **Dim** statement with the following syntax:

Dim variablename [*As* type]

The **As** clause in the **Dim** statement lets you specify the data type when the variable is declared, as shown in the following example code:

```
Dim strUserInput As String
Dim intProcCount As Integer
```

After the variable is created with the **Dim** statement, Visual Basic automatically initializes numeric variables to 0, and text strings or variants to empty ("").

When a variable is explicitly declared, Visual Basic automatically converts variable names to match the case used in the declaration statement, as shown in the following example code. If a variable is declared as:

```
Dim intVar As Integer
```

Then, when the variable is typed as:

```
intvar = 5
```

Visual Basic automatically converts it to:

```
intVar = 5
```

This is a quick way to confirm that the variable name typed is correct. It is especially useful when working with long variable names.

Note Variables declared using the **Dim** statement within a procedure exist only as long as the procedure is executing. When the procedure finishes, the variable disappears. In addition, the value of a variable in a procedure is local to that procedure—that is, you can't access a variable in a particular procedure from another procedure. Local variables allow you to use the same variable names in different procedures without worrying about conflicts or accidental changes. This is an example of scope. For more information, see "Scope of Variables" on page 99 in this chapter.

Using the Option Explicit Statement

Although it may be convenient to declare variables implicitly, it can cause logic errors if you make mistakes while typing. For example, assume that the variable curSalary holds an employee's annual salary. A procedure uses this variable in a formula that calculates the employee's bonus. Assume that the curSalary variable was typed incorrectly, as shown in the following example code:

```
CurBonus = curSalry * .10
```

This calculation will always result in a bonus of $0.00 because the variable curSalry will be implicitly declared and will be initialized to empty. When curSalry is used in the calculation, Visual Basic will automatically convert it to 0. If this calculation was performed multiple times within a looping structure, your application would run noticeably slower because it would take time for Visual Basic to create, initialize, and convert the variable.

To prevent errors of this nature, you can require that all variables be declared before they are used. You do that by placing the **Option Explicit** statement in the General Declarations section of a module. The General Declarations section lists certain options that apply to all procedures contained in the code module.

The following illustration shows the General Declaration section in the Code Editor window.

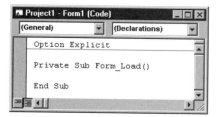

The **Option Explicit** statement instructs Visual Basic to check the module for any variables that are not explicitly declared. If an undeclared variable is used, an error message appears ("Variable not defined"), prompting you to correct the error.

Note It is recommended that you always use the **Option Explicit** statement in your Visual Basic projects.

▶ **To automatically place Option Explicit at the top of each new code module**

1. On the **Tools** menu, click **Options**.

2. Click the **Editor** tab.

3. Click **Require Variable Declaration**, and then click **OK**.

Note This option applies to new code modules only. The **Option Explicit** statement must be entered manually in the General Declarations section for existing code modules.

▶ **To manually enter Option Explicit in the General Declarations section**

1. Activate the Code Editor window.

2. In the **Object** list, click **General**.

3. In the **Procedure** list, click **Declarations**.

4. Type **Option Explicit**.

Variable Scope

In this section, you will learn about how variables can have a different visibility, called scope, depending on how and where they are declared. The **Dim, Public, Private,** or **Static** keywords are used to define the visibility of a variable. Certain rules apply when using these keywords.

Scope of Variables

The scope of a variable determines which parts of the code in your application are aware of the variable's existence. For example, when you declare a variable within a procedure, only code within that procedure can access or change the variable's value. The variable's scope is limited to the procedure containing the variable. When you want a variable to be available only to procedures within the same module, or to all procedures within a project, you need a variable with broader scope.

To see the demonstration "Declaring a Local Variable," see the accompanying CD-ROM.

The following table describes the scoping levels in Visual Basic.

Scoping level	Visibility
Local	A variable declared within a procedure that is visible only to that specific procedure.
Module/Form	A variable declared at the module or form level that is visible to all procedures within the module or form in which it is declared. This is done in the General Declarations section by using the **Dim** or **Private** keywords.
Public	A variable declared at the module or form level that is visible to all procedures within the project. This is done in the General Declarations section by using the **Public** keyword.

The following illustration shows the scope of variables declared at different locations.

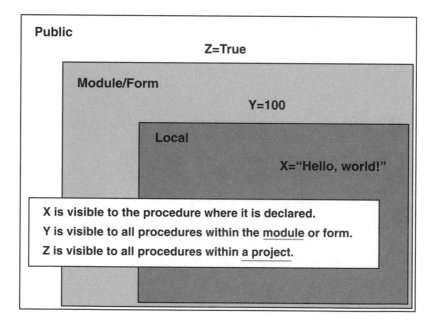

Declaring Local Variables

A local variable is declared inside of a procedure. Because its scope is limited to the procedure, the value of a local variable is not available to other procedures within the application. To declare a local variable by using the **Dim** statement, use the following syntax:

    Dim *varname* [**As** *type*]

The following example code declares a local variable by using the **String** data type, places the contents of a text box into the variable, and then uses the variable as part of the prompt in a message box:

```
Sub cmdShowMessage_Click()
    Dim strTempName As String
    strTempName = frmInfo.txtName.Text
    MsgBox "Welcome Back, " & strTempName & "!"
End Sub
```

Local variables exist in a procedure only while it is executing. By default, when a procedure is finished executing, the values of its local variables are not preserved and the memory used by the local variables is reclaimed. The next time a procedure is executed, all its local variables are initialized to zero (0) or empty. You can, however, preserve the value of a variable between calls to a procedure if you declare it as a static variable.

For more information about static variables, see "Declaring Static Variables" in this chapter.

Declaring Static Variables

You use the **Static** keyword to have a local variable retain its value between calls to the procedure. To declare a local variable by using **Static**, use the following syntax:

    Static *varname* [**As** *type*]

Static variables are useful for maintaining counters that are used only within a procedure. For example, the following example code declares the variable intCount by using the **Static** keyword. Each time the procedure runs, 1 is added to the value stored in intCount.

```
Sub cmdAddtoCount_Click()
    Static intCount As Integer

  'Add 1 to the counter
    intCount = intCount + 1

    'Use the ampersand(&) to combine two strings
    MsgBox "The count is now " & intCount
End Sub
```

Note The same results could be produced by declaring intCount as a module-level variable. However, other procedures would have access to the variable and might change it, making the value stored there subject to change. As a rule, if the value stored in a variable is not needed by other procedures in the application, declare the variable as local by using the **Static** statement.

Declaring Module, Form, and Public Variables

To declare variables with broad scope, such as module or project level, you use the General Declarations section in a module or form. By default, variables declared in the General Declarations section of a module or a form with the **Dim** or **Private** keyword are visible to the entire form or module in which they are declared, but are invisible to other modules or forms. To increase the scope of the variable and make it visible to the entire application, you must declare it with the **Public** keyword.

Note The **Dim** statement is provided for backward compatibility with earlier versions of Visual Basic. The **Private** keyword is preferred when declaring module variables.

The following table describes the visibility of private and public scope, and shows the syntax for declaring variables by using either form.

Scope	Visibility	Syntax
Private	Private to the module or form in which they are declared	**Dim** *varname* [**As** *type*] or **Private** *varname* [**As** *type*]
Public	Available to all modules in the project	**Public** *varname* [**As** *type*]

Although module-level and form-level variables are declared within the General Declarations section, you cannot assign values to them. The value of a variable must be set within a procedure.

Note Public variables declared in a form module must be prefixed with the form name when called from another form or standard module (for example, frmForm1.X).

Using Arrays

In this section, you will learn how to use arrays to store groups of related variables. Arrays enable you to refer to a series of variables by the same name and to use a number (an index) to tell them apart. By using arrays in this manner, you can use loop constructs to access or easily store like values.

Fixed-Size Arrays

In Visual Basic there are two types of arrays: a fixed-size array, which always remains the same size, and a dynamic array, whose size can change at run time.

All the elements in an array have the same data type. You can declare an array of any of the fundamental data types (including variant, user-defined types, and object variables).

Note Visual Basic allocates space for each index number, so you should avoid declaring an array that is larger than necessary.

Declaring Fixed-Size Arrays

Arrays have upper and lower bounds, with the individual array elements contiguous within those bounds. When declaring a fixed-size array, follow the array name by the upper bound in parentheses. The upper bound cannot exceed the range of a **Long** data type (–2,147,483,648 to 2,147,483,647). These array declarations can appear in the General Declarations section of a module, as shown in the following example code:

```
'15 elements
Dim Counters(14) As Integer
'21 elements
Dim Sums(20) As Double
```

To create a public array, you use **Public** in place of **Dim,** as shown in the following example code:

```
Public Counters(14) As Integer
Public Sums(20) As Double
```

To declare the same arrays in a procedure, use the **Dim** statement, as shown in the following example code:

```
Dim Counters(14) As Integer
Dim Sums(20) As Double
```

The first declaration creates an array with 15 elements, with index numbers running from 0 to 14. The second creates an array with 21 elements, with index numbers running from 0 to 20.

Changing Array Bounds

The default lower bound for an array is 0. To specify a different lower bound, provide it explicitly by using the **To** keyword, as shown in the following example code:

```
Dim Counters(1 To 15) As Integer
Dim Sums(100 To 120) As String
```

Note To change the default lower bound of an array from 0 to 1, you can use the **Option Base** statement in the General Declarations section of your form or module.

Multidimensional Arrays

To keep track of related information in an array, you can use a multidimensional array to store the values. For example, to keep track of each pixel on your computer screen, you need to refer to its x-coordinates and y-coordinates.

The statement in the following example code declares a two-dimensional, 10-by-10 array within a procedure:

```
Dim MatrixA(9, 9) As Double
```

Either dimension, or both, can also be declared with explicit lower bounds, as shown in the following example code:

```
Dim MatrixA(1 To 10, 1 To 10) As Double
```

You can extend this to more than two dimensions, as shown in the following example code:

```
Dim MultiD(3, 1 To 10, 1 To 15)
```

In the previous example, the declaration creates an array that has three dimensions with sizes 4 by 10 by 15. The total number of elements is the product of these three dimensions, or 600.

Note When you start adding dimensions to an array, the total storage needed by the array increases dramatically, so use multidimensional arrays with care. Be especially careful with **Variant** arrays, because the memory required to store **Variant** data types is larger than that required for other data types.

Dynamic Arrays

If you don't know exactly how large to make an array, use a dynamic array, which can be resized at any time. After a dynamic array is initially declared, you can add new elements as needed, rather than establishing the size of the array at the time the code is written.

Declaring Dynamic Arrays

You declare the array as dynamic by giving it an empty dimension list, as shown in the following example code:

```
Dim DynArray()
```

Then, you allocate the actual number of elements with a **ReDim** statement. The following example code allocates the number of elements based on the value of a variable, X:

```
ReDim DynArray(X + 1)
```

The **ReDim** statement can appear only in a procedure. Unlike the **Dim** and **Static** statements, **ReDim** is an executable statement—that is, **ReDim** makes the application carry out an action at run time.

The **ReDim** statement supports the same syntax used for fixed arrays. Each **ReDim** statement can change the number of elements, as well as the lower and upper bounds, for each dimension. However, the number of dimensions in the array cannot change. The following example code declares a single-dimensional, dynamic array that has nine elements:

```
ReDim DynArray(4 to 12)
```

In the following example code, the dynamic array Matrix1 is created by first declaring it at the module level:

```
Dim Matrix1() As Integer
```

A procedure then allocates space for the array, as shown in the following example code:

```
Sub CalcValuesNow ()
  ReDim Matrix1(19, 29)
End Sub
```

The **ReDim** statement shown in the previous example code allocates a matrix of 20 by 30 integers (at a total size of 600 elements). Alternatively, the bounds of a dynamic array can be set by using variables, as shown in the following example code:

```
ReDim Matrix1(X, Y)
```

Preserving the Contents of Dynamic Arrays

Each time you execute the **ReDim** statement, values currently stored in the array are lost. Visual Basic resets all the elements to their default initial values. This can be useful if you want to prepare the array for new data, or to reduce the size of the array.

However, sometimes you might want to change the size of the array without losing the data in the array. This is done by using **ReDim** with the **Preserve** keyword. For example, you can increase an array by one element without losing the values of the existing elements, as shown in the following example code:

```
ReDim Preserve DynArray(UBound(DynArray) + 1)
```

Note Only the upper bound of the last dimension in a multidimensional array can be changed when you use the **Preserve** keyword; if you change any of the other dimensions or the lower bound of the last dimension, a run-time error occurs.

User-Defined Data Types

You can combine variables of several different types to create user-defined types (known as structures in the C programming language). User-defined types are useful when you want to create a single variable that records several related pieces of information.

The Type Statement

You create a user-defined type with the **Type** statement, which must be placed in the General Declarations section of a module or form. User-defined types in a standard module can be public or private. However, user-defined types in a form can only be private.

For example, you could create a user-defined type that stores information about employees, as shown in the following example code:

```
'Declarations Section
Private Type EmployeeInfo
    lngEmployeeID As Long
    strFirstName As String
    strLastName As String
    dtBirthDate As Date
    curSalary As Currency
End Type
```

Declaring a User-Defined Type

To declare a variable that uses a user-defined type, use the **Dim** statement along with the variable name. Like regular data types, arrays can also be declared. To create a public variable of a user-defined type, declare it in the General Declarations section of a code module. If you declare a user-defined type in a form, the variable must be private.

User-defined types can contain any Visual Basic data type, including **Variant** and **Object,** or they can contain fixed and dynamic arrays. They can also contain other user-defined types. The following example code shows how to declare an array of user-defined types:

```
Dim MyVariable As EmployeeInfo
Dim MyVariable(10) As EmployeeInfo
```

—or—

```
Dim MyVariable() As EmployeeInfo
ReDim MyVariable(10)
```

Referencing a User-Defined Type

You can reference a user-defined type by using the variable name that you created along with the item in the Type block, separated by a period. The following example code uses the value contained in the FirstName user-defined type to set the **Text** property of an edit box:

```
txtFirstName.Text = MyNewVariable.strFirstName
```

Passing User-Defined Types to Procedures

Passing a user-defined type to a procedure allows you to easily pass many related items as one argument. You can even pass an array of user-defined types, as shown in the following example code:

```
'Passing a User-defined Type
Private Sub MyProc(Employees As EmployeeInfo)
    txtFirstName.Text = Employees.strFirstName
    txtLastName.Text = Employees.strLastName
End Sub

'Passing a User-defined Type Array
Private Sub MyProc(Employees() As EmployeeInfo)
    txtFirstName.Text = Employees(1).strFirstName
    txtLastName.Text = Employees(1).strLastName
End Sub
```

Converting Data Types

In this section, you will learn about converting data types. Visual Basic can perform some data type conversions automatically, such as converting some strings to integers. Automatic conversions may yield unexpected results, and code may run slower as a result. You will learn how to use the type conversion functions of Visual Basic to explicitly convert values before they are used, thus avoiding bugs in your code. You will also learn about localization issues to be aware of when using strings in code to represent dates and currencies.

Automatic Conversion

Most programming languages handle data typing quite rigidly. For example, if numbers stored as a string are needed in a calculation, the C programming language requires you to perform a conversion of the string data to a numerical type before performing the calculation.

Visual Basic, however, can perform some data-type conversions automatically. For instance, if you place the string "1234" in an **Integer** variable, Visual Basic automatically converts the string to an integer. Or, if a string such as "100" is added to a numeric value by using the formula "100" + 10, Visual Basic converts the string to the integer value 100 and adds it to 10.

There are disadvantages to relying on Visual Basic to perform automatic conversions. Automatic conversions may yield unexpected results. For example, when two strings are added together, Visual Basic concatenates the strings regardless of their contents; so, "100" + "10" = "10010." Moreover, when Visual Basic performs automatic conversions, the code runs slower because of the extra work that Visual Basic must perform.

To avoid bugs in the code that you write, use the conversion functions of Visual Basic to explicitly convert the values before they are used.

To see the demonstration "Using Conversion Functions," see the accompanying CD-ROM.

The following code is used in the demonstration. To copy this code for use in your own projects, see "Data Conversion" on the accompanying CD-ROM.

```
Private Sub cmdCalculate_Click()
    Dim feet As Double, inches As Double
    Dim millimeters As Double, meters As Double

    'First, extract feet and inches from the text boxes.
    'The text property returns a string, but we need a double,
    'so CDbl() is used to perform the conversion.
    feet = CDbl(txtFeet.Text)
    inches = CDbl(txtInches.Text)

    'Next, convert feet and inches to millimeters.
    millimeters = (inches * MILLIMETERS_PER_INCH) + _
        (feet * MILLIMETERS_PER_INCH * INCHES_PER_FOOT)

    'Convert millimeters to meters.
    meters = millimeters / 1000

    'Display the result in a label. Since the caption
    'property is a string, use CStr() to convert the double.
    lblMeterResult.Caption = Format(CStr(meters), "#.##")
End Sub
```

Using Conversion Functions

Visual Basic offers an extensive list of conversion functions.

The following illustration shows a simple application and the functions it uses to convert string values into numeric values to perform a calculation, and then to convert the resulting numeric value into a string.

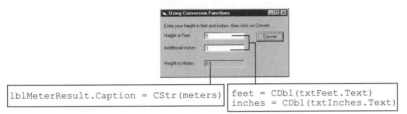

```
lblMeterResult.Caption = CStr(meters)
```

```
feet = CDbl(txtFeet.Text)
inches = CDbl(txtInches.Text)
```

The following table lists each of the conversion functions in Visual Basic.

Type of conversion	Function
Boolean	CBool
Byte	CByte
Currency	CCur
Date	CDate
Decimals	CDec
Double	CDbl
Integer	CInt
Long	CLng
Single	CSng
String	CStr
Variant	CVar
Error	CVErr

To use a conversion function, you place it on the right side of a calculation statement and use the following syntax:

    variable = CFunction (formula)

The following example code uses a conversion function:

```
dblArea = CDbl(txtLength.Text * txtWidth.Text)
```

For more information about using functions, see "Working with Procedures" on page 113 in this chapter.

Note Use the **Is** functions, such as **IsNumeric** or **IsDate**, to determine the data type of a variable.

Localization Issues

To make your code easier to localize, avoid typing dates and currencies as strings in code. Even locale-aware conversion functions may affect strings in unexpected ways. For example, the following example code won't run in any locale where the dollar sign ($) is not the currency symbol:

```
Money = "$1.22"
NewMoney = CCur(Money)
```

Instead, you should use decimal numbers, as shown in the following example code. (This example assumes that the period is the decimal separator in the locale, but the code runs correctly no matter what the decimal separator is in the user's locale.)

```
Money = 1.22
NewMoney = CCur(Money)
```

Using Constants

Constants, like variables, are named storage locations in memory with local, form, module, or global scope. Visual Basic prevents the value of a constant from being changed during program execution. Visual Basic uses constants more efficiently than variables, so if you plan to use a value that never changes, you should create a constant. To create a constant, use the **Const** statement with the following syntax:

[Public | Private] Const constname [As type] = expression

You declare constants by following the same rules that variables follow for declaring local, module, or global data. Constants may only be declared as public within the General Declarations section of a standard module. For more information, see "Declaring Module, Form, and Public Variables" on page 102 in this chapter.

The following example code declares and uses a public constant:

```
'General Declarations of a standard module
Public Const PI As Double = 3.1415

'Code within a procedure
dblArea = PI * dblRadius ^ 2
dblCircum = 2 * PI * dblRadius
```

Tip To distinguish constants from variables in your program, use all capital letters for constant names. Using this convention serves as a reminder that you're working with a value that can't be changed in the execution of your program.

Visual Basic provides predefined constants that are extremely useful in coding an application. For more information about using predefined constants, see "Predefined Visual Basic Constants" on page 76 in Chapter 3, "Working with Code and Forms."

Working with Procedures

Any large task is simplified by breaking it into smaller tasks. Programming is no exception. Programming an application, especially a large project, is made easier by breaking it into smaller logical components. In Visual Basic, these components are called procedures. In this section, you will learn about using procedures.

Procedures are useful for condensing repeated or shared tasks, such as frequently used calculations, and text and database manipulation.

When procedures are used effectively, there are two major benefits:

◆ You can more easily check code for errors, because each unit can be checked individually.

◆ You can reuse existing code. Procedures used in one program can be used in other projects, often with little or no modification.

Understanding Procedure Types

There are three main types of procedures used in Visual Basic: event, general, and property.

Event procedures are invoked automatically in response to a user or system action or when called by another statement. If an event procedure contains an argument, you cannot change the argument's name, nor can you add arguments to Visual Basic event procedures. Event procedures are subroutines stored in form modules and are private by default.

General procedures are functions or subroutines that you create within a module. General procedures can help divide complex application code into more manageable units. If a general procedure is public, it can be called from any number of other procedures within an entire project. However, if the procedure is private, the procedure or function can be called only by other procedures within the same module. The purpose of general procedures is to provide modularity and reuse of code.

Property procedures are used within class modules to assign or access property values. (Property procedures are beyond the scope of this course.)

Using Event Procedures

When Windows informs Visual Basic that an event has taken place for one of its objects, Visual Basic automatically runs the event procedure that corresponds to the event. For example, when a form is loaded into memory, the **Load** event for that form is automatically executed.

The event's name establishes an association between the object and the code.

An event procedure for a control combines the control's actual name (specified in the **Name** property), an underscore (_), and the event name. For instance, an event procedure called **cmdExit_Click** is executed when a command button named **cmdExit** is clicked.

An event procedure for a form combines the word "Form," an underscore, and the event name. To invoke an event procedure when the form is clicked, you use the procedure **Form_Click**. (Like controls, forms have unique names, but they are not used in the names of event procedures.)

All event procedures use the same general syntax. For controls, use the following syntax:

Private Sub controlname_eventname (arguments)

'*Statements*

End Sub

For forms, use the following syntax:

> **Private Sub Form_**eventname (arguments)
>
> '*Statements*
>
> **End Sub**

Visual Basic automatically creates procedures for forms and controls. You can view and edit the code for an event procedure in the Code Editor window. For more information about selecting, viewing, and writing event procedures, see "Working with Code Statements" on page 76 in Chapter 3, "Working with Code and Forms."

> **Tip** When writing procedures for new controls, it's a good idea to set the **Name** property immediately after creating the control. Because code procedures are attached to the controls, changing the name of the control after a procedure is written breaks the association between the code and the control. When Visual Basic cannot match the procedure name to a control, it becomes a general procedure.

Using General Procedures

A general procedure is a block of code that isn't bound to any particular event. Instead, a general procedure can be invoked from another procedure. General procedures can help divide complex application code into more manageable units.

There are two types of general procedures: **Sub** procedures and **Function** procedures. General procedures can be stored in a form module or in a standard module. If you want to reuse your code, general procedures can also be copied to, and used in, other projects.

To see the demonstration "Using General Procedures," see the accompanying CD-ROM.

Creating a General Procedure

There are two methods for adding general procedures to a code module:

- Use the **Add Procedure** dialog box.
- Define a procedure in the Code Editor window.

▶ **To create a general procedure by using the Add Procedure dialog box**

1. Open the Code Editor window for the module for which you want to write the procedure.

2. On the **Tools** menu, click **Add Procedure**.

3. In the **Name** box, type a name for the procedure. (Spaces are not allowed in the procedure name.)

4. In the **Type** group, select **Sub** to create a **Sub** procedure, or select **Function** to create a **Function** procedure.

5. In the **Scope** group, click **Public** to create a procedure that can be invoked from outside the module, or click **Private** to create a procedure that you can invoke only from within the module, and then click **OK**.

When you use the preceding method, Visual Basic sets up a procedure template for you, which you can modify to fit your needs.

You can also create a general procedure by typing the procedure definition directly in the Code Editor window.

▶ **To create a general procedure by using the Code Editor window**

1. In the Code Editor window, place the insertion point outside any existing procedures.

2. Type **Sub** or **Function**, followed by the procedure's name, and then press ENTER.

The syntax for the procedure depends on whether it is a **Sub** procedure or a **Function** procedure.

For **Sub** procedures, use the following syntax:

Sub ProcedureName (Param1 As Type, Param2 As Type, ...)
    [Sub procedure code]

End Sub

For **Function** procedures, use the following syntax:

Function ProcedureName (Param1 As Type, Param2 As Type, ...) As Type
    [Function procedure code]

End Function

Note The parameters shown in the preceding syntax example give you the capability to define arguments that can be passed to the procedure. For each argument, you provide a variable name and a data type. For more information on arguments, see "Passing Arguments to Procedures" on page 121 in this chapter.

Creating a Standard Module

The code in standard modules is public by default, so placing a general procedure in a standard module gives it the broadest scope. Public code in a standard module can be called from within event procedures or general procedures in any module or form. Standard modules can store general procedures but, by definition, can't store event procedures.

▶ **To create a standard module**

◆ On the **Standard** toolbar, click the **Add Module** icon.

 – or –

◆ Right-click in the Project window, click **Add,** and then click **Module** from the submenu that appears.

Calling a General Procedure

Unlike event procedures, general procedures run only when explicitly called. In the following example code, an event procedure calls a **Sub** procedure named PrintReport:

```
'An event procedure
Sub cmdReport_Click()
  'Run the procedure PrintReport
  PrintReport
End Sub

'A general procedure
Sub PrintReport()
  [code for printing a report]
End Sub
```

Note To call a public general procedure that resides in a form module from another module, you must place the form name before the procedure name (for example: frmCustomers.UpdateValues.)

Using Sub Procedures

A **Sub** procedure is a block of code that performs a task and does not return a value. After the **Sub** procedure executes its code, it returns program execution to the line of code following the line that called the **Sub** procedure.

A **Sub** procedure is referred to as a unit of code because each **Sub** procedure has a distinct beginning, body, and end. Each **Sub** procedure starts with the **Sub** statement and ends with the **End Sub** statement. The following example code creates a **Sub** procedure:

```
Sub SetData()
  [statement block]
End Sub
```

To call a **Sub** procedure that does not have any arguments, you type its name on a line by itself in your code. The following example code shows an event procedure that calls the **Sub** procedure **SetData**:

```
Sub cmdData_Click()
  SetData
End Sub
```

If the **SetData Sub** procedure had three arguments of type **Integer,** the syntax would be the **Sub** procedure name followed by the arguments, as shown in the following example code:

```
'Sub procedure is defined in the General Declarations
Private Sub SetData(intNumberOfCars, _
  intNumberofTrucks, intNumberOfVans)

End Sub

Sub cmdData_Click()
  'Call the SetData Sub procedure
  SetData 10, 20, 30
End Sub
```

Sub procedures do not return a value to the calling statement. A **Sub** procedure can, however, pass information back to the calling code by modifying any arguments passed by reference. You could also write code in your **Sub** procedure that modifies values in form-level variables, as shown in the following example code:

```
Public blnValid As Boolean

Public Sub Validate()
  If [condition] = True Then
      blnValid = True
  Else
      blnValid = False
  End If
End Sub
```

Using Function Procedures

The major difference between **Function** procedures and **Sub** procedures is that **Function** procedures have a return value while **Sub** procedures do not. To create a **Function** procedure, use the following syntax:

Function FunctionName() As DataType

{statement block]

FunctionName = [ReturnValue]

End Function

Note The default value returned by a **Function** procedure is a **Variant**. For more efficient code, specify a data type for the return values by using the **As** keyword.

Because **Function** procedures are able to return values just as the built-in functions of Visual Basic do, they are often used to perform a calculation. The following example code returns the square of an integer:

```
Function Square (intSquareVal As Integer) As Integer
  Square = intSquareVal * intSquareVal
End Function
```

The following example code uses the **Square** function to assign a value of 36 to the intNewValue variable:

```
intNewValue = Square(6)
```

You can also use call a function within a statement, as shown in the following example code:

```
'Set intNewValue to 61
intNewValue = Square(6) + 25
```

Function procedures are also useful for checking for errors. The following example code shows a **Function** procedure that opens a file. If the **Function** procedure is able to open the file, **True** is returned to the procedure that called the function. Otherwise, **False** is returned.

```
Function OpenFile () As Boolean
  [Attempt to open a file]
  If [operation was successful] Then
      OpenFile = True
  Else
      OpenFile = False
  End If
End Function
```

The **OpenFile** function is called from another procedure in the following example code:

```
If OpenFile() = True Then
  MsgBox "Success"
Else
  MsgBox "Fail to Open"
End If
```

Because the **OpenFile** function returns a value of **True** or **False**, the return value for **OpenFile** can be evaluated in an **If...Then** statement, as shown in the following example code:

```
If OpenFile() Then
  MsgBox "Success"
Else
  MsgBox "Fail to Open"
End If
```

Passing Arguments to Procedures

When you need to pass information to a **Sub** and **Function** procedure, you use its arguments.

The following illustration shows the relationship between parameters defined in the procedure and the arguments that are used when the procedure is called.

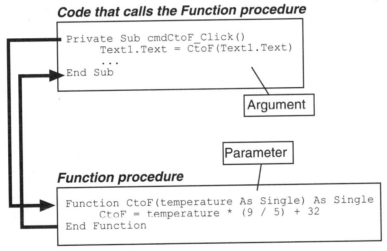

Code that calls the Function procedure

```
Private Sub cmdCtoF_Click()
    Text1.Text = CtoF(Text1.Text)
    ...
End Sub
```

Argument

Parameter

Function procedure

```
Function CtoF(temperature As Single) As Single
    CtoF = temperature * (9 / 5) + 32
End Function
```

The arguments that can be passed to a procedure are specified when the procedure is defined. For more information, see "Using General Procedures" on page 115 in this chapter.

Note The argument names used when calling the **Sub** or **Function** procedure do not have to match the parameter names used to define the procedure. Many **Sub** and **Function** procedures also support named arguments. Unless named arguments are used, the number, data type, and order of the arguments must match the parameters in the procedure definition. For more information about using named arguments, see Chapter 3, "Named Arguments" on page 77.

The following illustration shows an application that uses passed arguments to convert a temperature from Celsius to Fahrenheit or Fahrenheit to Celsius.

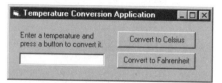

In the following example code, the functions accept a parameter called Temperature. The Temperature parameter is converted from Fahrenheit to Celsius or from Celsius to Fahrenheit, and the new value is returned from the function.

```
Function FtoC(sglTemperature As Single) As Single
    'Convert Fahrenheit to Celsius
    FtoC = (sglTemperature - 32) * (5 / 9)
End Function

Function CtoF(sglTemperature As Single) As Single
    'Convert Celsius to Fahrenheit
    CtoF = sglTemperature * (9 / 5) + 32
End Function
```

The functions are called from the **Click** event procedures for each command button. In the following example code, the contents of a text box are passed to the appropriate function, and the value is then converted and placed back in the text box:

```
Private Sub cmdFtoC_Click()
    txtDegrees.Text = FtoC(CSgl(txtDegrees.Text))
End Sub

Private Sub cmdCtoF_Click()
    txtDegrees.Text = CtoF(CSgl(txtDegrees.Text))
End Sub
```

Working with Dates and Times

In this section, you will learn how to perform calculations and operations involving dates and times. Visual Basic provides many date and time functions that you can use in your applications.

Overview of Date and Time Functions

In Visual Basic, dates and times are stored internally as numbers. The whole-number portion of the number represents the date between January 1, 100, and December 31, 9999, inclusive, with each day incrementing the number by one. The decimal portion of the number represents the time (the fractional part of a day) between 0:00:00 and 23:59:59, inclusive.

Because numbers are used to represent the date and time, you can perform calculations involving time. The following example code adds five days to today's date:

```
Dim dtNewDate As Date
dtNewDate = dtDate + 5
```

Visual Basic provides built-in date and time functions that can return the system's current date and time and generate a date value based on a string or other expression. For example, the **Now, Date,** and **Time** functions return the system's current date and time. The statements in the following example code display message boxes that show the system date and time:

```
MsgBox "The current date and time is " & Now()
MsgBox "The date is " & Date()
MsgBox "The time is " & Time()
```

Note The **Date** and **Time** functions can also be used to set the system clock, as shown in the following example code:

```
Date = date
Time = time
```

Visual Basic also provides functions that extract portions of the date or time value. The following table lists functions that are used to return portions of a given value.

Function	Example	Value displayed
Year()	Year(Now)	1999
Month()	Month(Now)	2
Day()	Day(Now)	22
Weekday()	Weekday(Now)	7
Hour()	Hour(Now)	11
Minute()	Minute(Now)	38
Second()	Second(Now)	9

The remaining date and time functions are calculation and conversion functions, as described in the following table.

Function	Description
DateSerial	Returns a **Variant** (**Date**) for a specified year, month, and day.
TimeSerial	Returns a **Variant** (**Time**) for a specified hour, minute, and second.
DateValue	Converts a string to a **Variant** (**Date**).
TimeValue	Converts a string to a **Variant** (**Date**).
DateAdd	Returns a **Variant** (**Date**) containing a date to which a specified time interval has been added.
DateDiff	Returns a **Variant** (**Long**) specifying the number of time intervals between two specified dates.
DatePart	Returns a **Variant** (**Integer**) containing the specified part of a given date.

DateSerial and DateDiff Functions

Visual Basic provides functions that you can use to perform complex operations with dates. These functions include the **DateSerial** and **DateDiff** functions.

The DateSerial Function

The **DateSerial** function returns the date for a specified year, month, and day. To use the **DateSerial** function, use the following syntax:

*DateSerial(*year, month, day*)*

The following example code uses the **DateSerial** function:

```
Dim dtMyBday As Date

dtMyBday = DateSerial(1956, 9, 23)
```

The **DateSerial** function can also be used in calculations. The following example code calculates the last day of the current month by generating the serial number for the first day of the next month and subtracting one day:

```
Dim dtLastDayofMonth As Date
dtLastDayofMonth = _
  DateSerial(Year(Now), Month(Now) + 1, 1) - 1
```

The DateDiff Function

The **DateDiff** function returns the number of time intervals (for example, year, month, or day) between two dates. To use the **DateDiff** function, use the following syntax:

*DateDiff(*interval, date1, date2[, firstdayofweek[, firstweekofyear]]*)*

The following example code calculates the number of days between two specified dates, while accounting for the uneven number of days in each month:

```
Dim dtTheDate As Date
Dim strMsg As String

dtTheDate = InputBox("Enter a date")
strMsg = "Days from today: " & DateDiff("d", Now, dtTheDate)
MsgBox strMsg
```

Using the Format Function

In this section, you will learn how to use the **Format** function. There are a number of universally accepted formats for numbers, dates, and times. Visual Basic provides a great deal of flexibility in displaying number formats, as well as date and time formats. An added benefit is that the international formats are easily displayed for numbers, dates, and times without recoding for each nationality.

Format Function Syntax

In general, the **Format** function accepts a numeric value and converts it to a string in the format specified by the format argument. To use the **Format** function, use the following syntax:

   Format(expression[, format[, firstdayofweek[, firstweekofyear]]])

The format argument can be a string of symbols, such as "$#,###.00", or a named format. (For more information about formats used with the **Format** function, see "Named Formats" on page 127 in this chapter.) The most commonly used symbols are listed in the following table.

Symbol	Description
0	Digit placeholder. Prints a trailing or leading zero in this position, if appropriate.
#	Digit placeholder. Never prints trailing or leading zeros.
.	Decimal placeholder.
,	Thousands separator.
- _ $ ( ) space	Literal character. Characters are displayed exactly as typed into the format string.

Note The **firstdayofweek** argument is a constant that specifies the first day of the week; the **firstweekofyear** argument is a constant that specifies the first week of the year. Both arguments are optional.

Printing Formatted Dates and Times

To print formatted dates and times, use the **Format** function with symbols representing the date and time. The examples in the following table use the **Now** and **Format** functions to identify and format the current date and time. The examples assume that Regional Settings in the **Regional Settings Properties** dialog box of Windows Control Panel is set to **English(United States)**.

Format syntax	Result
Format(Now, "m/d/yy")	1/27/99
Format(Now, "dddd, mmmm dd, yyyy")	Wednesday, January 27, 1999
Format(Now, "d-mmm")	27-Jan
Format(Now, "mmmm-yy")	January-99
Format(Now, "hh:mm AM/PM")	07:18 AM
Format(Now, "h:mm:ss a/p")	7:18:00 a
Format(Now, "d-mmmm h:mm")	3-January 7:18

By using the **Now** function with the format "ddddd" and "ttttt," you can print the current date and time in a format appropriate for the selection in the **Regional Settings** dialog box of Windows Control Panel, as shown in the following table.

Country	Format syntax	Result
Sweden	Format(Now, "ddddd ttttt")	1998-12-31 18.22.38
United Kingdom	Format(Now, "ddddd ttttt")	31/12/98 18:22:38
Canada (French)	Format(Now, "ddddd ttttt")	98-12-31 18:22:38
United States	Format(Now, "ddddd ttttt")	12/31/98 6:22:38 PM

Named Formats

Visual Basic provides several standard formats for use with the **Format** function. The format name will always be enclosed in double quotation marks (""). The following example code displays a message box containing "$80,000.00":

```
MsgBox Format(80000, "Currency")
```

In the following examples, the **Format** function is used to change the way a value appears in a text box.

The following example code displays today's date in format:

```
txtDate.Text = Format(Now, "Long Date")
```

The following example code displays the value 1,000 as "$1,000.00":

```
txtCost.Text = Format(1000, "Currency")
```

Tip	
Format	**Description**
General Number	Displays number as is, with no thousand separators.
Currency	Displays number with thousand separator, if appropriate; display two digits to the right of the decimal separator. Note that output is based on system locale settings.
Fixed	Displays at least one digit to the left and two digits to the right of the decimal separator.
Percent	Displays number multiplied by 100 with a percent sign (%) appended to the right; always display two digits to the right of the decimal separator.
General Date	Displays a date and/or time. For real numbers, display a date and time (for example, 4/3/93 05:34 P.M.); if there is no fractional part, display only a date (for example, 4/3/93); if there is no integer part, display time only (for example, 05:34 P.M.). Date display is determined by your system settings.
Long Date	Displays a date according to your system's long date format.
Medium Date	Displays a date by using the medium date format appropriate for the language version of Visual Basic.
Short Date	Displays a date by using your system's short date format.

table continued on next page

Format	Description
Long Time	Displays a time by using your system's long time format: includes hours, minutes, seconds.
Medium Time	Displays time in 12-hour format by using hours and minutes and the A.M./P.M. designator.
Short Time	Displays a time by using the 24-hour format (for example, 17:45).
Yes/No	Any nonzero numeric value (usually − 1) is Yes. Zero is No.
True/False	Any nonzero numeric value (usually − 1) is True. Zero is False.
On/Off	Any nonzero numeric value (usually − 1) is On. Zero is Off.

For more information about formatting a number or string, search for "Format Function" in MSDN Help.

Manipulating Text Strings

In many cases, strings require some type of manipulation, formatting, or evaluation. For example, a person's name may be typed in with the last name appearing before the first name, or a file may contain fields that are separated by commas. The string functions of Visual Basic can parse and manipulate strings in applications. These functions are used to return information about a string, extract only a certain portion of a string, or display information in a particular format.

The following table lists and describes common functions used when working with text strings.

Action	Function
Compare two strings	**StrComp**
Convert to lowercase or uppercase	**Format, LCase, Ucase**
Create string of repeating character	**Space, String**

table continued on next page

Action	Function
Find length of a string	Len
Format a string	Format
Justify a string	LSet, RSet
Manipulate strings	InStr, InStrRev, Left, LTrim, Mid, Right, RTrim, Trim
Convert strings	StrConv

In the following example code, the **Len** function returns the number of characters in a string:

```
Len(strCustomerName)
```

In the following example code, the **Left** function returns a specified number of characters from the left side of a string:

```
Left(strCustomerName, 5)
```

The following example code uses the **Len** and **Left** functions to remove the filename extension (the last four characters) from a file name:

```
strFileName = Left(strFileName, Len(strFileName) - 4)
```

The following sample code extracts the first and last name from a string (for example, "Nancy" and "Davolio" from "Nancy Davolio"). To copy this code for use in your own projects, see "Extracting Text from a String" on the accompanying CD-ROM.

```
Private Sub cmdReverse_Click()
    Dim strFirst As String
    Dim strLast As String
    Dim intSpace As Integer
    Dim intLastSpace As Integer
    Dim strName As String

    strName = txtName.Text

    'find the last space in the full name
    intSpace = 0
    Do
        intLastSpace = intSpace
        intSpace = InStr(intLastSpace + 1, strName, " ")
    Loop While intSpace <> 0

    'separate out the last name and everything before it
    strFirst = Left(strName, intLastSpace - 1)
    strLast = Right(strName, Len(strName) - intLastSpace)

    'set the reversed name
    lblReversed.Caption = strLast & ", " & strFirst
End Sub
```

Lab 4: Writing Procedures

In this lab, you will add functionality to the loan application project started in Lab 2 and continued in Lab 3. In this lab, you will start to implement the main form of the loan application. The purpose of this application is to compute monthly payments and the total amount repaid for a loan.

You will start by writing a function that computes the monthly payment of a loan; assume, for this lab, a 30-year term at an interest rate of 6.5 percent. In a subsequent lab, you will add controls to retrieve this information from the user. You can continue to work with the files that you created in the previous lab, or you can work with files provided for you in the *<install folder>*\Labs\Lab04 folder.

To see the demonstration "Lab 4 Solution," see the accompanying CD-ROM.

Estimated time to complete this lab: **45 minutes**

Objectives

After completing this lab, you will be able to:

◆ Create a function procedure.

◆ Call a function procedure from within another procedure.

u Add a module to a project.

To complete the exercises in this lab, you must have the required software. For detailed information about the labs and setup for the labs, see "Labs" in "About This Course."

The solution for this lab is located in the *<install folder>*\Labs\Lab04\Solution folder.

Prerequisites

There are no prerequisites for this lab.

Exercises

The following exercises provide practice in working with the concepts covered in this chapter:

◆ Exercise 1: Creating the User Interface

In this exercise, you will create a simple user interface to test the functions that you write.

◆ Exercise 2: Writing a Function

In this exercise, you will write a function to compute the amount of monthly payments for a loan.

◆ Exercise 3: Calling the **MonthlyPayment** Function

In this exercise, you will call the **MonthlyPayment** function, which you wrote in Exercise 2, from the **Monthly Payment** command button on frmMain.

◆ Exercise 4: Adding a Module File

In this exercise, you will add a module to your project. The new module will contain a function that computes the total amount to be repaid over the term of a loan. You will call this function to display the loan payment amount.

◆ Exercise 5: Adding MsgBox Formatting

In this exercise, you will add formatting for the message boxes in your application.

Exercise 1: Creating the User Interface

In this exercise, you will create a simple user interface to test the functions that you write.

▶ **Open the loan application project**

◆ Open either the loan application project that you have been working on or the loan application project located in the *<install folder>*\Labs\Lab04 folder.

▶ **Customize the code environment**

1. On the **Tools** menu, click **Options**.

2. Select **Require Variable Declaration**, and then click **OK**.

▶ **Add Option Explicit to the existing forms**

1. Open the Code Editor window for frmLogon.

2. In the **Object** list box, select **General**, and in the **Procedure** list box, select **Declarations**.

   Your cursor should be in the General Declarations section. This is the section at the top of the Code Editor window, preceding any event procedures or general procedures.

3. Add the following line of code:

   ```
   Option Explicit
   ```

Note Because this form was created before you set the environment option of requiring variable declarations, you need to add the code yourself. All subsequent forms and modules added to the project will contain this line of code automatically.

4. Add the **Option Explicit** statement to the General Declarations section of frmMain.

▶ **Add controls to frmMain**

1. Add controls to frmMain so it looks like the following illustration.

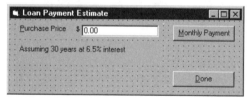

2. Name the text box and command button with names that reflect their purposes, such as **txtPurchase** and **cmdMonthly**.

3. Set the **TabIndex** property of the **txtPurchase** control to 0.

Exercise 2: Writing a Function

In this exercise, you will write a function to compute the amount of monthly payments for a loan.

Monthly payments for a loan depend on the length of the loan, the interest rate, and the amount borrowed.

▶ **Create a function to compute the monthly payments**

1. Open the Code Editor window for frmMain.

2. On the **Tools** menu, click **Add Procedure**.

3. Set the name of the procedure to **MonthlyPayment**, set the type to **Function,** set the scope to **Public,** and click **OK**.

   A function template should be added to the form:

   ```
   Public Function MonthlyPayment()

   End Function
   ```

4. Set the return type of the function to be Double by adding the keywords **As Double** to the function template:

   ```
   Public Function MonthlyPayment() As Double
   ```

5. Complete the body of the function:

   a. Declare a Double variable to hold the monthly interest rate, dblMonthRate.

   b. Declare an Integer variable to hold the number of payments, intNumPayments.

   c. Declare a Double variable to hold the amount of the loan, dblLoanAmt.

   d. Convert the text in the purchase price text box to a Double and save the value as dblLoanAmt.

   e. Declare a form-level constant to represent the number of months in a year (12) in several places.

   ```
   Private Const CONV_PERIOD As Integer = 12
   ```

   f. Assume that this will be a 30-year loan; calculate the number of payments that will be made (30 * CONV_PERIOD), and save this value as intNumPayments.

   g. Assuming that the interest rate is 6.5 percent, or .065, calculate the monthly interest rate (.065 / 12 or use the constant declared above .065 / CONV_PERIOD), and save this value as dblMonthRate.

   ```
   dblMonthRate = .065 / CONV_PERIOD
   ```

h. Use the Visual Basic **Pmt** function to calculate the monthly payment amount, and set this amount as the return value of the function:

```
MonthlyPayment = Pmt(Rate:=dblMonthRate, _
    NPer:=intNumPayments, PV:=-dblLoanAmt)
```

To see an example of how your code should look, see Hint 4.1 in Appendix B.

Exercise 3: Calling the MonthlyPayment Function

In this exercise, you will call the **MonthlyPayment** function, which you wrote in Exercise 2, from the **Monthly Payment** command button on frmMain.

▶ **Display monthly payments**

1. Double-click the **Monthly Payment** command button on frmMain.

   The Code Editor window should open, with a template for the **Click** event procedure.

2. Complete the body of the **Click** event procedure with code that calls the **MonthlyPayment** function and displays the result in a message box:

   a. Declare a Double variable to hold the return value of the **MonthlyPayment** function, dblMonthly.

   b. Call the **MonthlyPayment** function and store the return value in the variable dblMonthly.

   c. Create a message box displaying the monthly payment value.

   The full **Click** event procedure should look something like this:

```
Private Sub cmdMonthly_Click()
    Dim dblMonthly As Double
    dblMonthly = MonthlyPayment()
    MsgBox "Your monthly payments will be: " & dblMonthly
End Sub
```

3. Save and test your work.

Exercise 4: Adding a Module File

In this exercise, you will add a module to your project. The new module will contain a function that computes the total amount to be repaid over the term of a loan. You will call this function to display the payments total of the loan.

The function to compute total payments has already been written. It is named **TotalPaid** and is in module Totalpd.bas in the *<install folder>*\Labs\Lab04 folder.

▶ **Add a module to your project**

1. On the **Project** menu, click **Add Module**.

2. Click the **Existing** tab.

3. Open the *<install folder>*\Labs\Lab04 folder, select the file Totalpd.bas, and click **Open**.

    This adds the module to your project. To view the procedure in the module, right-click the module in the Project window and click **View Code**.

4. Look at the function **TotalPaid** in the new module. Note that it accepts an Integer parameter, the number of years for the loan, and returns a Double value, the total amount that will be repaid over the term of the loan.

▶ **Display the total of the payments for the loan**

1. Add a command button to frmMain to display the total amount paid for the loan.

2. Set the **Name** property of the command button to a name that represents its function, such as **cmdTotal**.

3. Fill in the **Click** event procedure for this command button to call the **TotalPaid** function and display the result in a message box:

    a. Declare a Double variable to hold the return value of the **TotalPaid** function, dblTotal.

    b. Call the **TotalPaid** function, pass the value 30, and store the return value in the variable dblTotal.

    c. Create a message box that displays the total payment value.

    The finished event procedure should look like the following example code:

    ```
    Private Sub cmdTotal_Click()
        Dim dblTotal As Double
        dblTotal = TotalPaid(30)
        MsgBox "The total you will pay will be: " & dblTotal
    End Sub
    ```

When you run your finished application, it should look like the following illustration.

4. Save and test your work.

Exercise 5: Adding MsgBox Formatting

In this exercise, you will add formatting for the message boxes in your application.

When displaying a currency value, you should format it in the accepted format for the locale where your application is running. For example, you would use "$" in the United States, and "DM" in Germany. The Visual Basic **Format** function makes this easy.

▶ **Format before outputting**

1. Edit the **cmdMonthly_Click** event procedure.

2. Change the MsgBox string to include a call to the **Format** function before displaying the monthly payment value:

```
MsgBox "Your monthly payments will be: " _
    & Format(dblMonthly, "currency")
```

3. Edit the **cmdTotal_Click** event procedure, and repeat step 2 before outputting the value of the total payments.

4. Save and test your work.

When you run your finished application, it should look something like the following illustration.

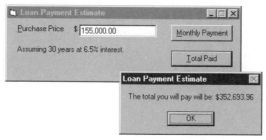

Self-Check Questions

See page 380 for answers.

1. **What is the scope of the variable intImageCount if it is declared by using the following syntax within the Genreal Declations section of frmProcImage?**

   ```
   Dim intImageCount As Integer
   ```

   A. Only in procedures within the frmProcImage form
   B. Only the Declarations section of frmProcImage
   C. All forms in the project
   D. All modules in the project

2. **Your program is supposed to add the contents of two text boxes. Testing the application shows that instead of the expected value of 78, the program returns 3,543. How can you solve this problem?**

   A. Use an '&' to combine the strings.
   B. Create a separate variable to hold the result.
   C. Use conversion functions to convert the strings to integers.
   D. Have the values entered into labels instead of text boxes.

3. **Which of the following code statements calls the CheckPassword function and passes the contents of the txtPassword text box?**

   A. blnValid = CheckPassword.Text(txtPassword)
   B. TxtPassword.Text(CheckPassword)
   C. CheckPassword() = txtPassword.Text
   D. blnValid = CheckPassword(txtPassword.Text)

Student Notes:

Chapter 5:
Controlling Program Execution

In this chapter, you will learn how to implement control structures in your Microsoft Visual Basic programs. Visual Basic provides many ways to control program flow and execution. Conditional statements make it possible for your program to selectively perform tasks based on values generated by your program or by the user. Looping statements contain blocks of code that execute repeatedly for a fixed or variable number of times. The logic of your Visual Basic program is implemented through the use of these control structures.

Objectives

After completing this chapter, you will be able to:

◆ List techniques for comparing variables and object properties by using Visual Basic code.

◆ Explain the difference between **If...Then** and **Select Case** statements, and describe the circumstances in which you use each statement.

◆ Explain the difference between the **For...Next** and **Do...Loop** statements.

◆ Choose the appropriate conditional or looping structure to control program flow.

Comparison and Logical Operators

After a value has been placed in a variable or an object's property, such as the **Text** property of a text box, your Visual Basic application will eventually need to evaluate the value. For example, you may want to ask the user to enter the quantity of items that a customer ordered. If the value entered is less than or equal to zero, you may want to display a warning that the user has entered an invalid number. To do this, you can use a comparison operator to evaluate the value provided by the user. Comparison operators evaluate numeric or string values that are part of an expression.

In addition to evaluating string or numeric values, Visual Basic provides a set of logical operators that you can use to compare different expressions. You can write conditional statements that rely on the results of those operations.

Comparison Operators

There are six comparison operators used in testing expressions.

Operator	Description
<	Less than
<=	Less than or equal to
>	Greater than
>=	Greater than or equal to
=	Equal to
<>	Not equal to

The following example code shows the use of comparison operators:

```
Dim blnResult as Boolean
Dim intAge1 as Integer, intAge2 as Integer

blnResult = (25 < 15) ' Returns False

intAge1 = 5: intAge2 = 3 ' Initialize variables
blnResult = (intAge1 > intAge2) ' Returns True
```

For more information, search for "Comparison Operators" in MSDN Help.

Comparing String Values

Strings, as well as numbers, can be compared. One string equals another only if both strings are the same length and if both contain exactly the same sequence of characters. When Visual Basic compares the two strings, it compares each string, character by character, until the first mismatch occurs. Consider the two strings, "different" and "difference." When these strings are compared, "different" is considered to be greater than "difference" because the first character mismatch occurs at "t" in different and the "c" in difference, and "t" is considered greater than "c."

Note Every character is assigned a code established by ANSI (American National Standards Institute). For example, the capital "A" is assigned the ANSI code of 65, a "B" is 66, and so forth. Therefore A<B is true and B<A is false. Also, because uppercase letters are assigned ANSI codes that are different from their lowercase counterparts (ANSI codes for lowercase are greater than those for uppercase), comparisons are case-sensitive.

Logical Operators

When Visual Basic compares two expressions, it returns one of two values: **True** or **False**. Visual Basic doesn't understand **True** and **False**, but uses numbers to represent them. **True** and **False** are Boolean values, with 0 for **False** and –1 for **True**. (Comparison operators also use this method to evaluate values to **True** or **False**.)

In addition to comparison operators, there are six logical operators.

Operator	Function
And	Combines two expressions. Each expression must be true for the entire expression to be true.
Or	Combines two expressions. If either expression is true, the entire expression is true.
Not	The negative of a single expression.
Xor	Combines two expressions. The entire expression is considered true if the two expressions are not both true or both false.

table continued on next page

Operator	Function
Eqv	Combines two expressions. Both expressions must be true or both expressions must be false for the entire expression to be true.
Imp	Combines two expressions. The entire expression is true except when the first expression is true and the second expression is false.

Combining Comparison and Logical Operators with Conditional Statements

The most common of these operators are the **And, Or,** and **Not** operators. The following examples combine common operators with the **If... Then** conditional statement (for more information, see "If...Then Statements" on page 145 in this chapter):

```
If (intDaysOverDue >= 60) And (blnActiveCustomer = True) Then
    MsgBox "Customer takes too long to pay."

If Not blnActiveCustomer Then
    MsgBox "Customer is not active."
```

Note The Xor, Eqv, and **Imp** operators are considered advanced operators and are not covered in this course.

Using If...Then Statements

Conditional structures allow applications written in Visual Basic to respond to different situations depending upon the result of a test condition. The condition can be a comparison or any expression that evaluates to a numeric value.

To see the animation "Conditional Structures," see the accompanying CD-ROM.

In this section, you will learn about the three types of conditional structures based on the **If...Then** statement: **If...Then, If...Then...Else,** and **If...Then...ElseIf.**

If...Then Statements

In general, you use an **If...Then** statement when your program must make an either/or decision. When your program must select from more than one alternative, use an **If...Then...Else** statement, an **If...Then...ElseIf** statement, or a **Select Case** statement.

You choose the structure that is most efficient for your needs. These other statements are covered in subsequent topics.

Syntax

If...Then statements evaluate whether a condition is true or false and direct the program's flow accordingly. **If...Then** statements can use either single-line or block-form syntax.

To use an **If...Then** statement, you can use the following single-line syntax:

If condition *Then* clause

Or, you can use the following block-form syntax:

If condition *Then*

[statements]

End If

Notice that the single-line version doesn't require the use of an **End If** statement. The single-line **If...Then** statement is usually used to execute only one statement conditionally. The multiple-line version can execute one or more statements and is often easier to read.

In both cases, the essential principle involved is, "If this is true, then do this...," as shown in the following example code:

```
If intCPUTemp > 125 Then MsgBox "CPU is Overheating!"
```

This example compares the value of an integer, intCPUTemp, to 125. If the value exceeds 125, a message box displays the overheating message. If the value of intCPUTemp does not exceed 125, the part of the instruction after **Then** is ignored and the message box is not displayed.

Note There are six operators that you can use in the condition portion of the **If...Then** block: = (Equal), <> (Not equal), < (Less than), <= (Less than or equal to), > (Greater than), and >= (Greater than or equal to). For more information, see "Comparison and Logical Operators" on page 142 in this chapter.

If more than one of the conditions in a conditional structure is true, only the code statements enclosed by the first true condition are executed.

If...Then...Else Statements

If...Then...Else statements are an elaboration on the **If...Then** concept. An **If...Then...Else** block allows you to define two blocks of code and have your program execute one based upon the result of a condition. If more than one of the conditions in a conditional structure is true, only the code statements enclosed by the first true condition are executed.

Syntax

Syntactically, an **If...Then...Else** statement includes a condition that evaluates to **True** or **False,** one or more statements that execute depending on the result of the test condition, and an **End If** statement in the case of a block **If...Then...Else** statement.

To employ an **If...Then...Else** statement, use the following syntax:

> *If* condition *Then*
>
> >   [statements]
>
> *Else*
>
> >   [statements]
>
> *End If*

Note For more efficient code, organize your conditional structures so that the most likely alternative is evaluated first.

The following example code tests whether a user's password is valid by comparing it to the correct password. If the password is valid, the user is allowed access. If the password is false, the user sees a message indicating that the password is invalid.

```
' Password is Espresso
If strUserPassword = "Espresso" Then
  ' Code allowing access
  [Allow user into the system]
Else
  ' Password invalid
  ' Inform user
  MsgBox "Password is invalid!"
End If
```

If...Then...ElseIf Statements

If...Then...ElseIf statements are like If...Then...Else statements, but they allow for your program to choose from more than two alternatives. To employ an If...Then...ElseIf statement, use the following syntax:

If condition *Then*

[statements]

ElseIf condition2 *Then*

[statements]

Else

[statements]

End If

In the following example code, a program determines a user's authority level based upon the password provided:

```
'Level 1 user password is "Espresso"
'Administrator password is "Latte"
If strUserPassword = "Espresso" Then
  ' Code allowing access
  [Allow Level 1 user into the system]
ElseIf strUserPassword = "Latte" Then
  ' Code allowing access
  [Allow administrator into the system]
Else
  ' Inform user
  MsgBox "Password is invalid!"
End If
```

Note Your program is not limited to three alternatives. However, when your program must select from several options, or cases, it's more efficient to use the **Select Case** structure.

Using Select Case Statements

In this section, you will learn how to use an alternative conditional structure to an **If...Then** statement — the **Select Case** statement. You will learn the syntax of **Select Case** as well as how to apply it to two different programming tasks: testing the value of an expression against a range of values, and testing a value returned by a function and choosing an action based on the result.

Understanding the Select Case Structure

Select Case structures are similar to **If...Then...ElseIf** structures in that they allow your program to choose from more than two alternatives. However, the **Select Case** structure can be more efficient because it evaluates the test expression only once. The result of the expression is then compared against multiple values to determine which code block is invoked.

The following example shows the code syntax for the **Select Case** structure. One of several groups of statements is run, depending on the value of an expression.

> *Select Case testexpression*
>
> [*Case* expressionlist1]
>
> [statements]
>
> [*Case* expressionlist2]
>
> [statements]
>
> [*Case Else*]
>
> [elsestatements]
>
> *End Select*

The following example code examines the contents of the strUserName variable and then compares the string with the different **Case** statements to determine if the user gets administrator, user, or guest privileges:

```
Select Case strUserName
  Case "Administrator"
      [Give the user adminstrator privileges]
  Case "User"
      [Give the user user-level privileges]
  Case Else
      [Give the user guest-level privileges]
End Select
```

Although this same structure could be written by using the **If...Then...ElseIf** structure, the **Select Case** statement is easier to read and more efficient. Compare the previous code, which uses a **Select Case** structure, with the following example code, which uses an **If...Then** statement:

```
If strUserName = "Administrator" Then
  [Give the user adminstrator privileges]
ElseIf strUserName = "User" Then
  [Give the user user-level privileges]
Else
  [Give the user guest-level privileges]
End If
```

Using the Select Case Statement to Test Ranges

The **Select Case** structure is ideal for testing the value of an expression against ranges of possible values. The following example code shows how to use the **Select Case** structure to evaluate a number against four different ranges and determine a bonus based on an individual range of values:

```
Dim sngBonus As Single
Dim intTestNumber As Integer

[Set intTestNumber value]
..
```

code continued on next page

code continued from previous page

```
Select Case intTestNumber
    ' If equal to 1
    Case 1
        ' Bonus is 0
        sngBonus = 0
    ' If either 2 or 3
    Case 2, 3
        ' Bonus is 5%
        sngBonus = 0.05
    ' If between 4 and 6
    Case 4 To 6
        ' Bonus is 10%
        sngBonus = 0.1
    ' If anything else
    Case Else
        ' Bonus is 20%
        sngBonus = 0.2
End Select
```

Using Select Case to Test a Returned Value

In the following example code, the **Select Case** statement examines the value returned by the **MsgBox** function and performs a task based on the button that the user clicks:

```
intButtonPressed = _
  MsgBox(prompt:="Save changes before exiting?", _
  buttons:=vbYesNo)

Select Case intButtonPressed
  Case vbYes
      SaveChanges
  Case vbNo
      Unload Me
End Select
```

Overview of Looping Structures

Looping structures allow you to specify the conditions under which you would like your program to execute a set of instructions repetitively. Your program can continue to execute an instruction based on whether a condition evaluates to true or false.

Visual Basic supports the following looping structures:

◆ Do...Loop

◆ For...Next

For more information on looping structures supported in Visual Basic, search for "Loop Structures" in MSDN Help.

Do...Loop

Do...Loop structures give your program the ability to execute a block of code an indeterminate number of times. Although there are several variations of the **Do Loop** structure, they fall into two major categories: loops in which an expression is evaluated at the end of the loop, and loops in which the expression is evaluated at the beginning. The first category ensures that the code in the loop is executed at least once. In the second category, the code in the loop may be bypassed entirely, depending upon the initial value of the expression.

Use **Do** loops when the specific number of times a block of code should execute isn't known, but the condition that determines when execution of the code block should stop is known.

Note Visual Basic also supports the **While...Wend** structure, but the same functionality is provided by the **Do...Loop** structures.

For...Next

If you know how many times a code block will execute, it is easier to write and maintain a **For...Next** statement. The **For...Next** statement executes a code block a specific number of times, using a counter variable to keep track of the number.

To see the animation "Looping Structures," see the accompanying CD-ROM.

Using Do...Loop Structures

In this section, you will learn how to use **Do...Loop** structures. Selecting the appropriate structure can be confusing because of the similarities of the names of the individual looping structures. You will learn which type of loop to use, depending on whether the code must execute while a condition is true or until that condition is true. You will also learn the correct looping structure to use, depending on whether the code must execute at the beginning or the end of the loop.

Do...Loop While

Do...Loop While structures check the condition after executing the code and repeat a code block until the test expression evaluates as false. To use a **Do...Loop While** structure, use the following syntax:

> *Do*
>
> [statements]
>
> *Loop While* [condition]

The following example code will loop until the correct password is entered:

```
Do
  strPassword = InputBox("Enter your password")
Loop While strPassword <> "Lefty"
```

Do...Loop Until

Do...Loop Until structures check the condition after executing the code and repeat a code block until the test expression evaluates as true. To employ a **Do...Loop Until** structure, use the following syntax:

> *Do*
>
> [statements]
>
> *Loop Until* [condition]

The following example code will loop until the **No** button is clicked in a message box:

```
Dim intLoopCount As Integer

Do
    intLoopCount = intLoopCount + 1
Loop Until MsgBox("Loop?", vbYesNo) = vbNo
```

Do While...Loop

Do While...Loop structures check the condition before executing the code. The code in the loop is executed only if the condition evaluates as true, and the code repeats until the test expression evaluates as false. To employ a **Do While...Loop** structure, use the following syntax:

Do While condition

[statements]

Loop

The following example code will ask the user for a password until the correct password is typed into the input box:

```
Dim strPasswordTry As String
Const PASSWORD As String = "password"

Do While strPasswordTry <> PASSWORD
    strPasswordTry = InputBox("Enter password")
Loop
```

Do Until...Loop

Do Until...Loop structures check the condition before executing the code. The code in the loop is executed only if the condition evaluates as false, and the code repeats until the test expression evaluates as true. To employ a **Do Until...Loop** structure, use the following syntax:

Do Until condition

[statements]

Loop

The following example code tests for the EndOfFile condition and reads lines until the end of the file is reached.

```
Dim intValue As Integer
Dim strInput As String

Do Until intValue = 3
    strInput = InputBox("Pick a number between 1 and 5")
    intValue = Val(strInput)
Loop
```

The following example code uses a **Do Until...Loop** to find all of the files in a directory that match a file specification entered by the user (for example, "C:\Windows*.txt"). The example uses the **Dir** function, which returns the first file name that matches a specified path. To get any additional file names that match *pathname*, the **Dir** function is called again with no arguments. When no more file names match, **Dir** returns a zero-length string. The **Do Until...Loop** produces a true condition when there are no more files and the length of the string returned by **Dir** is equal to zero.

```
Dim strMsg As String
Dim strFilespec As String
Dim strMatch As String

strMsg = "Enter a file specification."
'Get file extension
strFilespec = InputBox(strMsg)
'Find first match
strMatch = Dir(strFilespec)
Do Until Len(strMatch) = 0
    'Display matching files
    MsgBox strMatch
    'Find next match
    strMatch = Dir()
Loop
MsgBox "There are no more matching files."
```

For...Next Statement

If both the condition and the number of times a code block will execute is known, use a **For** loop. A **For** loop is easier to write and maintain than a **Do** loop.

To employ a **For...Next** statement, use the following syntax:

For counter = start *To* end [Step increment]

[statements]

Next [counter]

The following example code displays an input box that prompts the user to enter a number. It then executes the code in the **For...Next** loop the specified number of times, calculating and displaying a result.

```
Dim intNumStudents As Integer
Dim intCounter As Integer
Dim sglScore As Single
Dim sglTotalScore As Single
Dim sglAverage As Single

intNumStudents = InputBox(prompt:="How many students?")

For intCounter = 1 To intNumStudents
    sglScore = CSng(Val(InputBox(prompt:="Enter score")))
    sglTotalScore = sglTotalScore + sglScore
Next intCounter

sglAverage = sglTotalScore / intNumStudents
```

Note The counter value in a **For...Next** structure can either increase or decrease, depending on whether *step* is positive or negative.

The following illustration shows the use of the **For...Next** loop. The code generates a 10x10 multiplication table and, by using the **Print** method, displays the table on the form as shown.

1	2	3	4	5	6	7	8	9	10
2	4	6	8	10	12	14	16	18	20
3	6	9	12	15	18	21	24	27	30
4	8	12	16	20	24	28	32	36	40
5	10	15	20	25	30	35	40	45	50
6	12	18	24	30	36	42	48	54	60
7	14	21	28	35	42	49	56	63	70
8	16	24	32	40	48	56	64	72	80
9	18	27	36	45	54	63	72	81	90
10	20	30	40	50	60	70	80	90	100

Generate Table

The first **For...Next** loop generates each new line within the table. The second **For...Next** loop is nested within the first and generates each column within a row, as shown in the following example code:

```
Dim intOuter As Integer, intInner As Integer
Dim strOut As String
' Outer Loop
For intOuter = 1 To 10
    ' Inner Loop
    For intInner = 1 To 10
        ' Concatenate Outer * Inner results to strOut
        strOut = strOut & " " & Format(intOuter * intInner, "@@@")
    Next intInner
    ' Add a carriage return and linefeed to end of line
    strOut = strOut & vbCrLf
Next intOuter
' Monospaced font
Me.Font = "Courier New"
' Display strOut on form
Me.Print strOut
```

Exiting a Loop

The **Exit** statement allows you to exit directly from a **For** loop, **Do** loop, **Sub** procedure, or **Function** procedure. The syntax for the **Exit** statement is simple: **Exit For** can appear as many times as needed inside a **For** loop, and **Exit Do** can appear as many times as needed inside a **Do** loop. To employ the **Exit** statement, use the following syntax:

Do Until [condition]

[statements]

  If [condition] *Then*

   Exit Do

  End If

Loop

For counter = start *To* end [Step increment]

[statements]

code continued on next page

code continued from previous page

> *If* [condition] *Then*
>
> > *Exit For*
>
> *End If*
>
> *Next* [counter]

The **Exit Do** statement works with all versions of the **Do** loop syntax.

Exit For and **Exit Do** are useful because sometimes it's appropriate to quit a loop immediately, without performing any further iterations or statements within the loop.

Lab 5: Controlling Program Flow

In this lab, you will add password validation functionality to the loan project that you started in Lab 2. The frmMain form will check for a valid password on the frmLogon form and exit the application if the password is invalid. You will also limit the number of times that a user can type an invalid password.

You can continue to work with the files that you created in Lab 4, or you can work with the files provided in the *<install folder>*\Labs\Lab05 folder.

To see the demonstration "Lab 5 Solution," see the accompanying CD-ROM.

Estimated time to complete this lab: **45 minutes**

Objectives

After completing this lab, you will be able to:

♦ Add an **If** statement to verify the logon password.

♦ Use a static variable to count the number of logon attempts.

♦ Reset controls back to an original state.

♦ Use a public variable to pass information between two forms.

To complete the exercises in this lab, you must have the required software. For detailed information about the labs and setup for the labs, see "Labs" in "About This Course."

The solution for this lab is located in the *<install folder>*\Labs\Lab05\Solution folder.

Prerequisites

There are no prerequisites for this lab.

Exercises

The following exercises provide practice in working with the concepts covered in this chapter:

♦ Exercise 1: Validating Logon Information

  In this exercise, you will add password validation of the logon form to the main form.

◆ Exercise 2: Limiting Logon Attempts

In this exercise, you will limit the number of times that a user can try to log on to your application.

◆ Exercise 3 (Optional): Modifying Cancel Button Handling

In this exercise, you will change the way that the logon form reacts to the user clicking the **Cancel** button. Currently, clicking **Cancel** ends the application. However, some applications can continue even if the user doesn't successfully logon by allowing the user limited permissions. You will set a flag so that when the **Cancel** button is clicked, the main form will determine what action to take.

Exercise 1: Validating Logon Information

In this exercise, you will add password validation of the logon form to the main form.

▶ **Open the loan project**

1. If Visual Basic isn't running, start it.

2. Either continue with your project from Lab 4, or open the project provided for you in the *<install folder>*\Labs\Lab05 folder.

▶ **Add a form-level constant**

1. Open the Code Editor window for the frmMain form and move to the **General Declarations** section.

2. Declare a String constant, PASSWORD, and set it equal to "password":

```
Const PASSWORD As String = "password"
```

Note For this application, the only valid password is "password." In a production-quality application, each user would have a different password, and this information would reside in a database.

▶ **Validate the logon password from the frmMain form**

1. In the Code Editor window for frmMain, move to the **Form_Load** event procedure. Currently, this event procedure displays the **frmLogon** form modally.

2. Declare a static integer variable, sintLogonAttempts, to count the number of times that a user has tried to log on:

```
Static sintLogonAttempts As Integer
```

3. Write a loop that continues until the password typed into the **txtPassword** text box on frmLogon is equal to the constant PASSWORD.

4. Fill the body of the loop with code that:

    a. Increments the static counter, sintLogonAttempts, by 1.

    b. Posts a message box stating that the password is invalid.

    c. Clears out the **txtPassword** text box on frmLogon.

    d. Redisplays frmLogon modally.

To see an example of how your code should look, see Hint 5.1 in Appendix B.

▶ **Hide frmLogon instead of unloading it**

To retrieve the value of the **txtPassword** text box from the frmLogon form after it has been dismissed, the form must be hidden instead of unloaded.

1. Open the Code Editor window for frmLogon.

2. In the **cmdOK_Click** event procedure, hide the form instead of unloading it:

```
frmLogon.Hide
```

▶ **Save and test your application**

1. Save your project.

2. Run your application. The valid password is "password." Try typing an invalid password and clicking **OK**. What happens? Now type the valid password and click **OK**. What happens?

    To see the answers to the questions in step 2, see Hint 5.2 in Appendix B.

3. Close the running application.

Exercise 2: Limiting Logon Attempts

In this exercise, you will limit the number of times that a user can try to log on to your application.

▶ **Limit the number of logon attempts**

1. Open the Code Editor window for frmMain, and declare an Integer constant called MAX_LOGON_ATTEMPTS in the **Form_Load** event procedure as follows:

```
'This is the maximum number of times the application will allow a
'user to try to log on.
Const MAX_LOGON_ATTEMPTS As Integer = 3
```

2. Inside the loop that checks the validity of the password, after you increment the static counter sintLogonAttempts, add an **If** statement to compare sintLogonAttempts to the constant MAX_LOGON_ATTEMPTS:

```
sintLogonAttempts = sintLogonAttempts + 1
If sintLogonAttempts < MAX_LOGON_ATTEMPTS Then
```

3. If the number of attempts is less than the constant, handle the invalid attempt, as you currently are, by posting a message box and redisplaying **frmLogon**.

4. If the number of attempts is greater than or equal to the maximum attempts allowed, then post a message box stating that the user has tried too many times, and end the application:

```
Else
    MsgBox Prompt:= _
            "Too many invalid logon attempts. Good-bye.", _
            Buttons:=vbOKOnly + vbExclamation
    End
End If
```

5. Save and test your application.

Exercise 3 (Optional): Modifying Cancel Button Handling

In this exercise, you will change the way the logon form reacts to the user clicking the **Cancel** button. Currently, clicking **Cancel** ends the application. However, some applications can continue even if the user doesn't successfully logon by allowing the user limited permissions. You will set a flag so that when the **Cancel** button is clicked, the main form will determine what action to take.

▶ **Set a Global variable if Cancel is clicked**

1. Open the Code Editor window for frmLogon.

2. In the General Declarations section, declare a public Boolean variable, gblnCancel:

```
Public gblnCancel As Boolean
```

3. In the **cmdCancel_Click** event procedure, remove the **End** statement and, instead, set gblnCancel to **True** and unload the form:

```
Private Sub cmdCancel_Click()
    gblnCancel = True
    Unload frmLogon
End Sub
```

4. In the **cmdOK_Click** event procedure, set gblnCancel to **False** before hiding the form:

```
Private Sub cmdOK_Click()
    MsgBox "User Name = " & txtUserName.Text & _
        ", Password = " & txtPassword.Text
    gblnCancel = False
    frmLogon.Hide
End Sub
```

▶ **Check for Cancel in the frmMain Form_Load event procedure**

1. Edit the **Form_Load** event procedure for frmMain.

2. Add code to the body of the loop to check the value of the global variable, gblnCancel.

3. If gblnCancel is **True**, then end the application:

```
If frmLogon.gblnCancel = True Then
    End
End If
```

4. Save and test your application.

Self-Check Questions

See page 383 for answers.

1. The value of a variable can contain one of five different STRING values. Which of the following statements should be used to evaluate the variable?

    A. If...Then...ElseIf

    B. Select Case

    C. If...Then

    D. For...Next

2. In the statement, "If X < Y Then blnCheck = True" and X=5 and Y=3, what is the value of blnCheck?

    A. blnCheck is set to True.

    B. blnCheck is set to False.

    C. The value of blnCheck remains unchanged.

    D. The value of blnCheck is unknown.

3. When it is known how many times a set of statements should be executed, use the:

    A. Do...Loop structure.

    B. Loop Until structure.

    C. For...Next structure.

    D. While...Wend structure.

Student Notes:

Chapter 6:
Debugging

As programs become bigger and more complex, a certain number of errors are inevitable. Even careful programmers inadvertently introduce program errors, called bugs, into their syntax or logic. Finding and removing these bugs is called debugging.

In this chapter, you will learn about the debugging tools provided with Microsoft Visual Basic. Although Visual Basic cannot find and correct these errors, it provides several tools to help diagnose problems. Debugging tools assist in determining program errors by helping to examine the program execution flow, as well as the variable and property changes.

Objectives

After completing this chapter, you will be able to:

- Stop program execution by using breakpoints and watch expressions.
- Monitor variable values in the Watch window.
- Test data and a procedure's results in the Immediate window.
- Use the Locals window to evaluate variables.
- Distinguish among Run, Design, and Debug modes in Visual Basic.
- Trace the program execution sequence by using the **Call Stack**.

Types of Errors

Programming errors generally fit into three categories:

◆ Syntax

◆ Run-time

◆ Logic

The following illustration shows common error messages that appear due to run-time and syntax errors. A logic error will usually not generate an error message.

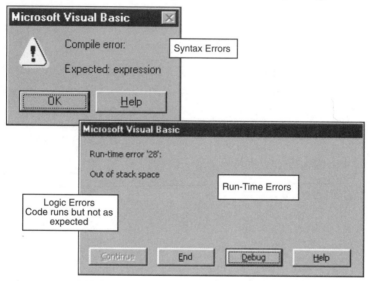

Syntax Errors

Syntax errors occur when code is constructed incorrectly. Examples include an incorrectly typed keyword, omission of required punctuation, or an incorrect construct (such as a **For** statement without a corresponding **Next** statement, or the **If** keyword on a line without a conditional operator).

Visual Basic includes an **Auto Syntax Check** option that can detect and correct syntax errors while you write your code. With this option enabled, Visual Basic interprets your code while you type it. When it spots an error, Visual Basic highlights the code and displays a message box explaining the error and offering help. This lets you correct the syntax error before moving on.

▶ **To set or clear the Auto Syntax Check option**

1. On the **Tools** menu, click **Options**.

2. In the **Options** dialog box, click the **Editor** tab.

3. Click **Auto Syntax Check**.

Run-Time Errors

Run-time errors occur when a statement attempts an operation that is impossible to carry out — for example, referencing an object that is inaccessible.

One common run-time error is attempting to read data from a nonexistent file. Another is an attempt to divide by zero. Consider the following example code:

```
Speed = Miles / Hours
```

If the variable Hours is equal to zero, the division is an invalid operation, even though the statement itself is syntactically correct. The application must run before this error is detected. It's important to provide error handlers and error-handling routines in your code to respond to these errors. For more information about error handlers, see Chapter 10, "Error Trapping."

Logic Errors

Logic errors occur when an application doesn't perform in the way it was intended. These errors are especially difficult to find because an application can have syntactically valid code, run without performing any invalid operations, and still produce incorrect results. The only way to verify an application's performance is to test it and analyze the results.

Break Mode

When you develop an application in Visual Basic, you work primarily in two modes: Design mode and Run mode. In Design mode, code is created and edited, although the effects cannot be checked until the code is run. In Run mode, the program's execution can be checked, but no changes can be made to the code. A third mode, Break mode, halts the operation of an application and gives you a snapshot of its condition at any moment.

In this section, you will learn the advantages of using Break mode while creating applications. You will learn how to set breakpoints, use the **Stop** statement, and use the **Debug.Assert** method. You will also learn when it is appropriate to use a **Watch** expression.

Overview of Break Mode

While in Break mode, you can:

◆ Modify the application's code.

◆ Determine the active procedures that have been called.

◆ Watch the values of variables, properties, and expressions.

◆ Change the values of variables and properties.

◆ Change the program flow.

◆ Execute Visual Basic statements.

Visual Basic will enter Break mode if:

◆ It encounters a breakpoint while running your code.

◆ It encounters a **Stop** statement.

◆ A watch expression that you have placed is triggered.

◆ You press CTRL+BREAK or click the **Break** button while your program is running.

◆ A statement in a line of code generates an untrapped run-time error, and you click **Debug** on the dialog box that appears.

◆ A **Debug.Assert** statement evaluates to **False**.

Note For information about error trapping and handling, see Chapter 10, "Error Trapping."

To see the demonstration "Entering Break Mode," see the accompanying CD-ROM.

Setting Breakpoints

A breakpoint is a marker in your code that tells Visual Basic to suspend execution. To stop your program and use debugging tools at a location in your code where you suspect a problem, set a breakpoint at that location. Breakpoints are temporary and are not saved with your code.

▶ **To set a breakpoint**

1. Position the insertion point anywhere in a line of the procedure where program execution should halt.

2. Use any of the following methods to add the breakpoint:

    ◆ On the **Debug** menu, click **Toggle Breakpoint**.

    ◆ Press F9.

    ◆ On the **Debug** toolbar, click the **Toggle Breakpoint** button.

    ◆ Right-click a line of code and click **Toggle Breakpoint** on the shortcut menu.

    ◆ Click the **Margin Indicator** bar next to the line of code.

Any of the previous methods adds the breakpoint; the line is set to the breakpoint color defined in the **Format Options** dialog box. You can use the same procedure to clear a breakpoint from the code. Alternatively, on the **Debug** menu, click **Clear All Breakpoints** to remove all breakpoints.

Using a Stop Statement

The **Stop** statement is similar to a breakpoint, except that it remains a part of the code until removed. Use **Stop** statements with caution. During compilation, **Stop** statements act just like **End** statements. Consequently, misuse of **Stop** statements can cause unintended run-time errors.

In the following example code, the **Stop** statement halts execution and enters Break mode:

```
Sub cmdSubmit_OnClick()
  'Enter Break mode
  Stop
End Sub
```

Using a Debug.Assert Method

You can conditionally enter Break mode by using the **Debug.Assert** method. This method uses a Boolean expression to determine whether or not to enter Break mode. To employ the **Debug.Assert** method, use the following syntax:

Debug.Assert *booleanexpression*

In the following example code, the **Debug.Assert** statement will cause Visual Basic to enter Break mode when the variable intCounter is greater than or equal to five:

```
Private Sub cmdCount_Click()
    Dim intCounter As Integer

    For intCounter = 1 To 10
        Debug.Assert intCounter < 5
    Next
End Sub
```

Note Assert invocations work only within the development environment. When the module is compiled into an executable, the method calls on the **Debug** object are omitted.

Using the Debug Toolbar

When execution of your program is halted near a point at which you think a problem is occurring, you can use the extensive debugging tools provided by Visual Basic to investigate the problem.

The **Debug** toolbar offers quick access to a number of the most frequently used debugging features. If the **Debug** toolbar isn't visible, right-click any toolbar while in Design or Break mode, and then click **Debug**.

The following illustration shows the **Debug** toolbar.

The following table describes the buttons on the **Debug** toolbar.

Button name	Description
Start	Runs the application from the Startup form (or Sub Main) specified on the **General** tab of the **Project Properties** dialog box. If in Break mode, the tooltip text of the **Start** button changes to **Continue**.
Break	Stops execution of a program temporarily. Click the **Continue** button to resume running the program.
End	Stops running the program and returns to Design mode.
Toggle Breakpoint	Creates or removes a breakpoint. A breakpoint is a place in the code where Visual Basic automatically halts execution and enters Break mode.
Step Into	Runs the next executable line of code, stepping through each line of code that follows. If the code calls another procedure, **Step Into** steps through each line in that procedure also.
Step Over	Runs the next executable line of code, stepping through each line of code that follows. If the code calls another procedure, that procedure runs completely before stepping to the next line of code in the first procedure.
Step Out	Executes the remainder of the current procedure and breaks at the next line in the calling procedure.
Locals Window	Displays the current value of local variables.
Immediate Window	Displays the Immediate window, if it is not already displayed. The Immediate window allows you to execute code or query values while the application is in Break mode.
Watch Window	Displays the Watch window, if it is not already displayed. The Watch window displays the values of selected expressions.
Quick Watch	Displays the current value of the expression that the cursor is on (while in Break mode). The expression can easily be added to the Watch window.

table continued on next page

Button name	Description
Call Stack	Displays the **Call Stack** dialog box, if it is not already displayed. While in Break mode, the **Call Stack** button lists the currently active procedure calls by presenting a dialog box that shows all procedures that have been called but not yet run to completion.

Using the Watch Window

The Watch window allows you to monitor the behavior of a variable or expression while the program executes. In this section, you will learn about using the Watch window. You will learn how to add, edit, and delete Watch expressions, and you will learn how to use the Quick Watch feature.

Overview of the Watch Window

You enter watch expressions to tell Visual Basic which variable or expressions to watch, as well as the context (procedure, module or modules) and, if you want, the conditions under which you want Visual Basic to break execution. Visual Basic will monitor the expressions that you choose and, when the program enters Break mode, tell you their values (if they are in context). You can also tell Visual Basic to enter Break mode when one of the watch expressions evaluates to **True** or changes value. This is especially useful if the variable changes inside a loop. When used in conjunction with the Quick Watch feature, the Watch window is an effective tool for detecting and fixing errors. For information about Quick Watch, see "Using Quick Watch" and "Using the Immediate Window" in this chapter.

To see the demonstration "Using the Watch Window," see the accompanying CD-ROM.

Note Watch expressions are not saved with the code.

Adding a Watch Expression

To add a watch expression, open the **Add Watch** dialog box and specify an expression, a context, and a watch-type option.

The following illustration shows the **Add Watch** dialog box with some values already entered.

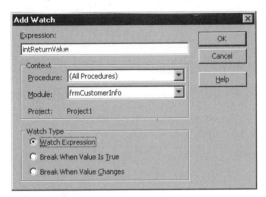

Expression

The expression can be a variable, a property, a function call, or any other valid expression. The **Add Watch** dialog box in the previous illustration uses the intReturnValue variable as an expression. Visual Basic watches the value of this variable while the program is running.

▶ **To add a watch expression by using the Add Watch command**

1. On the **Debug** menu, click **Add Watch**.

2. In the **Expression** box, type the name of the expression to evaluate.

▶ **To add a watch expression from the Code Editor window**

1. In the Code Editor window, select the expression to watch.

2. Use one of the following methods:

   ◆ On the **Debug** menu, click **Add Watch**.

   ◆ Right-click on the selected expression and click **Add Watch**.

   ◆ Drag the selected expression to the Watch window.

Note The drag-and-drop technique adds the expression to the Watch window without displaying the **Add Watch** dialog box.

Context Option Group

The values that you choose here set the scope, or context, in which Visual Basic will monitor the value of the watch expression. Be as precise as possible; Visual Basic can evaluate an expression in a narrow context more quickly.

▶ **To set the scope of the expression watched**

- ◆ Under **Context,** select the appropriate procedure and module name.

> **Note** When selecting a context for a watch expression, use the narrowest scope that fits your needs. Selecting all procedures or all modules could slow down execution considerably, because the expression is evaluated after the execution of each statement. Selecting a specific procedure for a context affects execution only while the procedure is in the list of active procedure calls, which can be seen by clicking the **Call Stack** command on the **View** menu. For more information about **Call Stack,** see "Tracing Program Flow with the Call Stack" on page 183 in this chapter.

Watch Type Option Group

This group of options sets how Visual Basic responds to the watch expression.

▶ **To determine how Visual Basic should respond to the watch expression**

- ◆ Under **Watch Type,** select an option button, and then click **OK.**

An icon appears at the left of each expression in the Watch window to indicate the expression's type. The following table shows the icon for each watch type and describes the function of each type.

Icon	Type	Description
👓	Watch Expression	Tells Visual Basic to watch the expression and display its value in the Watch window any time the application enters Break mode.
⬚	Break When Value Is True	Tells Visual Basic to break execution any time the value of the expression evaluates to a **True** (nonzero) statement.
⬚	Break When Value Changes	Tells Visual Basic to enter Break mode when the value of the expression changes.

Editing or Deleting a Watch Expression

Any watch expression listed in the Watch window can be edited or deleted.

▶ **To edit a watch expression**

1. In the Watch window, select the watch expression that you want to edit. From the **Debug** menu, click **Edit Watch**.

   −or−

   In the Watch window, right-click on the watch expression that you want to edit, and then click **Edit Watch** from the pop-up menu that appears.

   −or−

   Press CTRL+W.

   The **Edit Watch** dialog box appears.

2. Make any changes to the expression, the scope for evaluating variables, or the watch type, and then click **OK**.

The following illustration shows the **Edit Watch** dialog box. It contains a sample expression and options for context and watch type.

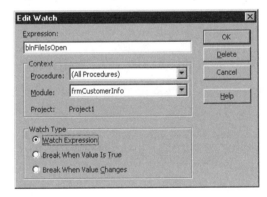

▶ **To delete a watch expression**

1. In the Watch window, select the watch expression to delete.

2. Press DELETE.

Using Quick Watch

To check the value of a property, variable, or expression for which a watch expression has not been defined, use the Quick Watch feature. To continue watching the expression, you can quickly add it to the Watch window.

The following illustration shows the **Quick Watch** dialog box.

Note If Visual Basic cannot determine the value of the current expression, the **Add** button in the **Quick Watch** dialog box is disabled.

▶ **To display the Quick Watch dialog box**

1. In the Code Editor window, select an expression.

2. On the **Debug** toolbar, click the **Quick Watch** button.

▶ **To add a watch expression from the Quick Watch dialog box**

1. In the Code Editor window, select the expression to watch.

2. On the **Debug** toolbar, click the **Quick Watch** button.

   Quick Watch displays the value of a selected expression without adding it to the Watch window.

3. In the **Quick Watch** dialog box, click **Add**.

   The expression is added to the Watch window.

Using the Immediate Window

In this section, you will learn about the Immediate window. You can use the Immediate window to query variables and object property values, and to run code. For example, when debugging or experimenting with code, you can use the Immediate window to test procedures, evaluate expressions, or assign new values to variables or properties. The Immediate window displays information that results from debugging statements that you've placed in the code or that you request by typing commands directly in the window. You will learn how to print from the Immediate window and use the **Debug.Print** statement. You will also learn how to set the value of properties in the Immediate window and display error messages. Finally, you will learn about Immediate window shortcuts.

Printing from the Immediate Window

To evaluate expressions, you print their values. Any valid expression, including expressions involving properties, can be evaluated by using the Immediate window.

There are two ways to print to the Immediate window:

◆ In Break mode, enter **Print** methods directly in the Immediate window.

◆ Include **Debug.Print** statements in the application code.

This topic focuses on using the **Print** method. For more information about using the **Debug.Print** statement, see "Using the Debug.Print Statement," on page 179 in this chapter.

To see the demonstration "Debugging in the Immediate Window," see the accompanying CD-ROM.

The scope of the Immediate window is limited to the current procedure only. This includes any local variables declared within the current procedure, module variables declared within the current code module, and global variables. Any variables or properties out of scope are not displayed.

When a program is in Break mode, the focus can be moved to the Immediate window to examine data. You can use the Immediate window to evaluate any valid expression, including expressions involving properties. The currently active form or module determines the scope. If the execution halts within code that is attached to a form or class, you can refer to the properties or local variables of that form (or one of its controls) without specifying the form or class.

For example, assume that, in the following example code, **txtCompanyName** is a control on the currently active form:

```
Print BackColor
Print txtCompanyName.Height
```

The first statement prints the numeric value of the current form's background color to the Immediate window. The second statement prints the height of **txtCompanyName**.

If execution is suspended in another module or form, you must explicitly specify the form name, as in the following example code:

```
Print  frmMain.BackColor
Print  frmMain.txtCompanyName.Height
```

A question mark (?) is useful shorthand for the **Print** method. The question mark means the same thing as **Print** and can be used in any context in which **Print** is used.

```
?  BackColor
?  txtCompanyName.Height
```

Note Referencing an unloaded form in the Immediate window (or anywhere else) loads that form.

▶ **To examine data in the Immediate window**

1. Click on the Immediate window (if visible).

   –or–

   On the **View** menu, click **Immediate Window**.

2. Type or paste a statement into the Immediate window, and then press ENTER.

   The Immediate window responds by carrying out the statement.

The following illustration shows how to use the Immediate window to examine data. The value of the expression intTestNumber * 40 is displayed in the Immediate window.

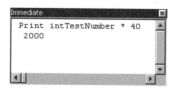

Tip Placing the cursor over a variable in the Immediate window or Code Editor window displays the variable's current value.

Using the Debug.Print Statement

The **Print** method of the **Debug** object, sends output to the Immediate window without entering Break mode. This printing technique offers several advantages over watch expressions:

◆ Execution of the program does not need to be broken for you to get feedback on how the application is performing. The data or other messages are displayed while the application runs.

◆ Feedback appears in a separate area (the Immediate window), so it does not interfere with the output that a user sees.

◆ The debug code is saved as part of the form, so the statements do not need to be redefined the next time the application is loaded.

To track variable values at full execution speed, while creating a history of the values in the Immediate window, use the following syntax:

Debug.Print [items][;]

where [*items*] is an expression or list of expressions to print. If omitted, a blank line is printed. [;] will use columns to separate multiple values.

The following example code prints the value of curSalary to the Immediate window every time the statement is executed:

```
Debug.Print "Salary = " & curSalary
```

Note The preceding technique works best if there is a particular place in the application's code at which the variable (in this case, curSalary) is known to change.

Note The ampersand (&) shown in the previous example is used to concatenate two strings to create one string. For example, the previous string might appear as Salary = 36000 when displayed in the Immediate window.

> **Important Note** Debug.Print statements are removed when an application is compiled into an .exe file. However, Visual Basic does not strip out function calls appearing as arguments to **Debug.Print**. Any side effects of those functions continue in a compiled .exe file, even though the function results are not printed.

Further Uses of the Immediate Window

Employing the **Print** method and the **Debug.Print** statement are the most common uses of the Immediate window. However, you can use the Immediate window to test your code in other ways.

Setting Values of Properties and Variables

In isolating the possible cause of an error, you sometimes need to test the effects of particular data values. The following example code shows how you can use statements in the Immediate window to set values when in Break mode:

```
frmMain.BackColor = 255
vsbRate.Value = 100
intMaxRows = 50
```

After the values of one or more properties or variables are changed, you can resume execution to see the results.

Testing a Procedure's Results

You can also use the Immediate window to make calls to **Sub** and **Function** procedures. This allows you to test a procedure with any given set of arguments. To test a procedure, enter a statement in the Immediate window, as in the following example code:

```
dblResult = Quadratic(2, 8, 8)
DisplayGraph 50, intArrayGraphVals
Form_MouseDown
```

When ENTER is pressed, Visual Basic switches to Run mode to execute the statement, and then returns to Break mode.

> **Note** If Option Explicit is in effect, any variables entered in the Immediate window must already be declared within the current scope. Scope applies to procedure calls just as it does to variables. Any procedure within the currently active form can be called. For more information about scope, see "Scope of Variables" on page 99 in Chapter 4, "Variables and Procedures."

Displaying Error Messages

You can use the Immediate window to get information about a specific error number.

▶ **To display the error message by using the Immediate window**

1. Type the error number in the Immediate window, as in the following example code:

```
error 58
```

2. Press ENTER.

   The associated error message appears, as shown in the following illustration.

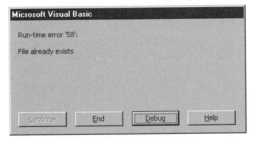

Immediate Window Shortcuts

The following are some shortcuts that you can use in the Immediate window:

◆ After you enter a statement, you can execute it again by moving the insertion point back to that statement and pressing ENTER.

◆ Before pressing ENTER, you can edit the current statement to alter its effects.

◆ You can use the mouse or the arrow keys to move around in the Immediate window. Don't press ENTER unless you are at a statement that you want to execute.

◆ Pressing CTRL+HOME moves the cursor to the top of the Immediate window; pressing CTRL+END moves it to the bottom.

◆ Pressing HOME moves the cursor to the beginning of the current line; pressing END moves the cursor to the end of the current line.

Using the Locals Window

Another debugging tool that can be used during Break mode is the Locals window. The Locals window shows the values of any variables within the scope of the current procedure. While the execution switches from procedure to procedure, the contents of the Locals window change to reflect only the variables that are applicable to the current procedure.

The following illustration shows the Locals window.

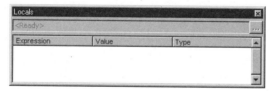

▶ **To access the Locals window**

◆ On the **View** menu, click **Locals window**.

The Locals window has four elements that you can use to evaluate the state of the application:

◆ **Call Stack** button

Opens the **Call** dialog box that lists the procedures in the Call Stack.

◆ Expression

Lists the name of the variables.

◆ Value

Lists the value of the variable. You can edit data in this column.

◆ Type

Lists the variable type. You cannot edit data in this column.

Tracing Program Flow with the Call Stack

The Call Stack feature creates a list of procedures that trace the flow of code through multiple active procedure calls. Active procedure calls are procedures in the application that were started but not completed. With this tool, the correct sequence of procedures can be verified.

The following illustration shows the **Call Stack** dialog box, which displays a list of currently active procedure calls during Break mode.

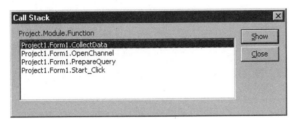

For example, one procedure can call a second procedure, which can call a third procedure—all before the first procedure is completed. Such nested procedure calls can be difficult to follow. The Call Stack shows this flow. You can display the Call Stack only when the code is in Break mode. There are four ways to invoke the Call Stack.

▶ **To display the Call Stack**

◆ On the **View** menu, click **Call Stack**.

   −or−

◆ While in Break mode, press CTRL+L.

   −or−

◆ On the **Debug** toolbar (when visible), click the **Call Stack** button.

   −or−

◆ In the Locals window, click the **Ellipsis (...)** button next to the **Procedure** box. The following illustration shows the **Ellipsis** button.

Tracing Nested Procedures

The **Call Stack** dialog box lists all the active procedure calls in a series of nested calls, placing the earliest active procedure call at the bottom of the list and subsequent procedure calls at the top of the list.

The information given for each procedure begins with the module or form name, followed by the name of the called procedure. Because the **Call Stack** dialog box doesn't indicate the variable assigned to an instance of a form, it does not distinguish between multiple instances of forms or classes.

You can use the **Call Stack** dialog box to display the statement in a procedure that passes control of the application to the next procedure in the list.

▶ **To display the statement that calls another procedure in the Call Stack dialog box**

1. In the **Call Stack** dialog box, select the procedure call to display.

2. Click the **Show** button.

The **Call Stack** dialog box closes, and the procedure appears in the Code Editor window. The cursor location in the Code Editor window indicates the statement that calls the next procedure in the **Call Stack** dialog box.

Lab 6: Using Visual Basic Debugging Tools

In this lab, you will explore the Visual Basic debugging tools and see the different types of assistance that these features can provide when debugging a program.

You will use a project provided for you, named Debug, located in the *<install folder>*\Labs\Lab06 folder.

To see the demonstration "Lab 6 Solution," see the accompanying CD-ROM.

Estimated time to complete this lab: **60 minutes**

Objectives

After completing this lab, you will be able to:

◆ Identify the main features of the Visual Basic debugging tools.

◆ Use Visual Basic debugging tools to step through an application, examine its variables, change data, and execute code dynamically.

◆ Use Visual Basic debugging tools to locate simple logic errors.

To complete the exercises in this lab, you must have the required software. For detailed information about the labs and setup for the labs, see "Labs" in "About This Course."

Prerequisites

There are no prerequisites for this lab.

Exercises

The following exercises provide practice in working with the concepts and techniques covered in this chapter:

◆ Exercise 1: Setting Breakpoints and Stepping Through Code

In this exercise, you will trace the logic of a procedure by stepping through its Visual Basic code one line at a time.

◆ Exercise 2: Stepping into and Stepping over Procedures

In this exercise, you will see the differences between stepping into, over, and out of a procedure. To step into a procedure means to run it one line at time. To step over a procedure means to run it as a unit. To step out of a procedure means to run it until it completes the current procedure and returns to the calling procedure.

◆ Exercise 3: Examining Variables in the Immediate Window

In this exercise, you will use the Immediate window to check the values stored in variables while your code is running. You will also change the values of variables from within the Immediate window.

◆ Exercise 4: Running Code from the Immediate Window

In this exercise, after clearing all of the breakpoints that you have added to the Debug project, you will run code from the Immediate window.

◆ Exercise 5: Outputting Text to the Debug Window

In this exercise, you will use the **Debug.Print** statement (the **Print** method of the **Debug** object) to display text in the Immediate window. This technique is helpful if you know of a particular place in your code where a variable changes repeatedly and you need to observe those changes. It is also helpful in places where calculations occur and you can't print the results of those calculations directly to a form.

◆ Exercise 6: Examining the Calls List

In this exercise, you will trace the flow of your code by examining the stack of procedure calls in the **Call Stack** dialog box.

◆ Exercise 7: Monitoring Variables with Watch Expressions

In this exercise, you will add a watch expression to test the value of a variable named intWordLength and to break when intWordLength equals 6.

◆ Exercise 8: Finding a Logic Error on Your Own

In this exercise, you will use the skills that you have learned to find and fix a logic error by yourself.

Exercise 1: Setting Breakpoints and Stepping Through Code

In this exercise, you will trace the logic of a procedure by stepping through its Visual Basic code one line at a time.

▶ **Open the project and display the debug form**

1. Open the Debug project located in the *<Install Folder>*\Labs\Lab06 folder.

2. View the form debug.frm.

3. On the **View** menu, point to **Toolbars**, and click **Debug**.

▶ Insert a breakpoint

1. Double-click the **Trace** button on frmDebug to view the **cmdLogic_Click** event procedure in the Code Editor window.

2. In the **cmdLogic_Click** event procedure, set a breakpoint on the first line of executable code:

```
picOutput.Cls
```

You can use one of the following methods to set a breakpoint:

- ◆ Place your insertion point in the line to break; then, on the **Debug** menu, click **Toggle Breakpoint**.
- ◆ Place your insertion point in the line to break and press F9.
- ◆ Place your insertion point in the line to break; then, on the **Debug** toolbar, click the **Toggle Breakpoint** button.
- ◆ In the Code Editor window, click the **Margin Indicator** bar next to the line on which to break.

Note Variable declarations are not executable statements. If you press F9 when the insertion point is in a declaration statement, Visual Basic displays an error message.

By default, the line's background color changes to red, and a red dot appears on the **Margin Indicator** bar in the Code Editor window. When you run the code, Visual Basic will stop at this line, and the program will switch to Break mode.

All of these methods toggle breakpoints. If any of them are repeated, the breakpoint will be deleted and the line will change back to its normal color.

▶ Run the application and step through the code

1. Click the **Start** button on the toolbar to run the application.

2. Move the mouse pointer over the nine buttons and watch the status bar.

   The status bar message reminds you which debugging feature each button demonstrates.

3. Resize the Visual Basic window so that it occupies only half of the screen. This allows you to see both the Visual Basic window and your application.

4. Click the **Trace** button of the form.

   The Code Editor window becomes the active window, and the line of code that is about to be executed is highlighted.

5. On the **Debug** toolbar, click the **Step Into** button to step through the procedure one line at a time. Watch the application's output appear in its window.

6. Continue stepping through the procedure until the **End Sub** statement is highlighted in the Code Editor window.

7. Click the **Continue** button on the toolbar to resume running the application normally.

8. Click the **End** button to end the program.

Exercise 2: Stepping into and Stepping over Procedures

In this exercise, you will see the differences between stepping into, over, and out of a procedure. To step into a procedure means to run it one line at time. To step over a procedure means to run it as a unit. To step out of a procedure means to run it until it completes the current procedure and returns to the calling procedure.

▶ **Insert a breakpoint and run the application**

1. On the **Debug** form, double-click the **Trace With Calls** button.

    Trace With Calls

2. Set a breakpoint on the first line of executable code in the **cmdLogicCalls_Click** event procedure.

3. Run the application.

4. Click the **Trace With Calls** button.

    The code does the same thing it did in the previous exercise, but this time it is broken into separate procedures instead of doing everything in a pair of nested **For** loops.

▶ **Step into and out of a procedure**

1. Click the **Step Into** button twice to step through two lines of code.

    The current line contains a call to the **PrintRow** procedure.

2. Click the **Step Into** button again.

    The debugger steps into the **PrintRow** procedure.

3. Click the **Step Into** button three more times.

    The debugger steps into the **PrintNumber** procedure.

4. Click the **Step Out Of** button to return to the calling procedure.

5. On the **Run** menu, click **Continue** to resume running the application normally.

▶ **Step over a procedure**

1. Click the **Trace With Calls** button in the **Debug** application again.

2. Click **Step Over** three times.

   When the call to **PrintRow** is highlighted, a **Step Over** operation runs that procedure and any other procedures that **PrintRow** calls, without forcing you to step into them — the debugger steps over the **PrintRow** procedure.

3. Continue clicking **Step Over** until the **End Sub** statement is highlighted.

4. Resume running the program normally.

5. Click the **End** button to end the program.

Exercise 3: Examining Variables in the Immediate Window

In this exercise, you will use the Immediate window to check the values stored in variables while your code is running. You will also change the values of variables from within the Immediate window.

▶ **Examine the values stored in variables**

1. In the Debug application, double-click the **Examine Variables** button.

2. Set a breakpoint on the first line of executable code in the **cmdExamine_Click** event procedure.

3. Run the application.

4. In the Debug application, click the **Examine Variables** button.

5. Step through the procedure until the **MsgBox** statement is highlighted.

6. Switch to the Immediate window.

7. Type **? a** and press ENTER.

   Visual Basic displays the number 1, which is the value currently in the variable *a*.

8. Use the same method to check the values in the variables *b*, *c*, *d*, *e*, and *sum*.

▶ **Assign a value to a variable**

1. Look at the value of the variable *sum*.

2. In the Immediate window, type **sum = 20** and press ENTER.

3. Type **? sum** and press ENTER.

   Notice that the value of *sum* has changed.

4. Resume running the program normally.

5. Click the **End** button to end the program.

Exercise 4: Running Code from the Immediate Window

In this exercise, after clearing all of the breakpoints that you have added to the Debug project, you will run code from the Immediate window.

▶ **Clear breakpoints**

◆ On the **Debug** menu, click **Clear All Breakpoints**.

▶ **Type code in the Immediate window and then run it**

1. On the Debug form, double-click the **Run Code On The Fly** button.

2. Add the following line of code to the **cmdCode_Click** event procedure:

```
Stop
```

When Visual Basic executes this line, it will enter Break mode.

3. Run the application.

4. In the Debug window, click the **Run Code On The Fly** button.

5. Type the following lines of code in the Immediate window to show that expressions can be evaluated and statements can be executed in the Immediate window:

```
x = sqr(2.0)
? x
x = x + 1
? x
```

6. Type the following lines of code in the Immediate window to show that properties can be queried or set in the Immediate window:

```
? me.height
me.height = me.height + 100
? cmdCode.caption
```

Observe that the height of the form changes.

7. Type the following lines of code in the Immediate window to show that code can be executed from Immediate window:

```
cmdLogic_Click
picOutput.cls
end
```

Exercise 5: Outputting Text to the Debug Window

In this exercise, you will use the **Debug.Print** statement (the **Print** method of the **Debug** object) to display text in the Immediate window. This technique is helpful if you know of a particular place in your code where a variable changes repeatedly and you need to observe those changes. It is also helpful in places where calculations occur and you can't print the results of those calculations directly to a form.

▶ **Print directly to the Debug window**

1. On the **Debug** form, double-click the **Use Debug.Print** button.

2. Set a breakpoint on the first line of executable code in the **cmdDebugPrint_Click** event procedure.

3. Run the application.

4. Click the **Use Debug.Print** button.

5. Step through several lines of code until the **Debug.Print** statement runs.

   The application displays directly to the Immediate window.

6. Continue stepping through code, and watch the application's output appear in the Immediate window.

7. When you reach the **End Sub** statement, click the **Continue** button on the toolbar.

8. Click the **End** button to end the application.

Exercise 6: Examining the Calls List

In this exercise, you will trace the flow of your code by examining the stack of procedure calls in the **Call Stack** dialog box.

▶ **Examine the calls list**

1. On the Debug form, double-click the **Examine Call Stack** button.

2. Set a breakpoint on the first line of executable code in the **cmdCallStack_Click** event procedure.

3. Run the application.

4. Click the **Examine Call Stack** button.

5. Click the **Step Into** button nine times, until you're in the most deeply nested procedure call, the **PrintNumber** procedure.

6. Click the **Call Stack** button on the toolbar.

   Visual Basic displays the **Call Stack** dialog box, which shows you the trail of calls leading to the **PrintNumber** procedure.

   How many levels deep is the **PrintNumber** procedure nested? See Hint 6.1 in Appendix B.

7. Click **Close,** and then resume normal program execution by clicking **Continue** on the **Run** menu.

8. Click the **End** button to end the application.

Exercise 7: Monitoring Variables with Watch Expressions

In this exercise, you will add a watch expression to test the value of a variable named intWordLength and to break when intWordLength equals 6.

▶ **Use the Variable Watch button**

1. Run the application.

2. On the Debug form, click the **Watch Variables** button.

   The application displays a message in its own output area, one word per line. The code assigned to this button extracts the words from a single string.

3. Click the **End** button to end the application.

▶ **Add a watch expression**

1. In the Debug application, double-click the **Watch Variables** button.

2. In the **cmdWatch_Click** event procedure, place the insertion point in the variable intWordLength, on the third line.

3. On the **Debug** menu, click **Add Watch.**

4. In the **Expression** box, type **intWordLength = 6.**

5. For Watch Type, select the **Break When Value Is True** option, and then click **OK.**

Setting this option tells Visual Basic to stop your code when intWordLength equals 6.

The Watches window appears, displaying the variables being watched.

▶ **Run the application with the added watch expression**

1. Run the application.

2. In the Debug application, click the **Watch Variables** button.

   The application stops on the second line of the **While** loop. Notice that four words are displayed in the application's output area, none of which is six letters long. Also, notice that the value of the expression in the Watches window is now **True**.

3. Resume running the application normally.

4. Click the **End** button to end the application.

Exercise 8: Finding a Logic Error On Your Own

In this exercise, you will use the skills that you have learned to find and fix a logic error by yourself.

▶ **Run the code with the logic error and then fix the error**

1. Run the application.

2. In the Debug application, click the **Trace** button and watch the output in its window. This is the correct output.

3. In the Debug application, click the **Fix Logic Error** button.

   Only two columns of output appear, not four.

4. Using your knowledge of the Visual Basic debugging tools, find the error and fix it.

For help in completing this exercise, see Hint 6.2 in Appendix B.

Self-Check Questions

See page 385 for answers.

1. To cause a Visual Basic program to enter Break mode when a value changes, use:

A. A **Stop** statement.

B. A breakpoint.

C. A **Debug.Break** statement.

D. A watch expression.

2. The scope of the Immediate window is:

A. Limited to the current procedure.

B. Limited to the current module.

C. Limited to the current form.

D. Global.

3. The output of a Debug.Print statement is sent to:

A. The default printer.

B. The Immediate window.

C. The Call Stack.

D. The txtDebug variable.

Chapter 7:
Working with Controls

At this point in the course, you should be familiar with the standard **TextBox** and **CommandButton** controls. In this chapter, you will learn how to use some of the more advanced standard controls that Microsoft Visual Basic provides. You'll also learn how to expand the functionality of your application by incorporating ActiveX controls.

Objectives

After completing this chapter, you will be able to:

◆ Identify and use the standard controls in Visual Basic.

◆ Define how an ActiveX control differs from a standard control.

◆ Add ActiveX controls to a project and use these controls in a program.

Types of Controls

The controls that you can use in Visual Basic fit into three categories: standard controls, ActiveX controls, and insertable objects. These categories are described in the following table.

Type	Description
Standard controls	These controls are contained in Visual Basic. Examples include the **CommandButton** and **TextBox** controls. Also called intrinsic controls, standard controls are always available from the toolbox and are the main focus of this course. These controls are covered in the topic "Overview of Standard Controls" in this chapter.
ActiveX controls	These controls are separate files with the .ocx extension. These controls can be added to the toolbox.
Insertable objects	These controls are typically OLE objects such as a Microsoft Excel **Worksheet** object. Insertable objects can be added to the toolbox and are covered briefly in the topic "Insertable Objects" on page 214 in this chapter.

Overview of Standard Controls

Standard controls are included with all editions of Visual Basic. Examples include the **TextBox, CommandButton, ListBox,** and **ComboBox** controls. For more information about the **TextBox** and **CommandButton** controls, see Chapter 2, "Visual Basic Fundamentals." You can use standard controls to add familiar Microsoft Windows features to your applications quickly and easily.

You can add standard controls to your application with minimum code. Other, more advanced controls, such as the **FileListBox** and **Timer** controls, require additional programming. For more information, see "Advanced Standard Controls" on page 205 in this chapter.

To see the demonstration "Using the PictureBox and Image Controls," see the accompanying CD-ROM.

The following table lists the standard controls in the Visual Basic toolbox.

Control	Description
A	The **Label** control most commonly displays text that the user cannot change. For more information, see "Label" on page 43 in Chapter 2, "Visual Basic Fundamentals."
|abl|	The **TextBox** control obtains information from the user or displays information provided by the application. For more information, see "TextBox" on page 45 in Chapter 2, "Visual Basic Fundamentals."
	The **CommandButton** control performs a task when the user clicks the control. For more information, see "CommandButton" on page 46 in Chapter 2, "Visual Basic Fundamentals."
	The **CheckBox** control presents a single option or several different options to the user, any or all of which can be selected. It can be turned on or off by the user.
	The **OptionButton** control presents a group of options from which the user can select only one. It can be turned on or off by the user.
	The **Frame** control groups related controls, either visually or functionally. A common use for the **Frame** control is to group several option buttons on a form.
	The **PictureBox** control displays a graphic or text. A **PictureBox** control can also be used to display animated graphics.
	The **Image** control displays a graphic, but it uses fewer system resources than a **PictureBox** control and supports fewer features.
	The **ComboBox** control combines the features of a **TextBox** control and a **ListBox** control. Users can enter information in the text box portion of the control or select an item from the list box portion. A **ComboBox** control can also be used to create a drop-down list box.
	The **ListBox** control displays a list from which the user can select one or more items.

Using ComboBox and ListBox Controls

In this section, you will learn how to use list boxes and combo boxes. List boxes and combo boxes present the user with choices.

You can use one of the drop-down lists to minimize the initial amount of space required to display the list on the form.

Populating a List

Generally, a combo box is appropriate when there is a list of suggested choices, and a list box is appropriate when you want to limit input to what is on the list. A combo box contains an edit field, so choices not on the list can be typed in this field.

The following illustration shows a form that uses several list boxes and combo boxes.

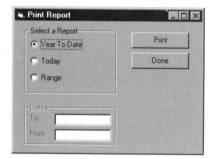

You can populate the list at design time or at run time.

Populating a List at Design Time

To add items to a combo or list box at design time, set the **List** property. In the **Property** box, click **List** and then add each item, pressing CTRL + ENTER after each one.

Populating a List at Run Time

To add items to a combo or list box at run time, use the **AddItem** method in code. To use the **AddItem** method, use the following syntax:

object.*AddItem* item, index

The *item* argument is a string that represents the text to add to the list.

The *index* argument is an integer that indicates where in the list to add the new item. If you do not provide an index, the item is added at the proper sorted position (if the **Sorted** property is set to **True**) or to the end of the list (if **Sorted** is set to **False**).

The following example code adds the string "Region A" to the **lstRegions** list box:

```
lstRegions.AddItem "RegionA"
```

Setting or Returning the Current Selection

To access items in a combo or list box, use the **ListIndex** and **List** properties.

The **ListIndex** property sets or returns the index number of the currently selected item. The first item in the list is index number 0. If no item is selected, **ListIndex** returns −1. The **ListCount** property is always one more than the index number of the last item in the list.

The **NewIndex** property returns the index of the last item added to the list. This property is useful when working with sorted lists. When you add an item to a sorted list, Visual Basic inserts the item in alphabetic order by default. This property tells you where the item was inserted. You can also use this value to select the newly added item.

The following example code adds an item to the list box and sets the new item as the current selection:

```
lstRegions.AddItem "West"
lstRegions.ListIndex = lstRegions.NewIndex
```

The **List** property sets or returns the text of an item in a list box. You pass an index number to the **List** property to specify which item to access. To return the text of the selected item, pass the **ListIndex** property, as shown in the following example code:

```
strSelection = lstRegions.List(lstRegions.ListIndex)
```

To return the string for a combo box, use the **Text** property of the control, as shown in the following example code:

```
strSelection = cboMyList.Text
```

Associating a Value with a List Item

Sometimes your application may require a specific value to be associated with an item in a list. For example, you may populate a combo box with a list of customer names. When the user selects a customer, the application looks up the record from a database. In this case, you may want to have the CustomerID returned when a customer is selected, instead of just their name. List boxes and combo boxes support the **ItemData** property for this purpose.

In the following example code, a combo box is populated with three customer names, and their associated CustomerIDs are loaded into the **ItemData** property. The **NewIndex** property is used to identify which item was just added.

```
cboCustomers.AddItem "Maria Anders"
cboCustomers.ItemData(cboCustomers.NewIndex) = 1000
cboCustomers.AddItem "Ana Trujillo"
cboCustomers.ItemData(cboCustomers.NewIndex) = 1010
cboCustomers.AddItem "Antonio Moreno"
cboCustomers.ItemData(cboCustomers.NewIndex) = 1020
```

The following example code returns the ItemData value of the selected record:

```
CustomerID = cboCustomers.ItemData(cboCustomers.ListIndex)
```

Removing Items from a List

Use the **RemoveItem** method to remove an item from a list box or combo box. The **RemoveItem** method uses the following syntax:

object.**RemoveItem** index

The following example code verifies that an item is selected in the list and then removes the selected item:

```
Private Sub cmdRemoveListItem_Click()
  If lstCustomers.ListIndex > -1 Then
      lstCustomers.RemoveItem lstCustomers.ListIndex
  End If
End Sub
```

Checking to make sure that the **ListIndex** property is greater than −1 keeps an error from occurring if you attempt to use **RemoveItem** when no items are selected.

Sorting the List

To cause a list to appear in alphanumeric order when displayed on a form, set the **Sorted** property to **True**.

To display list items in the order in which they are added to the list, set the **Sorted** property to **False**.

For more information on properties and methods of the **ComboBox** and **ListBox** controls, see "ComboBox" and "ListBox" in MSDN Help.

ComboBox Example

Combo boxes provide more versatility than simple list boxes. Some combo boxes allow the user to enter a new selection, rather than limiting the selection to only those items that are provided by the application.

There are three variations of combo boxes (the type is determined by the **Style** property):

◆ 0 (Drop-down combo box)

◆ 1 (Simple combo box)

◆ 2 (Drop-down list)

This topic provides example code that uses a **ComboBox** control. The example that follows displays the flag for a country selected from a list. An initial list of countries is displayed when the form loads. The user can then add and remove items from the list at run time.

The following illustration shows the form used in the example.

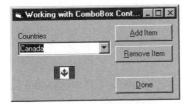

Note The sample code for this example, called FlagShow, can be found in the *<install folder>*\SampApps\Controls folder on the accompanying CD-ROM.

Building the Initial List

In the following example code, the **Form_Load** event uses the **AddItem** method to create the initial list:

```
Private Sub Form_Load()
  'Build the intial list
  cboCountries.AddItem  "Canada"
  cboCountries.AddItem  "United States"
  cboCountries.AddItem  "Mexico"
  cboCountries.AddItem  "Brazil"
  cboCountries.AddItem  "Chile"
End Sub
```

Changing the Flag when a Country Is Selected

When the user clicks a country name in the combo box, the example code uses the **Text** property of the combo box to retrieve the name of the selected country. This name is then passed to the function procedure **FindFile**. The **FindFile** function returns the file name of the flag image for the selected country. If the file name is not available, a blank flag image and a message appear. If an image is available for the selected country, it is loaded into **imgFlag**.

```
Private Sub cboCountries_Click()
  Dim strFileName As String
  strFileName = FindFile(cboCountries.Text)
  If strFileName <> "Not Available" Then
      imgFlag.Picture = _
        LoadPicture("C:\Program Files\Microsoft Visual Studio\" & _
          "Common\Graphics\Icons\Flags\" & strFileName)
      lblMessage.Visible = False
  Else
      imgFlag.Picture = imgNA.Picture
      lblMessage.Visible = True
  End If
End Sub
```

Adding Countries to the List

When the user clicks the **Add Item** button, the user is prompted for a new country name. The following example code adds the new name to the list and selects it:

```
Private Sub cmdAddItem_Click()
  Dim strNewItem As String
  strNewItem = InputBox(prompt:="Enter country name")
  cboCountries.AddItem strNewItem
  cboCountries.ListIndex = cboCountries.NewIndex
End Sub
```

Note   The **Sorted** property of the list box is set to **True** at design time, so the country names are displayed in alphabetical order.

Removing Countries from the List

When the **Remove Item** button is clicked, the **RemoveItem** method removes the selected item from the list. The application uses the index returned by **ListIndex** to determine which item is selected.

```
Private Sub cmdRemoveItem_Click()
  cboCountries.RemoveItem cboCountries.ListIndex
  imgFlag.Picture = imgNA.Picture
  lblMessage.Visible = False
End Sub
```

Using OptionButton and Frame Controls

Use the **OptionButton** control if you want the user to select one option from a group of available options. When a user clicks an option button, all other option buttons within the group are cleared.

To group option buttons, use a **Frame** or **PictureBox** control as a container control. All option buttons within a container control function as a group. The container control also provides a visual cue to the user that the options in each group are functionally distinct. You can also place option buttons directly on a form. All option buttons placed directly on a form function as a single group.

You cannot use the double-click technique of adding controls to a form to place an **OptionButton** control within a **Frame** or **PictureBox** control. Double-clicking the **OptionButton** button in the toolbox places the control in the middle of the form, rather than within the container.

The following illustration shows a form that contains a group of **OptionButton** controls within a **Frame** control.

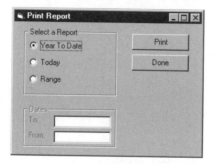

▶ **To create a group of option buttons**

1. Draw the **Frame** or **PictureBox** control to contain the option buttons.

2. Draw the option buttons within the container control.

 Note You should draw the container control before you draw the option buttons. You cannot drag an existing option button into a container.

Working with Selected Text

To access the text that has been selected in a control, use the **SelText**, **SelStart**, and **SelLength** properties.

The **SelText** property sets or returns the selected text. The following example code retrieves the selected text in a text box:

```
strMyText = txtMyTextBox.SelText
```

The **SelStart** and **SelLength** properties set or return integers that indicate the starting character and the length of the selected text, respectively.

The following example code selects all text in the **txtMyTextBox** text box:

```
With txtMyTextBox
    .SelStart = 0
    .SelLength = Len(txtMyTextBox.Text)
    .SetFocus
End With
```

 Note These properties are available at run time only and are not displayed in the Properties window.

Advanced Standard Controls

In this section, you will learn about some of the more advanced standard controls. These controls can be used for:

♦ Managing files (**FileListBox, DirListBox, DriveListBox**).

♦ Executing code at regular intervals (**Timer**).

Overview of Advanced Standard Controls

The following table describes each advanced control.

Advanced control	Description
📄	The **FileListBox** control displays a list of files in the directory specified by the **Path** property. Use this control to display a list of files selected by file type.
📁	The **DirListBox** control displays directories and paths. Use this control to display a hierarchical list of directories.
🗄	The **DriveListBox** control displays a list of all the valid drives in a user's system. Use this control to enable a user to select a disk drive at run time.
⏱	The **Timer** control is used to execute code at regular intervals by causing a **Timer** event.

> **Note** The FileListBox, DirListBox, and DriveListBox are provided in Visual Basic as one technique for accessing the file system. Consider using the **CommonDialog** control for file system operations such as opening or saving a file. For more information, about the **CommonDialog** control, see "Overview of the CommonDialog Control" on page 213 in this chapter.

Using File Management Controls

You can use the **DriveListBox, DirListBox,** and **FileListBox** controls to add file management features to your application.

The following illustration shows an Icon Viewer application that displays the image from a .bmp or .ico file.

The application uses the **DriveListBox, DirListBox,** and **FileListBox** controls to enable the user to select a file. The image from the selected file is then displayed in an image control.

To make these controls work together, you write code to change properties of the controls while the user interacts with the application. Only three lines of code are needed to implement the Icon Viewer application.

The following example code sets the **Path** property of the **DirListBox** control when the user selects a drive in the **DriveListBox** control:

```
Sub drvDrive_Change()
  dirDirectory.Path = drvDrive.Drive
End Sub
```

The following example code sets the **Path** property of the **FileListBox** control when the user selects a directory in the **DirListBox** control:

```
Sub dirDirectory_Change()
  filFileList.Path = dirDirectory.Path
End Sub
```

The following example code sets the **Picture** property of the **Image** control when the user selects a file name in the **FileListBox** control.

```
Sub filFileList_Click()
  imgSelectedImage.Picture = LoadPicture(dirDirectory.Path _
      & "\" & filFileList.FileName)
End Sub
```

Note For more information on using the **LoadPicture** function, see "LoadPicture" in MSDN Help.

File System Object

A new feature of Visual Basic is the File System Object (FSO) object model, which provides an object-based tool for working with folders and files. This tool allows you to use the familiar object.method syntax with a rich set of properties, methods, and events to process folders and files, in addition to using the traditional Visual Basic statements and commands. Implementing solutions by using FSO is outside the scope of this course. For more information, see "Introduction to the File System Object Model" in MSDN Help.

Using the Timer Control

You can use the **Timer** control to delay execution of code or to execute code at fixed intervals. For example, you can use the **Timer** control to run a task once a minute. The **Timer** control works by causing a **Timer** event to occur at a specified interval.

The following table lists some important properties of the **Timer** control.

Property	Description
Interval	The **Interval** property is measured in milliseconds and is represented by a value from 1 to 65,535. For example, a value of 10,000 milliseconds equals 10 seconds. The maximum value, 65,535 milliseconds, is equivalent to just over 1 minute.
Enabled	The **Enabled** property determines if the **Timer** control will invoke the **Timer** event in the time specified by the **Interval** property.

By using a **Timer** control, you can create a digital clock for your application, as shown in the following illustration.

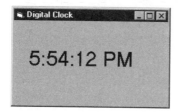

▶ **To add a digital clock to your application**

1. Add a **Label** control and a **Timer** control to the form.

2. Set the following properties of the **Timer** control at design time.

Property	Value
Enabled	True
Interval	1000 (equal to 1 second)

3. In the **Timer** event for the **Timer** control, add code to set the **Caption** property of a label to the current time, as shown in the following example code:

```
Private Sub Timer1_Timer()
    Label1.Caption = Time
End Sub
```

Note A **Timer** control can start disabled, be enabled by some event procedure during program execution, and then be disabled again when the **Timer** event is invoked.

ActiveX Controls

In this section, you will learn how ActiveX controls provide functionality beyond that of standard controls. Unlike standard controls, which are intrinsic to Visual Basic and appear in the toolbox by default, ActiveX controls are separate files and must be added to the toolbox before you can use them.

You can use ActiveX controls to greatly expand the capabilities of Visual Basic. In addition to the controls included with Visual Basic, a number of third-party controls are available separately. You can also create your own ActiveX controls for reuse or distribution.

Note Creating ActiveX controls is beyond the scope of this course. For more information, see *Mastering Visual Basic 6 Development*.

Adding ActiveX Controls to the Toolbox

Many ActiveX controls come with Visual Basic, and others are available for purchase. ActiveX controls are contained in files with the .ocx extension.

Controls with the extension .vbx use older technology and are found in applications written in earlier versions of Visual Basic. Visual Basic 6 does not support .vbx controls. When Visual Basic opens a project containing a .vbx control, the default behavior is to replace the .vbx control with an .ocx control, if an .ocx version of the control is available.

▶ **To add ActiveX controls to the toolbox**

1. On the **Project** menu, click **Components**.

   The **Components** dialog box appears.

2. On the **Controls** tab, select the controls that you want to add and click **OK**.

Microsoft Windows Common Controls

The Windows common controls let you build the appearance and functionality of Windows into your applications. The collection includes the controls listed in the following tables.

Microsoft Windows Common Controls 6.0

Name	Control	Description
TabStrip		Use the **TabStrip** control to create tabbed dialog boxes similar to those found throughout the Windows environment (for example, the **Display** dialog box in the Control Panel).
ToolBar		Use the **ToolBar** control to add a toolbar to a form. Typically, the buttons in a toolbar correspond to items in an application's menu, providing a more direct way for the user to access an application's commands.
StatusBar		Use the **StatusBar** control (at the bottom of an application window) to display information about the current state of the application. For example, in Microsoft Word, the status bar displays the current page and section number of a document.
Progress		Use the **Progress** control to let the user know that the application is processing information and how far the process has progressed. When you copy or move files in Windows, for example, a progress indicator gives you immediate feedback about the operation.
TreeView		Use the **TreeView** control to display a hierarchical list of entries, each of which consists of a label and an optional bitmap. A tree view is typically used to display the headings in a document, the entries in an index, the files and directories on a disk, or any other kind of information that might usefully be displayed as a hierarchy.

table continued on next page

Name	Control	Description
ImageList		Use the **ImageList** control to contain a collection of images that can be used by other controls. The **ToolBar** control, for instance, can retrieve the images for the toolbar buttons from an **ImageList** control.
ListView		Use the **ListView** control to display a collection of items, such as files or folders. A **ListView** control has four display modes: Large Icons, Small Icons, List, and Details. An example of a **ListView** control can be found in the right side of Windows Explorer; from the **View** menu, you can view the different modes by selecting the corresponding command.
Slider		Use the **Slider** control to display a slider and optional measurement marks. The user can move the slider by dragging it, clicking the mouse to either side of the slider, or using the keyboard. **Slider** controls are useful if you want the user to select a discrete value. Examples of the **Slider** control can be found in the **Mouse Properties** dialog box in the Control Panel in Windows.
ImageCombo		Use the **ImageCombo** control to implement a picture-enabled version of the standard Windows combo box. Each item in the list portion of the control can have a picture assigned to it.

Microsoft Windows Common Controls-2 6.0

Name	Control	Description
Animation		Use the **Animation** control to create buttons that display animations, such as .avi files, when clicked. The control can play only .avi files that have no sound. In addition, the **Animation** control can display only uncompressed .avi files or .avi files that have been compressed by using Run-Length Encoding (RLE).

table continued on next page

211

Name	Control	Description
UpDown		Use the **UpDown** control to create a pair of arrow buttons that the user can click to increment or decrement a value, such as a scroll position or a value in an associated control, known as a buddy control.
MonthView		Use the **MonthView** control to create applications that let users view and set date information via a calendar-like interface.
DateTimePicker		Use the **DateTimePicker** control to provide a formatted date field that allows easy date selection. In addition, users can select a date from a drop-down calendar interface, similar to the **MonthView** control.
FlatScrollBar		Use the **FlatScrollBar** control to provide a mouse-sensitive version of the standard Windows scroll bar that offers two-dimensional formatting options. This control can also replace the standard Windows three-dimensional scroll bar. The flat scroll bar provides increased interactivity when using the scroll arrows and the scroll box.

Microsoft Windows Common Controls-3 6.0

Name	Control	Description
CoolBar		Use the **CoolBar** control to contain a collection of objects used to create a configurable toolbar that is associated with a form.

▶ **To add Windows Common Controls 6.0 to a project**

1. On the **Project** menu, click **Components**.

2. On the **Controls** tab, click **Microsoft Windows Common Controls 6.0**, and then click **OK**.

The .ocx files in which the Windows common controls are stored are 32-bit ActiveX controls and can be used only with Windows 95 or later or Windows NT. If you use the Windows common controls in your project, you must include the appropriate .ocx file with your .exe file when you distribute your application.

Overview of the CommonDialog Control

A number of common dialog boxes have been implemented in an ActiveX control called **CommonDialog**. Using these common dialog boxes makes programming easier and gives users an interface that is consistent with those of other Microsoft applications.

Instant familiarity can be built into applications by using some of the dialog boxes provided by the operating system. Although a custom dialog box could be built to open a file, the user of the application might already be familiar with the open dialog box used by many existing applications, such as Microsoft Office.

The **CommonDialog** control works like an interface between an application and Comdlg32.dll, the dynamic-link library that generates the dialog boxes for Windows. Using the **CommonDialog** control, the following dialog boxes can be displayed:

- **Color**
- **Font**
- **Help**
- **Open**
- **Printer**
- **Save**

Using the CommonDialog Control

▶ **To add the CommonDialog control to a project**

1. On the **Project** menu, click **Components**.

   The **Components** dialog box appears.

2. On the **Controls** tab, click **Microsoft Common Dialog Control 6.0,** and then click **OK**.

The **CommonDialog** control has the following methods:

- **ShowColor**
- **ShowFont**
- **ShowHelp**
- **ShowOpen**
- **ShowPrinter**
- **ShowSave**

Each method lets you display a different standard dialog box. The following example code uses the **ShowOpen** method to display the **Open** dialog box:

```
dlgFileOpen.ShowOpen
```

The **Show** methods display the dialog boxes. You must write code to use the information provided by the user. For example, the **ShowOpen** method enables the user to select a file; you must write code to actually open the file.

Each type of dialog box has a set of properties that you use to set the initial state of the dialog box or to determine what the user enters.

The following example code sets some of the initial properties of the **Open** dialog box. The code sets the **DialogTitle** property to show the text "Select a file name" in the title bar and sets the **Filter** property to display only those files that have a .bmp or .ico extension. The code then displays the **Open** dialog box. When the user selects a file and clicks **Open**, the code verifies that the **FileName** property has a .bmp or .ico extension and loads the picture into the **Image** control.

```
Sub cmdSelectImage_Click()
  dlgFileOpen.DialogTitle = "Select a file name"
  dlgFileOpen.Filter = "Pictures(*.bmp;*.ico)|*.bmp;*.ico"
  dlgFileOpen.ShowOpen
  If dlgFileOpen.FileName Like "*.bmp" _
      Or dlgFileOpen.FileName Like "*.ico" Then
      imgSelectedImage.Picture = LoadPicture(dlgFileOpen.FileName)
  Else
      MsgBox prompt:="The selected file is invalid!", _
      Buttons:=vbOKOnly + vbExclamation
  End If
End Sub
```

Insertable Objects

Insertable objects are objects that you add to your application to provide functionality that is usually associated with the parent application. For example, you can add a Microsoft Excel **Worksheet** object that uses the sophisticated statistical analysis functions of Excel.

The following illustration shows an Excel chart object contained within a Visual Basic form.

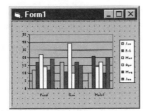

Using insertable objects is beyond the scope of this course. For more information, see "OLE Container Control" and "OLEObject Object" in MSDN Help.

Lab 7: Working with Controls

In this lab, you will add functionality to the loan project that you started in Lab 2. You can continue to work with the files that you have already created, or you can use the files that have been provided in the *<install folder>*\Labs\Lab07 folder.

In Lab 4, some assumptions were made about the length of the loan and the interest rate. In this lab, you will add controls to frmMain to retrieve this information from the user and then enter those values into the functions that you wrote in Lab 4.

Estimated time to complete this lab: **45 minutes**

To see the demonstration "Lab 7 Solution," see the accompanying CD-ROM.

Objectives

After completing this lab, you will be able to:

- Add controls to a form.
- Respond to control events.
- Retrieve values from controls.

To complete the exercises in this lab, you must have the required software. For detailed information about the labs and setup for the labs, see "Labs" in "About This Course."

The solution for this lab is located in the *<install folder>*\Labs\Lab07\Solution folder.

Prerequisites

Before working on this lab, you should be familiar with the following:

- Declaring variables.
- Setting control properties.
- Adding code to event procedures.

Exercises

The following exercises provide practice in working with the concepts and techniques covered in this chapter:

◆ Exercise 1: Creating the User Interface

In this exercise, you will add controls to frmMain to retrieve additional information about the loan from the user.

◆ Exercise 2: Implementing the User Interface

In this exercise, you will add code to save values from the **Loan Term** option buttons and to initialize the controls on frmMain when the form is loaded.

◆ Exercise 3: Retrieving User Values

In this exercise, you will use the values of the controls to compute the monthly payment and the total amount paid.

◆ Exercise 4 (Optional): Adding a Summary Button

In this exercise, you will add a command button that displays summary information.

Exercise 1: Creating the User Interface

In this exercise, you will add controls to frmMain to retrieve additional information about the loan from the user.

▶ **Open the loan project**

◆ Open the loan project on which you have been working, or open the loan project in the *<install folder>*\Labs\Lab07 folder.

▶ **Add controls to frmMain**

1. Add controls to frmMain so that it looks like the form in the following illustration.

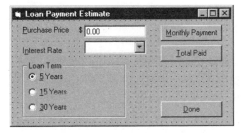

2. Set properties for the controls as listed in the following table.

Note To set the **List** property of a list box or combo box at design time, press CTRL+ENTER after entering each item in the list.

Control type	Property	Desired setting
ComboBox	Name	cboRate
	Style	0 - Dropdown Combo
	List	fill list with values: 4.5, 6.25, 7, 8.325, 9, 10
Label	Caption	I&nterest Rate
Frame	Name	fraTerm
	Caption	Loan Term
OptionButton	Name	optLength
	Caption	&5 Years
	Index	0
OptionButton	Name	optLength
	Caption	&15 Years
	Index	1
OptionButton	Name	optLength
	Caption	&30 Years
	Index	2

Exercise 2: Implementing the User Interface

In this exercise, you will add code to save values from the **Loan Term** option buttons and to initialize the controls on frmMain when the form is loaded.

▶ **Implement a group of option buttons in a control array**

1. Open the Code Editor window for frmMain.

2. In the General Declarations section, declare an Integer variable, mintLength, to hold the value of the selected option button, which indicates the term of the loan.

3. Edit the **Click** event for the **optLength** option buttons. Using a **Select Case** statement, set mintLength to the number of years corresponding to the selected control. For example, if the Index is 0, the number of years is 5.

```
Select Case Index
    Case 0
      mintLength = 5
    Case 1
      mintLength = 15
    Case 2
      mintLength = 30
End Select
```

For help in completing this exercise, see Hint 7.1 in Appendix B.

Note The option buttons are an example of a control array. A control array is a group of controls that share common names, types, and event procedures. Each control has a unique index. If a control in the array recognizes an event, it calls the event procedure for the group and passes the index as an argument, allowing your code to determine which control recognized the event. For more information about control arrays, see "Using Control Arrays" on page 339 in Chapter 13, "More About Controls."

▶ **Initialize controls in the Form_Load event procedure**

1. In the Code Editor window for frmMain, move to the **Form_Load** event.

2. After the loop, add initialization code that checks for a valid password.

    a. Initialize the **Text** property of **txtPurchase** to "0.00."

    b. Initialize the **Text** property of **cboRate** to "4.25."

    c. Set the **Value** property of the **5 Years** option button to **True**.

    d. Call the **Click** event for the **5 Years** option button, because the event procedure sets a form-level variable.

To see an example of how you code should look, see Hint 7.2 in Appendix B.

3. Save and test your application.

Exercise 3: Retrieving User Values

In this exercise, you will use the values of the controls to compute the monthly payment and the total amount paid.

Now that there are controls to obtain loan information from the user, delete the hard-coded values in the **MonthlyPayment** function, written in Lab 4, and enter the values from the controls.

▶ **Use control values in the MonthlyPayment function**

1. In the Code Editor window for frmMain, move to the **MonthlyPayment** function.

2. Declare a Double variable to hold the interest rate, dblRate.

3. Retrieve the interest rate from the drop-down combo box, convert it to a Double value, convert it to a percentage, and save it as dblRate:

   ```
   dblRate = CDbl(cboRate.Text) / 100
   ```

4. Use the value in the saved variable mintLength and the value of dblRate, instead of the constants 30 and .065, in the computation of intNumPayments and dblMonthRate.

5. Save and test your application.

▶ **Use control values in the TotalPaid function**

1. In the Code Editor window for frmMain, move to the **cmdTotal_Click** event procedure.

2. Pass the value in the saved variable mintLength, instead of the constant 30, to the **TotalPaid** function.

3. Save and test your application.

Exercise 4 (Optional): Adding a Summary Button

In this exercise, you will add a command button that displays summary information.

▶ **Add a Summary button**

1. Add a command button to display a summary of the information entered on the form.

2. In the **Click** event for the **Summary** button, display the values entered on the form in a message box.

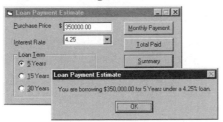

3. Save and test your application.

Self-Check Questions

See page 387 for answers.

1. Which of the following returns the value of the selected item in a combo box?

A. strSelection = cboCustomer.Text

B. strSelection = cboCustomer.IndexItem

C. cboCustomer.ListIndex = strSelection

D. cboCustomer.strSelection

2. In the following example, what happens if no item is selected in the list?

```
lstRegions.RemoveItem  lstRegions.ListIndex
```

A. The first item is removed.

B. The last item is removed.

C. The last item added to the list is removed.

D. None of the above.

3. When several option buttons are grouped into a container:

A. Only one can be selected at a time.

B. Multiple options can be selected at a time.

C. The value property of the container is **True** when an option is selected.

D. None of the above.

Chapter 8:
Data Access Using the ADO Data Control

Microsoft Visual Basic 6.0 includes a robust collection of tools for accessing data from a database. This course focuses on an introduction to accessing desktop databases by using the **ADO Data** control.

You can use the **ADO Data** control to quickly create an application that displays, adds, and updates data in a database. The **ADO Data** control is an excellent tool for creating basic database applications. The **ADO Data** control can also be used to create more advanced database applications, such as applications that use Microsoft SQL Server.

Objectives

After completing this chapter, you will be able to:

◆ Define the following terms: database, table, field, record, and key.

◆ Define ActiveX Data Objects (ADO).

◆ Use the **ADO Data** control to view records in a database.

◆ Use the **ADO Data** control to find, modify, delete, and add records.

◆ List the standard bound controls.

◆ Define Structured Query Language (SQL).

◆ Describe the purpose of the **Select** statement in SQL.

◆ Use the Data Form Wizard to design a simple data-entry form.

Overview of ActiveX Data Objects

A review of the evolution of Microsoft's data access technologies will help you understand the fundamental concepts behind ADO. You will also become familiar with data-access terminology.

Definition of ActiveX Data Objects

ADO is Microsoft's strategic application-level programming interface to data and information. It provides an easy-to-use, application-level interface to OLE DB, which provides the underlying access to data. ADO is implemented with a minimal number of layers between the front end and data source to provide a high-performance interface. ADO supports a variety of development needs, including the creation of front-end database client applications.

Note This course does not cover programming with ADO in detail. For more information about ADO, see *Mastering Microsoft Visual Basic 6 Development*.

Understanding OLE DB

This course focuses on ADO; however, it is important to have a high-level understanding of OLE DB before you learn about ADO. ADO provides its functionality through OLE DB—an open standard designed to allow access to all kinds of data. Conceptually, OLE DB has three components:

◆ Data providers

A data provider is any OLE DB provider that owns data and exposes its data in a tabular form. Examples of data providers include relational database management system (DBMS), spreadsheets, file systems, and e-mail.

◆ Data consumers

Data consumers are applications that use the data exposed by data providers. In other words, any application that uses ADO is an OLE DB consumer.

◆ Service components

Although data providers can provide some database functionality, OLE DB service components perform data processing and transport functionality between data consumers and data providers. In this scenario, neither the front-end application nor the back-end database is responsible for providing its own database functionality. Instead, service components provide functionality that any application can use when accessing data.

Visual Basic Data Access Features

The database functionality provided by Visual Basic is very flexible. By using Visual Basic, you can access all types of data. Data access is the process of viewing or manipulating information that originates in an external data source, such as Microsoft Access, SQL Server, or Microsoft Exchange.

Visual Basic Data Access Features

ADO provides quick, high-performance access to all types of data and information. You can incorporate data-access features into your Visual Basic program by using the following techniques:

◆ **ADO Data** control

The **ADO Data** control provides data access functionality with a limited amount of code. In this course, the discussion of data access focuses on using the **ADO Data** control.

◆ ADO

ADO provides a complete programming interface that gives you access to all types of data. For detailed information about ADO, search for "ADO Overview" in MSDN Help.

◆ Data Form Wizard

The Data Form Wizard is used in conjunction with the **ADO Data** control and is designed to automatically generate Visual Basic forms. These forms contain individual bound controls (see "Binding a Control" in ths chapter) and proce-dures used to manage information derived from database tables and queries. You can use the Data Form Wizard to create either single query forms to manage the data from a single table or simple query, or master/detail type forms used to manage more complex one-to-many data relationships.

◆ ADO Data Environment designer

The Data Environment designer provides an interactive, design-time environment for creating ADO objects, which can be used as a data source for data-aware objects on a form or report, or accessed programmatically as methods and properties.

◆ Query Designer

By using the Query Designer, you can create queries that modify a database by updating, adding, or deleting rows, or by copying rows. You can also create special-purpose queries, such as parameter queries in which search values are provided when the query is executed. If you are familiar with SQL, you can also enter SQL statements directly or edit the SQL statements created by the Query Designer.

◆ Third-party controls

Various third-party developers offer database connectivity options.

Although you can write code to take advantage of the functionality of ADO, this course focuses on the use of the **ADO Data** control to provide data access. The following illustration shows how the **ADO Data** control connects to a data provider.

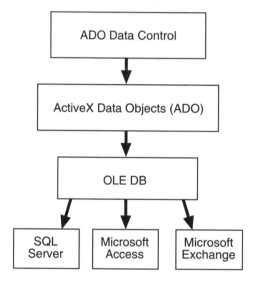

Relational Database Concepts

The Northwind.mdb database is a sample relational database that is included with Access and Visual Basic. This course includes the Visual Basic version of the Northwind database for your use during class.

The following illustration shows the Northwind database.

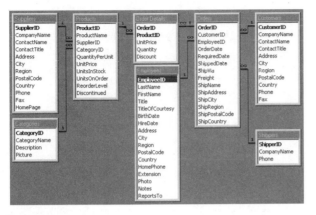

Tables

The relational database model presents data as a collection of tables. A table is a logical grouping of related information. For example, the Northwind database has a table that lists all of the employees and another table that lists all of the customer orders.

Tables are made up of rows and columns. Rows are often referred to as records, and columns are referred to as fields.

The following illustration shows the Employees table from the Northwind database.

Employees Table

	Employee ID	Last Name	First Name
Rows (records)	3	Leverling	Janet
	5	Buchanan	Steven
	• • •	• • •	• • •

Columns (fields)

Records

Each record in a table contains information about a single entry in the table. For example, a record in the Employees table would have information on a particular employee.

Fields

A record is composed of multiple fields. Each field in a record contains a single piece of information about the record. For example, an Employee record has fields for Employee ID, Last Name, First Name, and so forth.

Keys

To uniquely identify a row, each table should have a primary key. The primary key is a field or combination of fields whose value is unique for each row (or record) in the table. For example, the Employee ID field is the primary key for the Employees table. No two employees can have the same ID.

A table can also contain fields that are foreign keys. A foreign key points to a primary key field in a related table. For example, in the Northwind database, the Orders table contains a Customer ID field. Each Customer ID in the Orders table identifies which customer made the order.

The relationship between the Orders and Customers tables is a one-to-many relationship—that is, for each order, there is only one customer. However, one customer can have many orders.

Using the ADO Data Control to Access Data

In this section, you will learn about the **ADO Data** control. You can use the **ADO Data** control to easily link a Visual Basic form to a database. With the **ADO Data** control, you can create an application that displays and updates data from a database with very little code. You will also learn how to display data on a form by using bound controls.

Using the ADO Data Control

Implementing the ADO Data Control

When you use the **ADO Data** control, you connect to a database and specify a record source within the database. The associated records become available as a recordset. For more information about recordsets, see "Using a Recordset" on page 238 in this chapter.

The following illustration shows a form that uses the **ADO Data** control to display records.

To return a set of records by using the **ADO Data** control, you must set the **ConnectionString** and **RecordSource** properties of the control. You can set these properties at design time through the Properties window or at run time, typically in the **Form_Load** event.

> **Note** Before you can use the **ADO Data** control, you must first add it to the project. The **Data** control that is in the toolbox by default is the older **DAO** control. To add the **ADO Data** control to a project, open the **Components** dialog box and locate **Microsoft ADO Data Control 6.0 (OLEDB)**.

ConnectionString Property

The **ConnectionString** property of the **ADO Data** control contains the information used to establish a connection to a data source. This property can be set at design time by using the Properties window. The following illustration shows the three **ConnectionString** options when setting the value through the Properties window.

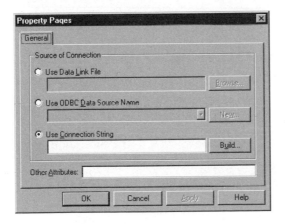

When you set the **ConnectionString** value through the Properties window, you have three connection options, as described in the following table.

Option	Definition
Use Data Link File	Specifies that you are using a custom connection string that connects to the data source. When this is selected, you can click **Browse** to access the **Organize Data Sources** dialog box, from which you can select your Data Link file.
Use ODBC Data Source Name	Specifies that a system-defined data source name (DSN) is used for the connection string. You can access a list of all system-defined DSNs set through the **ODBC** option in Windows Control Panel. You can click **New** to access the **Create New Data Source** wizard dialog box to add to or modify DSNs on the system.
Use Connection String	Specifies that you are using a connection string to access data. You can click **Build** to access the **Data Link Properties** dialog box. Use this dialog box to specify the connection, authentication, and advanced information required to access data by using an OLE DB provider.

▶ **To set the ConnectionString property value**

1. In the Properties window, click on the ellipsis location on the right side of the **ConnectionString** property.

2. Select the **Use Connection String** option and click **Build**.

3. Select the **Microsoft Jet 3.51 OLE DB Provider** option and click **Next**.

4. Click the **...** button to the right of the **Select or enter database name** text box to browse the database name.

5. In the **Select Access Database** dialog box, select **Nwind.mdb** and click **Open**.

6. In the Data Link Properties window, click **Test Connection**.

   A message box will appear, notifying you whether or not the connection succeeded.

7. Click **OK** to close the message box, and then click **OK** to close the Data Link Properties window.

A string value will be automatically generated for the Use Connection String value.

8. Click **OK** to close the ConnectionString Property Pages window.

RecordSource Property

The **RecordSource** property can be either an individual table in the database, a stored query, or a query string that uses SQL. For information about SQL, see "Structured Query Language (SQL)" on page 236 in this chapter.

The **RecordSource** property can be set at design time or at run time. The following illustration shows the dialog box used to set the **RecordSource** property at design time.

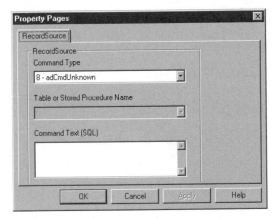

In the **RecordSource** settings dialog box, you set the command type parameter, which tells ADO which type of command object to use. The following table explains the different command type options.

Value	Description
adCmdUnknown	Signifies that the type of command in the **CommandText** property is not known. This is the default value.
adCmdText	Evaluates **CommandText** as a textual definition of a command or stored procedure call.

table continued on next page

Value	Description
adCmdTable	Evaluates **CommandText** as a table name whose columns are all returned by an internally generated SQL query.
adCmdStoredProc	Evaluates **CommandText** as a stored procedure name.

If you select either **adCmdTable** or **adCmdStoredProc**, you set the table or stored procedure name in the **Table or Stored Procedure Name** drop-down list box below the command type drop-down list box.

> **Note** A **Command** object is a definition of a specific command that you intend to execute against a data source and is not covered in this course. For more information on the **ADO Command** object, search for "Command Object" in MSDN Help.

You can set the **RecordSource** property to a string value at run time, as shown in the following example code:

```
adcEmployees.RecordSource = "Employees"
```

> **Note** To improve performance, avoid setting the **RecordSource** property to an entire table. Set the **RecordSource** to an SQL string that retrieves only the necessary records.

Binding a Control

After you set the **ConnectionString** and **RecordSource** properties for the **ADO Data** control, you can add a bound control to display data on your form.

A bound control is one that is data-aware. When an **ADO Data** control moves from one record to the next, either through code or when the user clicks the **ADO Data** control arrows, all bound controls connected to the **ADO Data** control change to display data from fields in the current record. In addition, if the user changes the data in the bound control, those changes are automatically posted to the database while the user moves to another record. Only one record of information can be edited and updated at a time. This record is the current record.

Using bound controls minimizes the amount of code that you must write. Because the value of the bound control is automatically retrieved from and written to the database, little or no programming is involved. The bound controls also enable you to add features that make your application easy to use. For example, instead of requiring the user to type each value for a field, you can provide a list of all the possible values from which the user can choose. Or, you can provide a selected or cleared check box instead of an edit box that displays **True** or **False**.

DataSource and DataField Properties

To bind a control to an **ADO Data** control, you must set the **DataSource** and **DataField** properties of the bound control, as shown in the following illustration.

The **DataSource** property specifies the **ADO Data** control through which the control is bound to the database (for example, Adodc1). The **DataSource** property is usually set at design time through the Properties window. However, if you want to set the **DataSource** property at run time, you must use the **Set** keyword because the **DataSource** property is an object.

The **DataField** property indicates which field is displayed in the bound control. The **DataField** property can be set at design or run time. The following example code sets the **DataSource** and **DataField** properties:

```
Set txtFirstName.DataSource = adcEmployees
txtFirstName.DataField = "FirstName"
```

Available Bound Controls

The data-aware controls found on the standard toolbox include the following:

- Label
- TextBox
- CheckBox
- ComboBox
- ListBox
- PictureBox
- Image

You can also add custom controls that are data-aware. The following data-aware custom controls are provided with Visual Basic:

- DBCombo
- DBList
- MSFlexGrid
- OLE Control
- RichTextBox
- DBGrid

New Data-Aware Controls

Several new ActiveX controls, specifically designed to view and edit data, have been included with Visual Basic:

- **DataGrid** control

  The **DataGrid** control is a new grid control that can work with the **ADO Data** control.

- **DataList** control

  The **DataList** control functions exactly like the **DBList** control but is optimized for use with OLE DB data sources.

- **DataCombo** control

  The **DataCombo** control functions like the **DBCombo** control but can use OLE DB data sources.

◆ Hierarchical FlexGrid control

The **Hierarchical FlexGrid** and **FlexGrid** controls present recordset data, from one or more tables, in a grid format.

◆ **DataRepeater** control

The **DataRepeater** control lets you use a user control to display data and repeats the control to view multiple records.

◆ **MonthView** control

The **MonthView** control displays dates graphically as a calendar.

◆ **DateTimePicker** control

Like the **MonthView** control, the **DateTimePicker** control displays dates in a text box; clicking the text box causes a graphic calendar to drop down for selection of a new date.

Data Binding Properties

Intrinsic controls, and many ActiveX controls, have specific data properties associated with them. The properties used for data binding include the following:

◆ **DataSource** property

Returns or sets the source of data for a control. You can now dynamically set the **DataSource** of a control or object at run time to any valid data source.

◆ **DataMember** property

Returns or sets the specific data set within the source to use. Data sources in Visual Basic 6.0 can contain multiple sets of data, and the **DataMember** property lets you specify which set of data to use. Visual Basic displays a list of available data members when this property is selected.

◆ **DataField** property

Returns or sets the specific field to bind a control to (same functionality as in previous versions of Visual Basic).

◆ **DataFormat** property

Lets you define the automatic formatting of data as it is retrieved from the data source.

Structured Query Language (SQL)

In this section, you will learn about SQL and syntax for basic SQL **Select** statements.

Before you can write an application that accesses a database, you should know a little bit about SQL. You use SQL to specify exactly which records to retrieve from a database.

> **Note** This course does not cover SQL in detail.

Overview of Structured Query Language

To retrieve data from a database, you use SQL. SQL is an industry-standard language that has evolved into the most widely accepted means to query and modify data in a database.

Earlier in this chapter, you learned how to set the **RecordSource** property for the **ADO Data** control to a table name to retrieve all records in the table. Rather than retrieving an entire table, you can set the **RecordSource** property to an SQL statement. With SQL, you can specify exactly which records you want to retrieve and in what order. You can create an SQL statement that retrieves information from multiple tables at once or that retrieves only one specific record.

The following example code retrieves the FirstName field from every record in the Employees table:

```
adcEmployees.RecordSource = "SELECT FirstName FROM Employees"
```

> **Note** SQL is defined by the ANSI standard, but most implementations of SQL differ slightly from the defined standard. The version of SQL supported by Microsoft Jet is generally ANSI-compliant; however, some things may be different when working with a SQL Server database.

Using the Select Statement

The **Select** statement returns specific fields from one or more tables in a database. To select all fields in the table, use the asterisk (*). To implement a **Select** statement within the property sheet of the **ADO Data** control, use the following syntax:

```
SELECT * FROM Employees
```

The following example code shows how to implement a **Select** statement:

```
adcEmployees.RecordSource = "SELECT * FROM Employees"
```

Where Clause

Use the **Where** clause to limit the selection of records. You can filter queries based on multiple fields.

Basic Where

The following example code retrieves all fields from all records in the Employees table where the last name is equal to "Davolio":

```
adcEmployees.RecordSource = "Select * FROM Employees " & _
  "WHERE LastName = 'Davolio'"
```

Where In

By using the **Where In** clause, you can return all employee last names from selected states, as shown in the following example code:

```
SELECT LastName FROM Employees WHERE Employees.State IN ('NY','WA')
```

Where Between

A selection of records between two criteria can also be returned. Note the use of the number signs (#) surrounding the dates in the following example code:

```
SELECT OrderID FROM Orders WHERE OrderDate BETWEEN #01/01/93# AND
#01/31/93#
```

Where Like

In the following example code, all records where the last name starts with the letter "D" are returned:

```
Select LastName FROM Employees WHERE LastName LIKE 'D%'
```

Order By

Use the **Order By** clause to return records in a particular order. The ASC option indicates ascending order; DESC indicates descending order. The following example code selects all fields from the Employees table, sorted by last name:

```
SELECT * FROM Employees ORDER BY LastName ASC
```

> **Tip** Use an application such as Access or Microsoft Query to generate your SQL statements. You can build the query by using the graphical user interface and then copy the SQL statement generated by the application into your program.

To see the demonstration "Using SQL Statements in the ADO Data Control," see the accompanying CD-ROM.

Manipulating Data

In this section, you will learn about manipulating data with the **ADO Data** control. The **ADO Data** control allows you to support viewing and editing records without writing any additional code. However, to support more advanced features, you will need to write some code. By using the **ADO Data** control — and a bound control's properties, methods, and events — you can gain complete control over how your application interacts with external data.

Using a Recordset

The **ADO Data** control has a property called a **Recordset**, which is a group of records. The **Recordset** property of the **ADO Data** control is an object itself and has its own properties and methods.

To retrieve a set of records, you set the **RecordSource** property of the **ADO Data** control. The **RecordSource** property is a string value that can be a query or table name within a database from which to retrieve records.

The **Recordset** object has properties, **BOF** and **EOF**, that indicate if you are at the beginning or end of the **Recordset**. If there are no records in the **Recordset**, the values of both **BOF** and **EOF** are **True**.

For more information, search for "ADO Recordset Object" in MSDN Help.

Modifying and Updating Records

The following paragraph describes how to use the **ADO Data** control to modify and update records.

Modifying Records

The **ADO Data** control can automatically modify and update records. You do not need to add any code to use the **ADO Data** control to modify records.

▶ **To modify a record with the ADO Data control**

1. Move to the record that you want to modify.

2. Change any of the information displayed in the bound controls.

3. Click any arrow on the **ADO Data** control to move to another record.

The **ADO Data** control automatically changes the record in the database.

Updating Records

You can also provide a command button that the user clicks to update the data instead of using the arrows on the **ADO Data** control. Using a command button allows you to add code to the **Click** event to verify the data on the form before updating the record.

The following illustration shows a form that contains an **Update** button to modify data by using the **Update** method.

To update the current record, use the **Update** method. For example, in the **Click** event for the **Update** button, you can add the following example code:

```
adcEmployees.Recordset.Update
```

If you want to cancel any changes made to the current record, or to a new record prior to calling the **Update** method, you can use the **CancelUpdate** method. The syntax for the **CancelUpdate** method is shown in the following example code:

```
adcEmployees.Recordset.CancelUpdate
```

Adding New Records

The following illustration shows a form that contains an **Add** button to modify data by using the **AddNew** method.

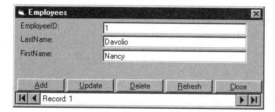

New records can be added to a recordset by calling the **AddNew** method, as shown in the following example code:

```
adcEmployees.Recordset.AddNew
```

The **AddNew** method initializes the bound controls, and the new record becomes the current record. If you call **AddNew** while editing another record, ADO automatically calls the **Update** method to save any changes and then creates the new record.

 Note You can use the **CancelUpdate** method to cancel any changes made to a new record prior to calling the **Update** method.

 Tip You can refine the user interface by disabling buttons that do not apply in certain situations. When the user clicks the **Add** button, disable all other buttons, except the **Update** button and a **Cancel** button.

Deleting Records

By using the **Delete** method, you can delete the current record or a group of records in a recordset. The **Delete** method has an **AffectRecords** parameter that is used to set how many records the **Delete** method will affect.

AffectRecords value	Definition
adAffectCurrent	This option will delete only the current record, it is also the default option.
adAffectGroup	This option can be used to delete all records that satisfy the current **Filter** property setting. You must set the **Filter** property in order to use this option.

Retrieving field values from the deleted record generates an error. When you delete the current record, the deleted record remains current until you move to a different record. After you move away from the deleted record, it is no longer accessible.

To invoke the **Delete** method, use the following syntax:

Adodc1.Recordset.Delete AffectRecords

You can check the **EOF** property to see if you have deleted the last record. If **EOF** is **True**, move to the last record in the recordset, as shown in the following example code:

```
adcEmployees.Recordset.Delete
adcEmployees.Recordset.MoveNext
If adcEmployees.Recordset.EOF = True Then
  adcEmployees.Recordset.MoveLast
End If
```

Note The Northwind database has defined referential integrity rules that prevent you from deleting certain records from the recordset. For example, you cannot delete a customer if the customer has records in the Orders table.

Searching for Records

To add a search feature to your application, you use the **Find** method for the recordset of the **ADO Data** control.

The **Find** method searches an existing recordset for the record that satisfies the specified criteria. If the criteria are met, the recordset is positioned on that record; otherwise, the position is set at the end of the recordset (EOF).

Find Method Syntax

The **Find** method has one required parameter, Criteria, and three optional parameters: SkipRows, SearchDirection, and Start.

The Criteria parameter is a string containing a statement that specifies the column name, comparison operator, and value to use in the search. The comparison operator in criteria may be ">" (greater than), "<" (less than), "=" (equal to), or "like" (pattern matching).

In the following example code, the first customer that resides in the state of Washington will be returned:

```
adcCustomers.Find "State = 'WA'"
```

Note The **Find** method can be slow unless you have limited the total number of records in the recordset. Another method for finding records is to use a SQL statement when setting the **RecordSource** property of the **ADO Data** control. You can also set the **Filter** property of the **ADO Data** control to limit the number of records in a recordset.

Verifying Find Results

When you search for records by using the **Find** method, you can use the **EOF** or **BOF** properties of the **Recordset** object to determine whether a particular record was found. If the search fails to find the record, you should return to the record where the search began. The following example code shows how to use the **EOF** and **BOF** properties:

```
'If the record isn't found
If .EOF Or .BOF Then
  'Return to the starting record
  .Bookmark = varBookmark
  MsgBox "Record not found."
End If
```

Building Criteria with Partial Values

When you add searching capabilities to an application, offering the user the ability to search on a partial value is typically preferable to requiring a complete value. For example, a user may not know the exact name of a company and may provide only a portion of the company name. You can perform a search based on a partial name.

To search based on a partial string, you can use the LIKE keyword in SQL. Remember, when searching on a string, that you must place single quotes around the string. If the comparison operator is "LIKE," the string value may contain "%" (one or more occurrences of any character) or "_" (one occurrence of any character). The following example code shows the use of the LIKE keyword:

```
'Match states such as Maine and Massachusetts
adcStates.Find "State LIKE 'M%'"
```

The value in criteria may be a string, floating point number, or date. String values are delimited with single quotes (for example, "state = 'WA'").

The following table describes the optional parameters for the **Find** method of a **Recordset** object.

Optional parameter	Value
SkipRows	An optional **Long** data type value, whose default value is zero. It is used to specify the offset from the current row or start bookmark to begin the search.
searchDirection	An optional value that specifies whether the search should begin on the current row or the next available row in the direction of the search. The search stops at the start or end of the recordset, depending on the value of searchDirection. It can be one of the following enumerated values: **adSearchForward** (0) - search forward from the current record, or **adSearchBackward** (1) - search backward from the current record.
start	An optional Variant bookmark to use as the starting position for the search. This argument is a Variant and can be either a bookmark or one of the following enumerated values: **adBookmarkCurrent** (0) - the current record, **adBookmarkFirst** (1) - the first record, or **adBookmarkLast** (2) - the last record.

The following example code implements the **Find** method of a **Recordset** object by using all four parameters:

```
Dim varBookmark As Variant
With adcFood.Recordset
    'Mark the current record
    varBookmark = .Bookmark
    'Specify the searh criteria, start and direction
    .Find "CategoryName = 'Condiments'", 0, _
        adSearchForward, adBookmarkCurrent
    'If the record isn't found
    If .EOF Or .BOF Then
        'Return to the starting record
        .Bookmark = varBookmark
        MsgBox "Record not found."
    End If
End With
```

Using the Data Form Wizard

The Data Form Wizard is an add-in that you can use to create database viewer applications.

By using the Data Form Wizard, you can create a form that displays, adds, deletes, and edits data in a database. The wizard reduces the task of adding the controls and setting properties to a few easy steps.

The Data Form Wizard:

◆ Creates and adds a new form to the current project.

◆ Adds an **ADO Data** control and sets the **RecordSource** property for your specification.

◆ Automatically sets the **ConnectionString** property of the **ADO Data** control.

◆ Performs the following tasks for each field selected in a table:

  • Adds a label with the field name.

- Adds a bound control. The type of control depends on the type of data stored in the field, as shown in the following table.

Data type	Control
String, date, and numeric	TextBox
Boolean	CheckBox
Memo fields	Multi-line TextBox
Binary data	OLE Container
Picture	PictureBox

- Adds command buttons to perform various data-access functions, including **Add, Delete, Refresh, Update,** and **Close.**
- Adds code behind the command buttons and **ADO Data** control, including comments.

▶ **To install the Data Form Wizard add-in**

1. On the **Add-Ins** menu, click **Add-In Manager.**
2. In the **Add-In Manager** dialog box, click **VB 6 Data Form Wizard,** click **Loaded/Unloaded** for the load behavior, and then click **OK.**

▶ **To use the Data Form Wizard to connect to the Nwind.mdb database**

1. On the **Add-Ins** menu, click **Data Form Wizard.**
2. Click **Next** to accept the default profile.
3. On the **Database Type** list, click **Access,** and then click **Next.**
4. Click **Browse,** select the Nwind.mdb file, and then click **Open.**

   The Database Name should be set to C:\Program Files\Microsoft Visual Studio\VB98\Nwind.mdb. If you cannot find the Nwind.mdb file in C:\Program Files\Microsoft Visual Studio\VB98, browse to the *<install folder>*\Labs folder.

5. Click **Next** to accept the database name.
6. Set the Form Layout to **Single Record,** set the Binding Type to **ADO Data Control,** and then click **Next.**
7. Select **Employees** for the Record Source, select the fields of your choice, and then click **Next.**
8. Select from the **Add, Update, Delete, Refresh,** and **Close** check boxes, and then click **Finish.**

Lab 8: Accessing Databases

In this lab, you will build a customer order information application. The main form of the application will display customer information, and a second form will display the order history for a selected customer.

To see the demonstration "Lab 8 Solution," see the accompanying CD-ROM.

Estimated time to complete this lab: **45 minutes**

Objectives

After completing this lab, you will be able to:

◆ Use the Data Form Wizard to create forms.

◆ Create an SQL statement.

◆ Work with the **ADO Data** control.

To complete the exercises in this lab, you must have the required software. For detailed information about the labs and setup for the labs, see "Labs" in "About This Course."

The solution for this lab is located in the *<install folder>*\Labs\Lab08\Solution folder.

Note The Data Form Wizard does not automatically handle referential integrity. If you attempt to delete a record by using the lab solution, a run-time error will occur. Additional code must be added to trap these run-time errors.

Prerequisites

There are no prerequisites for this lab.

Exercises

The following exercises provide practice in working with the concepts and techniques covered in this chapter:

◆ Exercise 1: Creating a Customer Information Form with the Data Form Wizard

In this exercise, you will use the Data Form Wizard to create a form that will display customer information.

◆ Exercise 2: Creating an Order Information Form with the Data Form Wizard

In this exercise, you will use the Data Form Wizard to design a form that will display order information. Then, you will add a command button to the frmCustomers form to show the frmOrders form.

◆ Exercise 3: Creating an SQL Statement

In this exercise, you will link the customer form and the orders form, so that only the orders for a selected customer are displayed in the frmOrders form.

◆ Exercise 4 (Optional): Reviewing Code Created by the Data Form Wizard

In this exercise, you will review the code created by the Data Form Wizard.

Exercise 1: Creating a Customer Information Form with the Data Form Wizard

In this exercise, you will use the Data Form Wizard to create a form that will display customer information.

▶ **Install the Data Form Wizard add-in**

1. Open Visual Basic and start a new Standard EXE Visual Basic project.

2. If the Data Form Wizard is not a menu item on the **Add-Ins** menu, on the **Add-Ins** menu click **Add-In Manager** to load the **VB 6 Data Form Wizard** add-in.

3. Double-click **VB 6 Data Form Wizard** in the **Available Add-Ins** list, or select **VB 6 Data Form Wizard,** and check **Loaded/Unloaded,** and then click **OK.**

Note The Load Behavior changes to **Loaded** when **VB 6 Data Form Wizard** is selected.

▶ **Build the customer information form**

1. On the **Add-Ins** menu, click **Data Form Wizard.**

2. On the Data Form Wizard Introduction screen, click **Next.**

3. From the list of database types, select **Access,** and click **Next.**

4. Click **Browse** and select the **Nwind.mdb** database, and then click **Next.**

5. Name the form **frmCustomers,** select **Single Record** as the **Form Layout, ADO Data Control** for the **Binding Type,** and then click **Next.**

6. In the **Record Source** list box, select **Customers**.

7. From the **Available Fields** list, add the CustomerID and the CompanyName fields to the **Selected Fields** list, and click **Next**.

8. Click **Select All** and then click **Next**.

9. Click **Finish**. Then, on the **Data Form Created** dialog box, click **OK**.

In this application, you will not be using the default form that Visual Basic created.

▶ **Remove the default form and set the startup form**

1. In the Project Explorer window, select **Form1**.

2. On the **Project** menu, click **Remove Form1**.

3. On the **Project** menu, click **Project1 Properties**.

4. Name the project **ADOProject**, and set the **Startup Object** to **frmCustomers**, the form you just created, and then click **OK**.

5. Save the Project to the *<install folder>*\Labs\Lab08 folder and test your application. Use the forward and backward buttons on the **ADO Data** control to cycle through some records in the database. Change the Company Name field of the database and click the **Update** button or move to another record to save the changes.

6. Click **Close** to end the application.

Exercise 2: Creating an Order Information Form with the Data Form Wizard

In this exercise, you will use the Data Form Wizard to design a form that will display order information. Then, you will add a command button to the frmCustomers form to show the frmOrders form.

▶ **Build the order information form**

1. On the **Add-Ins** menu, click **Data Form Wizard**.

2. On the Data Form Wizard Introduction screen, click **Next**.

3. From the list of database types, select **Access** and click **Next**.

4. Click **Browse** and select the **Nwind.mdb** database, and then click **Next**.

5. Name the form **frmOrders**, select **Grid (Datasheet)** in the **Format Layout** list box, click the **ADO Data Control** option button for the **Binding Type**, and click **Next**.

6. In the **Record Source** list box, select **Orders**.

7. From the **Available Fields** list, add **CustomerID, OrderID, OrderDate,** and **RequiredDate** to the **Selected Fields** list, and click **Next**.

8. Click **Select All,** and then click **Next**.

9. Click **Finish.** Then, on the **Data Form Created** dialog box, click **OK**.

▶ **Display the frmOrders form from the frmCustomers form**

1. Widen the frmCustomers form and add an **Orders** command button.

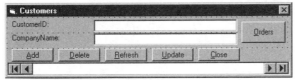

2. In the **Click** event of the **Orders** command button, display the frmOrders form as modal:

```
frmOrders.Show vbModal
```

▶ **Save and test your work**

1. Save the project.

2. Run the application. Click the **Orders** button, and scroll through some of the records in the Orders table and try resizing the form.

3. Click **Close** on the frmOrders form to return to the frmCustomers form.

4. Click **Close** to end the application.

Exercise 3: Creating an SQL Statement

In this exercise, you will link the customer form and the orders form so that only the orders for a selected customer are displayed in the frmOrders form.

▶ **Customize the frmOrders form**

1. Open the Code Editor window for frmOrders.

2. In the General Declarations section, create a public string variable, gstrCustomerID.

This variable will be set from the frmCustomers form.

3. In the **Form_Load** event procedure for frmOrders:

    a. Create an SQL string that selects all fields from the Orders table, where CustomerID is equal to the gstrCustomerID variable.

    b. Set the **RecordSource** property of the **ADO Data** control to the SQL string.

    c. Refresh the **ADO Data** control.

```
Dim strSQL As String
strSQL = "SELECT * FROM Orders " & _
        "WHERE CustomerID = " & Chr(34) &  _
        gstrCustomerID & Chr(34)
datPrimaryRS.RecordSource = strSQL
datPrimaryRS.Refresh
```

▶ Customize the frmCustomers form

1. Edit the **Click** event procedure for the **Orders** button on frmCustomers.

2. Before showing the frmOrders form, set the public variable gstrCustomerID in frmOrders equal to the current text in the CustomerID field:

```
frmOrders.gstrCustomerID = txtFields(0).Text
```

Note The Data Form Wizard assigns names to the controls it creates. Therefore, the names on your forms may be different from the names in the solution. For more information about control arrays, see "Using Control Arrays" on page 339 in Chapter 13, "More About Controls."

▶ Save and test your work

1. Save your project.

2. Run your application. Select several of the companies, and for each one, click the **Orders** button. Are all of the records displayed in the frmOrders form for the selected company?

3. On the frmOrders form, click **Close** to return to the frmCustomers form.

4. Click **Close** to end the application.

Exercise 4 (Optional): Reviewing Code Created by the Data Form Wizard

In this exercise, you will review the code created by the Data Form Wizard.

▶ **Review the code that is generated by the Data Form Wizard**

1. Look at the code for the **Add**, **Delete**, **Refresh**, **Update**, and **Close** buttons.

2. Look at the code written for the **ADO Data Control** event procedures: **Error**, **MoveComplete**, and **WillChangeRecord**.

▶ **Add a Find command to the frmCustomers form**

1. Add a **Find** command button to frmCustomer.

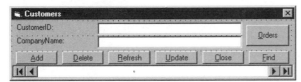

2. In the **Click** event of the **Find** command button:

   a. Use the **InputBox** function to ask the user for a company name to locate.

   b. Call the **Find** method of the **Recordset** property of **ADO Data** Control.

   c. If the **Find** method fails, reset the **ADO Data** control to the record on which it was positioned before executing the method.

   d. Save and test the application.

Self-Check Questions

See page 389 for answers.

1. Rows are often referred to as _____, and columns are referred to as _____.

    A. primary keys, foreign keys

    B. tables, keys

    C. fields, records

    D. records, fields

2. When using the ADO Data control, changes to a record are updated when:

    A. A different record is accessed.

    B. The **AddNew** method is used.

    C. The **Refresh** method for the **ADO Data** control must be invoked.

    D. The **RecordSource** property is changed.

3. What does the following code statement do?

```
adcEmployees.Recordset.Bookmark = varCurrentRecord
```

    A. Moves the record pointer to the record position stored in the varCurrentRecord variable

    B. Makes the current record equal to the value of the varCurrentRecord variable

    C. Sets a bookmark at the current record

    D. None of the above.

Chapter 9:
Input Validation

Multimedia

In most applications that you create, a user will have to enter information for the application to process. For example, you could create an application that calculates the cost of goods sold based upon income and expense values that a user enters. A well-written application prevents users from entering invalid data whenever possible. For example, a field for inventory cost would require a numeric value, and it is important to prevent users from entering alphabetic characters in this case.

In this chapter, you will learn how to validate user data at the field level and at the form level in your Microsoft Visual Basic applications, as well as how to use event procedures to validate data.

Objectives

After completing this chapter, you will be able to:

◆ Create an application that validates user data at the field level and at the form level.

◆ Create an application that uses the **Masked Edit** control.

◆ Create an application that enables or disables controls based on field values.

Field-Level Validation

In many cases, you will want to validate data entries while the user enters data in each field. In this section, you will learn how to validate data in fields.

Using the InputBox Function

The **InputBox** function displays a standard dialog box prompting the user to enter a string value. The user can type an alphanumeric value into a text box and click **OK** or **Cancel**.

When the user clicks **OK** or presses ENTER, the **InputBox** function returns a string value equal to the contents of the **TextBox** control within the **InputBox** dialog box. If the user clicks **Cancel**, the **InputBox** function will return an empty string ("").

To test whether the user entered a numeric value, you can use the **IsNumeric** function. The **IsNumeric** function returns a value of **True** if the argument is numeric. If the argument is not numeric, **False** is returned.

Note Other expressions can be checked by using functions similar to **IsNumeric**. **IsDate**, for example, checks a value to determine if it is a valid date.

The following example code checks to see if a numeric value has been entered into an input box:

```
Private Sub EvaluateInput()
    Dim strInputValue As String

    strInputValue = InputBox("Enter a value")
    If IsNumeric(strInputValue) Then
        MsgBox strInputValue & " is a number."
    Else
        MsgBox strInputValue & " is not a number."
    End If
End Sub
```

Using KeyPress to Modify Keystrokes

When a user enters a standard ASCII character, the **KeyPress** event occurs. By responding to the **KeyPress** event, you can restrict the characters entered or transform them as they are typed.

KeyPress does not work with special keys, such as function keys, the arrow keys, or DELETE, because these keys are not standard ASCII characters. To respond to these keys, you must use the **KeyDown** and **KeyUp** events.

The following example code shows that, by using the **KeyPress** event procedure for a **TextBox** control, you can translate characters to uppercase while the user types them:

```
Sub txtSubdivision_KeyPress(KeyAscii As Integer)
  'Use the Chr function to return the character
  'associated with the specified character code
  'After the character is converted to upper case,
  'convert the uppercase character back into an ASCII value
     KeyAscii = Asc(UCase(Chr(KeyAscii)))
End Sub
```

The following example code restricts a text box to receiving only digits, the BACK-SPACE key, or the other non-ASCII keys:

```
Private Sub txtOrganizationNumber_KeyPress(KeyAscii As Integer)
    If KeyAscii = 8 Then
        'Exit subroutine if backspace key is pressed
        Exit Sub
    End If

    'Only digits are valid characters
    If Chr(KeyAscii) < "0" Or Chr(KeyAscii) > "9" Then
        'Set character to null if out of range
        KeyAscii = 0
        Beep
    End If
End Sub
```

Using KeyUp and KeyDown to Trap Keystrokes

Any time there is keyboard activity, **KeyUp** and **KeyDown** events are triggered. Each **KeyUp** or **KeyDown** event provides a key code that identifies which key was pressed.

Because some keys (such as function keys) do not cause a **KeyPress** event to occur, code can be added to their **KeyDown** event procedures instead.

The following illustration shows the use of the **KeyDown** event.

```
Sub Text1_KeyDown(KeyCode As Integer,_
                  Shift As Integer)
    If KeyCode = vbKeyF1 Then
        MsgBox "You pressed F1!"
    End If
End Sub
```

The following example code uses the **KeyDown** event to check for the F1 key:

```
Sub txtOrganizationNumber_KeyDown(KeyCode As Integer, Shift As
Integer)
    If KeyCode = vbKeyF1 Then
        MsgBox "You pressed F1!"
    End If
End Sub
```

Note There is no guarantee that a **KeyUp** event will occur for every **KeyDown** event. If the user holds a key down, for example, you will receive multiple **KeyDown** events and a single **KeyUp** event.

For a list of all Visual Basic constants, click **Object Browser** on the **View** menu. In the **Object Browser** dialog box, click **VBRUN** in the **Project/Library** box, and then click **<globals>** in the **Classes** list.

Using the Validate Event

Focus is an object's ability to receive user input through a mouse or keyboard. In Microsoft Windows, although several applications can be running simultaneously, only the application that has focus has an active title bar and is able to receive user input. On a Visual Basic form with several text boxes, only the text box with focus can receive input through the keyboard. The **GotFocus** and **LostFocus** events occur when an object receives or loses focus. Forms and most controls support these events.

> **Note** Some controls—such as the **Frame**, **Line**, **Image**, and **Label** controls— cannot receive focus. Additionally, controls that are invisible at run time, such as the **Timer** control, cannot receive focus.

Using the LostFocus Event to Validate Input

The **LostFocus** event occurs when an object loses focus. This can occur as a result of a user action, such as tabbing to another field or clicking another object. Furthermore, you can change focus between controls programmatically by using the **SetFocus** method. It is possible to use the **LostFocus** event procedure to validate the data in a field; however, this validation technique can result in an infinite loop in which one or more controls are using the **SetFocus** method in the **LostFocus** event.

Using the Validate Event to Validate Input

Visual Basic 6.0 includes a **Validate** event for controls, which occurs before a control loses focus. This event occurs only when the **CausesValidation** property of the control that is about to receive the focus is set to **True**. The **Validate** event and **CausesValidation** property for a control are used together to evaluate input before allowing the user to move focus away from that control. The **Validate** event also includes a **Cancel** argument, which will cause the control to retain focus when set to **True**.

The **Validate** event is better for validating data entry than the **LostFocus** event, because the **LostFocus** event occurs after the focus has moved away from the control and can potentially force your program into an infinite loop. By using the **Validate** event, you can prevent the focus from ever shifting to another control until all validation rules have been met.

Possible uses for the **Validate** event include the following:

◆ A data entry application needs to perform more sophisticated data entry valida-tion than can be provided by the **Masked Edit** control, or the validation occurs in a business rule.

◆ A form needs to prevent users from moving off a control, by pressing TAB or an accelerator key, until data has been entered in a field.

The following illustration shows a form with three text boxes and a **Help** button.

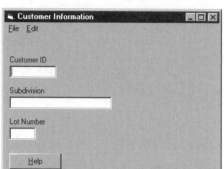

When one text box receives focus, you can prevent the user from changing focus to another until the text box contains valid data. Alternatively, you may want to allow users to click the **Help** button at any time. You can do this by writing data validation code in the **Validate** event procedure and then setting the **Causes Validation** property of the **Help** button to **False**. The following example shows how to use the **Validate** event to perform field-level validation:

```
Private Sub txtLotNumber_Validate(Cancel As Boolean)
  If Not IsNumeric(txtLotNumber.Text) Then
      MsgBox "Lot Number must be a number between 1 and 53."
      Cancel = True
  ElseIf txtLotNumber.Text < 1 Or txtLotNumber.Text > 53 Then
      MsgBox "Invalid Lot Number: Must be 1 - 53."
      Cancel = True
  End If
End Sub
```

The previous code example uses three controls to demonstrate the use of the **Validate** event and **Causes Validation** property. By default, the **Causes Validation** property of the three **TextBox** controls is set to **True**. Thus, when you try to shift the focus from one **TextBox** control to the other, the **Validate** event occurs. For example, if txtLotNumber does not contain a numeric value between 1 and 53, the shift of focus is prevented. However, because the **Causes Validation** property of the **CommandButton** control is set to **False**, you can always click the **Help** button.

Using Text Box Properties to Restrict Data Entry

Another way to validate data at the field level is by setting properties that restrict certain values from being entered in the field. Text boxes in Visual Basic offer several properties for this purpose, which can be set at design time.

The MaxLength Property

The **MaxLength** property can be used to set a maximum number of characters that can be entered into a text box. The system beeps when the user tries to type more characters than specified in the **MaxLength** property.

The PasswordChar Property

The **PasswordChar** property allows you to hide (or mask) characters that are entered into a text box. For example, if you set the **PasswordChar** property to an asterisk (*), the user will see only asterisk characters in the text box. This technique is often used to hide passwords on logon dialog boxes.

Although any character can be used, most Windows-based applications use the asterisk (*) character, Chr(42). The **PasswordChar** property does not affect the **Text** property; the **Text** property contains exactly what the user types or what was set.

The Locked Property

The **Locked** property setting determines whether users can edit the text in a text box. If the **Locked** property is set to **True**, users can view the text in the text box, but they cannot edit the text. In other words, the **Locked** property allows you to make a text box read-only for the user and still change the **Text** property programmatically.

Using the Masked Edit Control

In this section, you will learn how to set properties of the **Masked Edit** control to restrict the kind of data that can be entered and to format how that data is displayed.

The Mask Property

To define an input mask, use the **Mask** property, which you can set either at design or run time. Although you can use standard formats at design time, and the control will distinguish between numeric and alphabetic characters, you may want to write code to validate content such as the correct month or time of day. Each character position in the **Masked Edit** control corresponds to either a placeholder of a specified type or to a literal character.

The following example code shows how to use the **Mask** property of the **Masked Edit** control to create an input mask for entering a United States telephone number, complete with placeholders for area code and local number:

```
frmMain.mskPhone.Mask = "(###)###-####"
```

You can enter your own masks by using the special mask characters, or you can use one of the predefined masks. For more information about using specific characters for input masks, search for "Mask Property" in MSDN Help.

The **Masked Edit** control is included in Visual Basic Professional Edition as an ActiveX control and, therefore, does not appear by default on the toolbox.

▶ **To add the Masked Edit control to the toolbox**

1. On the **Project** menu, click **Components**.

   The **Components** dialog box appears.

2. On the **Controls** tab, select **Microsoft Masked Edit Control 6.0**, and then click **OK**.

The Format Property

The **Format** property defines the format that you want to use for displaying and printing the contents of a control, such as numbers, dates, times, and text. You use the same format expressions as defined by the Visual Basic **Format** function, except that you cannot use named formats such as "On/Off."

The **Format** property can have up to four parameters, separated by semicolons, as shown in the following syntax:

[form.]MaskedEdit.*Format* [= posformat$; negformat$; zeroformat$; nullformat$]

The four parameters of the **Format** property are described in the following table.

Parameter	Description
posformat$	Expression used to display positive values
negformat$	Expression used to display negative values
zeroformat$	Expression used to display zero values
nullformat$	Expression used to display null or empty values

If one of the parameters is not specified, the format called for by the first parameter is used. If multiple parameters appear, the appropriate number of separators must be used. For example, to specify *posformat$* and *nullformat$*, use the following syntax:

[form.]MaskedEdit.*Format* = posformat$;;; nullformat$

Text and ClipText Properties

The **Text** property returns the data that the user has typed, along with the mask. The **ClipText** property returns only the data that the user has typed. This is particularly important when implementing a **Masked Edit** control with a database.

The following example code sets a mask for a **Masked Edit** control that requires the user to enter only digits in the control:

```
mskPhoneNumber.Mask = "(###)###-####"
```

If the user enters a valid phone number (5555551234), the **mskPhoneNumber.Text** property returns (555)555-1234, while the **mskPhoneNumber.ClipText** property returns 5555551234.

The AutoTab Property

To make data entry easier for users, you can set the **AutoTab** property to **True**. When automatic tabbing is enabled and the user enters the maximum number of characters specified by the **Mask** property for the control, the insertion point automatically moves to the next control.

For example, if the **Mask** property is set to "???" (three characters), when the user enters a fourth character, that character will appear in the next field on the form.

For automatic tabbing to work properly, you must use the **Mask** property to limit the number of characters that the user can enter. If you use the **MaxLength** property instead of the **Mask** property, automatic tabbing will not occur, regardless of the setting of the **AutoTab** property.

Clearing a Masked Edit

When the value of the **Mask** property is an empty string (""), the control behaves like a standard text box control. When an input mask is defined, underscores appear beneath every placeholder in the mask. You can only replace a placeholder with a character that is of the same type as the one specified in the input mask.

To clear the **Text** property when you have defined a mask, you first need to set the **Mask** property to an empty string, and then the **Text** property to an empty string, as shown in the following code:

```
mskPhoneNumber.Mask = ""
mskPhoneNumber.Text = ""
```

The ValidationError Event

If a user enters an invalid character, you should provide feedback indicating that the error occurred and how to fix the problem. You can place code in the **ValidationError** event to provide this feedback.

The **ValidationError** event occurs if the user types an invalid character, or if the user does not enter all required characters into the **Masked Edit** control.

If you try to assign an invalid string value to a **Masked Edit** control, a **ValidationError** event occurs, the string is not assigned to the control, and the **Masked Edit** control retains the value it had prior to the attempted assignment.

Use the **ValidationError** event procedure when:

◆ Only numeric values can be accepted.

◆ There is a maximum number of characters that can be accepted.

◆ The data must match a particular format.

The **ValidationError** event has two arguments:

◆ **InvalidText**

The string that is invalid.

◆ **StartPosition**

A zero-based value that contains the position of the invalid character.

In the following example code, the error message "Limit 6 digits" appears if the user types more than six digits. The error message "Invalid entry" appears if the user types a value that is not a number.

```
Sub mskID_ValidationError(InvalidText As String, _
    StartPosition As Integer)

    If StartPosition = mskID.MaxLength Then
        lblError.Caption = "Limit 6 digits"
    Else
        lblError.Caption = "Digits Only"
    End If
End Sub
```

The **ValidationError** event will occur if the user enters an invalid character into the **Masked Edit** control. The user can press the TAB key to move away from the field without entering any characters.

For example, assume that the user enters a value of "123a" in a control that has a mask of "####". The **ValidationError** event will occur because the character "a" is invalid. The **InvalidText** argument will be set to "123a", and **StartPosition** will be set to a value of 3.

Form-Level Validation

In some situations, you may want to perform data validation only after all fields on a form have been filled in completely. In this section, you will learn form-level validation techniques.

A Form-Level Keyboard Handler

Sometimes it's useful to have a centralized keystroke handler for a form. For example, you could write code to respond to a user who presses a particular key, regardless of which control has focus. You can set the **KeyPreview** property for a form to do this.

KeyPreview Property

Forms have a **KeyPreview** property that determines whether the form receives keyboard events before any controls on the form.

If the **KeyPreview** property for a form is set to **True**, the form receives keyboard events before any controls on the form. For example, assume that there is a **KeyPress** event procedure written for a form and a **KeyPress** event procedure written for a **TextBox** control on that form. If the **KeyPreview** property for the form is set to **True**, the **Form_KeyPress** event procedure will execute first, as shown in the following example code:

```
'KeyPreview is set to True
'This procedure will execute first
Private Sub Form_KeyPress(KeyAscii As Integer)
    MsgBox "KeyPress event for the form."
End Sub

'This procedure will execute after Form_Keypress
Private Sub txtOrganizationNumber_KeyPress(KeyAscii As Integer)
    MsgBox "KeyPress event for the textbox."
End Sub
```

Note If the form's **KeyPress** event sets **KeyAscii** to 0, **KeyPress** events will not occur for any controls.

If the **KeyPreview** property for a form is set to **False**, the form does not receive the keyboard events.

Enabling an OK Button

When you implement form-level validation, it is important to provide visual cues to your users to allow them to determine which tasks they need to perform. For example, a form may contain multiple fields (such as first name, last name, address, city, state, and zip code) that need to be completely filled in before any further processing can take place. A good way to communicate that the user has not filled in all of the required information is to disable commands, such as an **OK** button. When the user has typed all required information, you can set the command button's **Enabled** property to **True**. This will let the users know that they have successfully completed their task.

One way to enable a command button when all fields have valid data is to loop through the **Controls** collection and validate each control. The **Controls** collection is a predefined collection provided by Visual Basic that contains all controls on a form.

The following sample code enables a command button when data has been entered into all fields on a form. To copy this code for use in your own projects, see "Enabling an OK Button" on the accompanying CD-ROM.

> **Note** The following code sequence uses the **For Each... Next** statement. This is covered in "Working with Collections" on page 335 in Chapter 13, "More About Controls."

```
Private Sub Form_Load()
  cmdOK.Enabled = False
End Sub

Private Sub Form_KeyUp(KeyCode As Integer, Shift As Integer)
    Dim ctrlVariable As Control

    For Each ctrlVariable In frmCustomerInfo.Controls
        'check to see if the current control is a textbox
        If TypeOf ctrlVariable Is TextBox Then
            'check to see if the textbox control
            'has been filled in by the user
            If Trim(ctrlVariable.Text) = "" Then
                'if the textbox has not been filled in,
                'disable the command button and exit
                'the subroutine
                cmdOK.Enabled = False
                Exit Sub
            End If
        End If
    Next

    'enable the OK command button
    cmdOK.Enabled = True
End Sub
```

Validating All Fields on a Form

In some situations, you might want to validate user input in a particular procedure. For example, you could have a form that requires customer information such as name, address, and phone number. For these fields, you can use text boxes to allow users to enter the information and provide an **OK** button for the user to click after filling in each field. You can then use the command button's **Click** event procedure to validate data from each text box on the form, and you can direct the user to any field that might have invalid data by setting focus to that field.

The following sample code performs this type of validation. To copy this code for use in your own projects, see "Validating All Fields on a Form" on the accompanying CD-ROM.

```
Private Sub cmdOK_Click()
    If txtFirstName.Text = "" Then
        lblError.Caption = "You must provide a first name."
        txtFirstName.SetFocus
        Exit Sub
    ElseIf txtLastName.Text = "" Then
        lblError.Caption = "You must provide a last name."
        txtLastName.SetFocus
        Exit Sub
    ElseIf mskDept.ClipText = "" Then
        lblError.Caption = "You must provide a department."
        mskDept.SetFocus
        mskDept.ForeColor = vbRed
        Exit Sub
    ElseIf CInt(mskDept.ClipText) < 50 Or CInt(mskDept) > 80 Then
        lblError.Caption = "Invalid Department " & _
            "Valid numbers are 50-80"
        mskDept.SetFocus
        mskDept.ForeColor = vbRed
        Exit Sub
    Else
        Unload Me
    End If
End Sub
```

Form Events Used When Validating Data

There are several **Form** event procedures that you can use to manage your forms, initialize controls and variables, and write termination code.

Activate and Deactivate Events

The **Activate** event occurs when the form receives focus. While a user changes from one form to another in a modeless environment, the **Activate** event fires. The **Deactivate** event occurs when the form loses focus. So, as the user changes from one form to another, both the **Activate** and **Deactivate** events will fire on the applicable form. These events will fire only if the form is loaded and focus is changing from forms within a single application. If focus changes to a different application, the **Deactivate** event will not fire. Likewise, if focus changes from a different application back to the Visual Basic program, the **Activate** event will not fire.

GotFocus and LostFocus Events

A form receives a **GotFocus** or **LostFocus** event only if there are no controls on the form capable of receiving the focus. Typically, you use a **GotFocus** event procedure to specify the actions that occur when a control or form first receives focus. For example, by attaching a **GotFocus** event procedure to each control on a form, you can guide the user by displaying brief instructions or status bar messages. You can also provide visual cues by enabling, disabling, or showing other controls that depend on the control that has the focus.

Load and Unload Events

The **Load** and **Unload** events occur when a form is loaded or unloaded. Any form that becomes visible must first be loaded. Use the **Load** event to initialize controls and variables, and use the **Unload** event to close files and save information.

When the **Form_Load** event procedure begins, the controls on the form have all been created and loaded. A form will be loaded automatically if:

◆ The form has been specified as the **Startup Object,** on the **General** tab of the **Project Properties** dialog box.

◆ The **Show** method is the first property or method of the form to be invoked, as in frmValidation.Show.

◆ The first property or method of the form to be invoked is one of the form's built-in members, as in the **Move** method.

QueryUnload Event

The **QueryUnload** event occurs just before the **Unload** event, when the form is unloaded. The **QueryUnload** event enables you to determine how the **Unload** event was initiated and to cancel the **Unload** event if desired.

The **QueryUnload** event has two arguments:

◆ The **UnloadMode** argument indicates how the **Unload** event was initiated.

◆ The **Cancel** argument cancels the unload. If you set **Cancel** to **True,** the application remains as it was before the close was attempted.

Note Executing the **End** statement unloads all forms and sets all object variables in your program to **Nothing**. However, this is an abrupt way to terminate your program. None of your forms will get their **QueryUnload**, **Unload**, or **Terminate** events, and objects that you've created will not get their **Terminate** events.

The following example code checks whether the **QueryUnload** event was triggered by the user clicking the **Control** menu and, if so, notifies the user and cancels the close:

```
Sub Form_QueryUnload(Cancel As Integer, UnloadMode As Integer)
    If UnloadMode = vbFormControlMenu Then
        MsgBox "Do not use Close from Control menu."
        Cancel = True
    End If
End Sub
```

For more information about using Visual Basic constants, search for "Visual Basic Constants" in MSDN Help.

Lab 9: Input Validation

In this lab, you will write code and set properties to control how the user interacts with your loan application. By implementing these steps, you will make it easier for users to enter valid data. In addition, you will add controls that provide visual feedback to further aid a user in using your interface.

You can continue to work with the loan project files that you've created, or you can use the files provided for you in the folder *<install folder>*\Labs\Lab09.

To see the demonstration "Lab 9 Solution," see the accompanying CD-ROM.

Estimated time to complete this lab: **30 minutes**

Objectives

After completing this lab, you will be able to:

◆ Set validation properties of a text box.

◆ Use the **Validate** event to validate user input.

◆ Validate the user-entered numeric data.

The solution for this lab is located in the folder *<install folder>*\Labs\Lab09\Solution.

To complete the exercises in this lab, you must have the required software. For detailed information about the labs and setup for the labs, see "Labs" in "About This Course."

Prerequisites

There are no prerequisites for this lab.

Exercises

The following exercises provide practice in working with the concepts covered in this chapter:

◆ Exercise 1: Adding Code to the Validate Event

In this exercise, you will add code to the **Validate** events of the **User Name** and **Password** text boxes. This code will verify that the user enters text in both fields.

◆ Exercise 2: Validating Numeric Data

The **MonthlyPayment** and **TotalPaid** functions require a numeric value in the **txtPurchase** text box. Calling either function with a string in the text box causes a run-time error. In this exercise, you will protect against this error by checking for a number in the text box before calling the functions.

Exercise 1: Adding Code to the Validate Event

In this exercise, you will add code to the **Validate** events of the **User Name** and **Password** text boxes. This code will verify that the user enters text in both fields.

▶ **Open the loan project**

◆ Open the loan project on which you have been working, or open the loan project in the *<install folder>*\Labs\Lab09 folder.

▶ **Code the Validate events**

1. Set the **CausesValidation** property of the **Cancel** button on frmLogon to **False**.

> **Note** The **Validate** event occurs only when the **CausesValidation** property of the control that is about to receive the focus is set to **True**. The **Validate** event also includes a **Cancel** argument, which, when set to **True**, allows the control to retain focus.

2. Add code to the **Validate** events for **txtUserName** and **txtPassword** that verifies that data was entered into each text box and sets the focus back to the corresponding text box if no data was entered:

```
Private Sub txtUserName_Validate(Cancel As Boolean)
  If txtUserName.Text = "" Then
    MsgBox "A user name is required."
    Cancel = True
  End If
End Sub

Private Sub txtPassword_Validate(Cancel As Boolean)
  If txtPassword.Text = "" Then
    MsgBox "A password is required."
    Cancel = True
  End If
End Sub
```

3. Save the project and test the application.

Exercise 2: Verifying Numeric Data

The **MonthlyPayment** and **TotalPaid** functions require a numeric value in the **txtPurchase** text box. Calling either function with a string in the text box causes a run-time error. In this exercise, you will protect against this error by checking for a number in the text box before calling the functions.

▶ **Check for an invalid value**

1. Run the loan application, type a nonnumeric value into the **txtPurchase** text box, and click **Monthly Payment**.

   The run-time error Type Mismatch should occur.

2. In the Visual Basic **Error** dialog box, click **End**.

3. Open the Code Editor window for frmMain and move to the **cmdMonthly_Click** event procedure.

4. Before calling the **MonthlyPayment** function, test to see if the value entered in the **txtPurchase** text box is a numeric value:

   ```
   If IsNumeric(txtPurchase.Text) Then
   ```

5. If the value is numeric, call the **MonthlyPayment** function and display the results in a message box.

6. If the value is not numeric:

   a. Display a message box instructing the user to type a numeric value.

   b. Set focus back to the **txtPurchase** text box.

   c. Highlight the invalid text in the text box.

> **Note** For more information about highlighting text, see "Working with Selected Text" on page 204 in Chapter 7, "Working with Controls."

7. Add the same type of error checking to the **cmdTotal_Click** event procedure.

8. Save and test your work.

To see an example of how your code should look, see Hint 9.1 in Appendix B.

Self-Check Questions

See page 391 for answers.

1. How do you make a text box read-only?

A. Set the **MaxLength** property to 0.

B. Set the **Cancel** property to **True**.

C. Set the **Locked** property to **True**.

D. Set the **Enabled** property to **True**.

2. What occurs if a user enters an invalid character in a Masked Edit control?

A. The invalid character is not accepted and the program continues.

B. The invalid character is not accepted and a **ValidationError** event occurs.

C. The invalid character is accepted, but the program ends.

D. The invalid character is accepted and a **ValidationError** event occurs.

3. Setting the KeyPreview property to True allows:

A. The key to be displayed but not used in a mask.

B. The form to receive keyboard events before the active control.

C. The key press to be trapped by the control before it is displayed.

D. None of the above.

Chapter 10:
Error Trapping

In this chapter, you will learn how to handle errors in ways that avoid disruption of the program and your users' work. Microsoft Visual Basic provides a number of tools that help prevent run-time errors in your applications. It is important to plan for possible errors due to invalid data or user interaction.

Objectives

After completing this chapter, you will be able to:

◆ Trap run-time errors.

◆ Create error handlers.

◆ See how errors are handled in the calling chain.

◆ Handle errors in an error-handling routine.

◆ Handle inline errors.

◆ Describe some common error-handling styles.

◆ Describe error-trapping options in the Visual Basic development environment.

Overview of Run-Time Errors

Errors that occur during the execution of an application are often a result of unforeseen actions. For example, a user might forget to insert a disk into a floppy drive, or a user could select an invalid input file. These errors are called run-time errors. You can prevent run-time errors, provide useful information to users, and exit the application gracefully by using error handlers. For a list of all errors that are trappable in Visual Basic, search for "Trappable Errors" in MSDN Help.

If a run-time error occurs when your program is running from the Visual Basic development environment, a message appears that lets you enter Debug mode, refer to Help, or end the application. If a run-time error occurs when your application is running as an executable file, Visual Basic displays an error message and the application ends. To prevent run-time errors, you can write error-handling code that traps errors and either corrects the problem, prompts the user for action, or saves data before ending the program.

Overview of the Error-Handling Process

In this section, you will learn how to use error handlers in Visual Basic. Occasionally, hardware problems or unanticipated actions by the user can cause run-time errors that stop your application. Other errors can cause your code to act unpredictably, although they might not interrupt your application. To avoid these situations, use the error-handling features in Visual Basic to intercept errors and take corrective action. The process of intercepting an error is also known as error trapping.

Introduction to Error Handling

An error handler is a routine for trapping and responding to errors in your application. You should add error handlers to any procedure in which you anticipate the possibility of a run-time error.

To see the demonstration "Error Handling," see the accompanying CD-ROM.

The process of designing an error handler involves three steps:

◆ Set, or enable, an error trap by telling the application where to branch to (which error-handling routine to execute) when an error occurs.

Visual Basic enables an error trap when it executes the **On Error** statement. The error trap remains enabled while the procedure containing it is active. Only one error trap can be enabled at any one time in any given procedure. In addition, the error trap must reside in the local procedure. You cannot use the **On Error** statement to branch to another procedure. To disable an error trap, use the **On Error GoTo 0** statement.

◆ Write an error-handling routine (an error handler) that responds to all anticipated errors.

The first step in writing an error-handling routine is adding a line label to mark the beginning of the error handler. The line label should have a descriptive name and must be followed by a colon. A common convention is to place the error-handling code at the end of the procedure with an **Exit Sub** or **Exit Function** statement immediately before the line label. This allows the procedure to avoid executing the error handler if no error occurs.

◆ Exit the error-handling routine.

You can exit an error-handling routine by using a **Resume** or **Resume Next** statement. The **Resume** statement will execute the line of code that caused the error, and the **Resume Next** statement will execute the line of code following the line of code that caused the error. Generally, you use **Resume** if the error handler can correct the error, and **Resume Next** when the error handler cannot. You can write an error handler so that the existence of a run-time error is never revealed to the user, or you can write an error handler to display error messages and allow the user to enter corrections.

The following illustration shows the error-handling process.

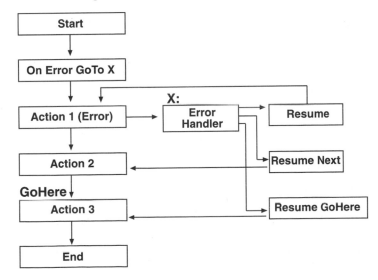

Implementing an Error Trap

Error handling requires careful consideration. The steps involve enabling the error trap, writing code to handle the error, and then exiting the error-handling routine.

Enabling an Error Trap

You can test and respond to trappable errors by using the **On Error** statement. If a run-time error occurs, you can force your application to jump to the label specified by the **On Error GoTo** statement. The statement in the following example code causes execution to jump to the portion of your program labeled ErrorHandler:

```
On Error GoTo ErrorHandler
```

Exiting the Error-Handling Routine

After an error trap has been set, it remains enabled until execution of the procedure ends or the error trap is disabled. You can use the **Resume** statement to specify where your application should resume processing after handling the error. The three variations of the **Resume** statement are described in the following table.

Statement	Description
Resume	Return to the statement that caused the error. Use this statement to repeat an operation after correcting the error.
Resume Next	Return to the statement immediately following the one that caused the error.
Resume *line* or *label*	Return to a specific line number or label.

The statement **On Error Resume Next** causes errors to be ignored. If a run-time error occurs, processing continues with the next line. This form of the **On Error** statement is used for inline error handling. For more information about handling errors inline, see "Inline Error Handling" on page 280 in this chapter.

The statement **On Error GoTo 0** disables the error trap.

In the following example code, the error-handling code follows the **Exit Sub** statement and precedes the **End Sub** statement to separate it from the procedure flow:

```
Sub InitializeMatrix()
  On Error GoTo ErrorHandler
  [statement block]
  Exit Sub
ErrorHandler:
  [statement block]
  Resume Next
End Sub
```

The Err Object

The **Err** object contains information about an error that just occurred. The **Err** object has properties and methods that you can use to check which error occurred, to clear an error value, or to cause an error.

Properties

The **Number** property is an integer that indicates the last error that occurred. In some cases, your error handler may be able to correct an error and continue processing without interrupting the user. Otherwise, it will notify the user of an error and then take action based on the user's response.

The **Description** property is a string that contains a description of the error.

The **Source** property contains the name of the application that generated the error. This is helpful when using Automation. For example, if you access Microsoft Excel and it generates an error, Excel sets **Err.Number** to the correct error code and sets **Err.Source** to Excel.Application.

The **Err** object has three additional properties, but they are beyond the scope of this course. For a list of all the properties for the **Err** Object, search for "Err Object" in MSDN Help.

Methods

The **Clear** method clears an error, setting the value of **Err.Number** back to 0. Use this method primarily when you handle errors inline. For more information about handling errors inline, see "Inline Error Handling" on page 280 in this chapter.

The **Raise** method causes an error. To keep from duplicating error-trapping code, use the **Raise** method to pass an error back to a calling procedure or to test your error-handling code. Visual Basic does not use all available numbers for its own errors. If you want to generate and trap your own errors, begin your numbering scheme with 32767 and work your way down, as in the following example code:

```
Err.Raise 32000
```

Errors and the Calling Chain

If an error occurs in a procedure that does not have an error handler enabled, the error is passed up the invocation, or calling chain.

The following illustration shows the calling chain.

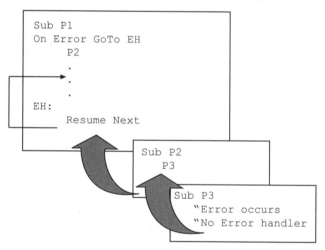

```
Sub P1
On Error GoTo EH
       P2
       .
       .
       .
EH:
      Resume Next
```

```
Sub P2
       P3
```

```
Sub P3
     "Error occurs
     "No Error handler
```

If no error handler is encountered, Visual Basic displays a message box and the application ends. If an error handler is encountered, the error-handling code is executed. If the error-handling code includes a **Resume** statement, the application resumes at the level of the error handler—not necessarily at the level at which the error occurred.

Note When you are debugging an application, you can use the Call Stack to see what procedures have been invoked at the point where an error occurs. For more information about viewing the sequence of procedure calls, see "Tracing Program Flow with the Call Stack" on page 183 in Chapter 6, "Debugging."

In a procedure, you can handle some errors locally and pass unknown errors back to the calling procedure. The following sample code implements this type of error handling. To copy this code for use in your own projects, see "Passing Errors to the Calling Procedure" on the accompanying CD-ROM.

```
Private Sub ProcA()
    On Error GoTo ErrorHandlerA
    ProcB
    Exit Sub
ErrorHandlerA:
    MsgBox Err.Description
End Sub

Private Sub ProcB()
    On Error GoTo ErrorHandlerB:
    Open "c:\myfile.txt" For Input As #1
    Exit Sub
ErrorHandlerB:
    If Err.Number = 53 Then
        'File Missing
        MsgBox "File Not Found"
        Exit Sub
    Else
        'Unknown Error Passed back to calling procedure
        Err.Raise Err.Number
    End If
End Sub
```

Errors in an Error-Handling Routine

If a run-time error occurs within an error-handling routine, the error is passed up to the calling procedure. If there is no calling procedure, the application displays a message and ends.

To prevent errors within an error handler, keep your error-handling code simple. If necessary, you can invoke other procedures from your error-handling code that contain their own error-handling code.

An **On Error** statement included in your error handler does not take effect until the end of the error-handling code, that is, until some form of the **Resume** or **Exit Sub** statement has executed.

Inline Error Handling

Instead of setting up an error handler that you branch to, you may want to handle an error inline (immediately after the error occurs).

▶ **To handle an error inline, perform the following steps:**

1. Include the **On Error Resume Next** statement in your code.

2. Check the value of **Err.Number** after each statement that may have an error.

3. Use **Err.Clear** to reset the error number.

Inline error-handling code does not contain labels or **Resume** statements.

Note that **Err.Number** contains the value of the last error that occurred. If a statement is successful, it does not change the value of **Err.Number**. For example, you can use the **Shell** function in Visual Basic to run an executable program. If the **Shell** function cannot start the executable program, a run-time error occurs. However, you can use inline error handling to test whether or not the **Shell** function failed, as shown in the following example code:

```
Dim strAppName As String

On Error Resume Next
strAppName = InputBox("To run the Calculator type 'calc'. " & _
  "To run Notepad type 'notepad'.")

'Use the Shell function to run an application
Shell strAppName, vbNormalFocus

'Check for an error
If Err.Number <> 0 Then
    MsgBox "Unable to find " & strAppName & _
        vbCrLf & "Run-time error.  Number " & Err.Number
End If
```

For more information about the **Shell** function, search for "Shell Function" in MSDN Help.

Exercise caution when using **On Error Resume Next**. Your error-handling code might ignore errors that you are not aware of.

The following sample code uses inline error handling. To copy this code of use in your own projects, see "Inline Error Handling" on the accompanying CD-ROM.

```
Sub cmdOpenFile_Click ()
Dim intTempErr As Integer
On Error Resume Next

Open "c:\AAA.txt" For Input As #1

Select Case Err.Number
  Case 0:
      'No error. Do nothing.
  Case 53:
      'File not Found
      'Code to prompt for file
  Case 55:
      'File already open
      'Code to correct
  Case Else
      intTempErr = Err.Number
      On Error GoTo 0
      Err.Raise intTempErr
End Select

'Reset Err.Number
Err.Clear

Open "c:\BBB.txt" For Input As #2
End Sub
```

Error-Handling Styles

Two styles of error handling are commonly used: functions with complete error handlers or centralized error-handling code.

Functions with Complete Error Handlers

Whenever possible, you should generalize your code into a standard function that contains full error-handling code. Then, invoke the function from elsewhere in your program. The function should return a value to indicate its success in handling errors that occur.

For example, instead of coding **Open** statements directly in your code, create a general function that opens a file and contains full error-handling code, and then invoke that procedure. The following sample code invokes a procedure. To copy this code for use in your own projects, see "Error Handling General Function" on the accompanying CD-ROM.

```vba
Sub cmdOpenFile_Click()
    Dim intFileHandle As Integer
    intFileHandle = stdFileOpen("c:\mytest.txt")
    If intFileHandle Then
        MsgBox "FILE WAS OPENED"
    Else
        MsgBox "FILE OPEN FAILED"
    End If
End Sub

Function stdFileOpen(strFileName As String) As Integer
    Dim intResponse As Integer
    Dim intFileNumber As Integer
    On Error GoTo stdFileOpenError
    intFileNumber = FreeFile
    Open strFileName For Input As intFileNumber
    stdFileOpen = intFileNumber

ExitStdFileOpen:
    Exit Function

stdFileOpenError:
    Select Case Err.Number
        Case 67:
            'Too many files open
            intResponse = MsgBox("Close files", vbRetryCancel, _
"Error")
            If intResponse = vbYes Then
                Resume
            Else
                stdFileOpen = 0
                Resume ExitStdFileOpen
            End If
        Case 53:        'File not found
            MsgBox "File not found"
            stdFileOpen = 0
            Resume ExitStdFileOpen
        Case Else
            MsgBox "Unknown Error " & Err.Description
            End
    End Select
End Function
```

For more information about error handling, search for "Handling Run-Time Errors" in MSDN Help.

Centralized Error-Handling Code

You can also centralize your application's primary error handling by creating a main error-handling function that tells procedures how to process errors. However, because **Resume** statements can only appear in procedures that contain an **On Error** statement, some error-handling code must remain within each procedure that needs error-handling capabilities.

The following sample code demonstrates centralized error-handling. To copy this code for use in your own projects, see "Centralized Error Handling" on the accompanying CD-ROM.

The following code implements an error handler that passes the error to a general-purpose error-handling routine.

```
Public Const MYRESUME As Integer = 1
Public Const MYRESUMENEXT As Integer = 2

Private Sub CodeWithErrorHandler()
  On Error GoTo ErrHandler
    '...Procedure code ...
    '...
Exit Sub

ErrHandler:
  'Pass error to general purpose error-handling routine
  intAction = HandleError(Err.Number)
  'Take action based on result of function
  If intAction = MYRESUME Then
    Resume
  ElseIf intAction = MYRESUMENEXT Then
    Resume Next
  End If
End Sub
```

code continued on next page

```
code continued from previous page
      'And here's the code for the general-purpose error handler.
   Dim intAnswer As Integer
   Private Function HandleError(intErrNum As Integer) As Integer
      Select Case intErrNum
      Case 53 'File not found
        intAnswer = MsgBox("File not found. Try again?", _
            vbYesNo)
      Case 76 'Path not found
        intAnswer = MsgBox("Path not found. Try again?", _
                     vbYesNo)



      Case Else 'unknown error
        MsgBox "Unknown error.  Quitting now."
        Unload Me
      End Select

      If intAnswer = vbYes Then
        HandleError = MYRESUME    'tell calling procedure
                                   'to resume
      ElseIf answer = vbNo Then
        HandleError = MYRESUMENEXT  'tell calling procedure
                                     'to resume next
      End If
   End Function
```

General Error-Trapping Options in Visual Basic

There are three general error-trapping options available as part of the Visual Basic development environment:

◆ Break on All Errors

◆ Break in Class Module

◆ Break on Unhandled Errors

Break on All Errors

If you set the **Break On All Errors** option, Visual Basic ignores any **On Error** statements and enters Break mode if any run-time errors occur. This option is useful for debugging while running your application within the Visual Basic development environment.

Break in Class Module

Set the **Break in Class Module** option when debugging a COM component project. This option causes the COM component to enter Break mode rather than passing the error back to the client application.

Break on Unhandled Errors

If you set the **Break on Unhandled Errors** option, Visual Basic enters Break mode on any error for which you do not have specific error-handling code. This is consistent with the behavior of a compiled application, which ends after it encounters a run-time error.

▶ **To set error-trapping options**

1. On the **Tools** menu, click **Options**.

2. In the **Options** dialog box, click the **General** tab.

3. Under Error Trapping, select the option you want, and then click **OK**.

The following illustration shows the **General** tab in the **Options** dialog box.

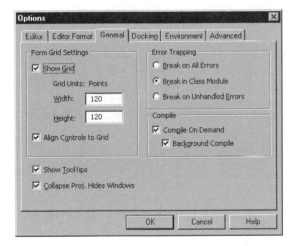

Lab 10: Error Trapping

In this lab, you will write code that uses the **Shell** statement to attempt to run another application. If the **Shell** statement fails, it can produce a run-time error. You can use a number of error-handling techniques to deal with this error.

To see the demonstration "Lab 10 Solution," see the accompanying CD-ROM.

Estimated time to complete this lab: **30 minutes**

Objectives

After completing this lab, you will be able to:

◆ Handle errors inline.

◆ Create an error handler.

◆ Determine how to exit the error handler.

◆ Create a centralized error handler.

To complete the exercises in this lab, you must have the required software. For detailed information about the labs and setup for the labs, see "Labs" in "About This Course."

The solution for this lab is located in the folder *<install folder>*\Labs\Lab10\Solution.

Prerequisites

Before working on this lab, you should be familiar with the following:

◆ Adding and working with procedures

Exercises

The following exercises provide practice in working with the concepts covered in this chapter.

◆ Exercise 1: Using Inline Error Handling

In this exercise, you will check for errors in your code by using inline error handling.

◆ Exercise 2: Creating an Error-Handling Routine

In this exercise, you will trap errors in the event procedure by using an error-handling routine.

◆ Exercise 3: Creating an Error-Handling Function

In this exercise, you will create a function for running applications. This function will return **True** if it was able to shell the application and **False** if it was not.

Exercise 1: Using Inline Error Handling

In this exercise, you will check for errors in your code by using inline error handling.

▶ **Open the loan project**

◆ Open either the loan project on which you have been working, or the loan project in the *<install folder>*\Labs\Lab10 folder.

▶ **Create event procedure**

1. Add a command button to the main form. Set the **Name** property to **cmdOtherApp** and the **Caption** property to **&Other Applications,** as shown in the following illustration.

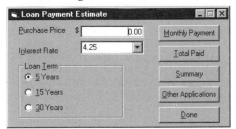

2. In the **Click** event procedure for the **Other Applications** button, add the code that prompts the user for an application name and uses the **Shell** statement to execute the application, as shown in the following code:

```
Dim strAppName As String
strAppName = InputBox("To run the Calculator type 'calc'. " & _
    "To run Notepad type 'notepad'.")
Shell strAppName, vbNormalFocus
```

3. Run the application and test the **Other Application** button by typing **calc** (the Windows calculator application).

4. Test the **Other Application** button again by typing an invalid application name, such as **XYZ.** This will produce a run-time error. Click the **End** button.

▶ **Add inline error-handling code**

1. At the beginning of the **cmdOtherApp_Click** event procedure, add the **On Error Resume Next** statement to prevent Visual Basic from raising an exception when an error occurs.

2. After the **Shell** statement, check the **Number** property of the **Err** object to see if an error occurred. For example, if an error occurred, display a message box with the error number.

```
Private Sub cmdOtherApp_Click()
'Keep running if error occurs
On Error Resume Next
Dim strAppName As String
strAppName = InputBox("To run the Calculator type 'calc'. " & _
    "To run Notepad type 'notepad'.")

Shell strAppName, vbNormalFocus
'Check the Number property to see if there was an error
If Err.Number <> 0 Then 'If an error occurred
    MsgBox "Unable to find " & strAppName & _
        vbCrLf & "Run-time error.  Number " & Err.Number
End If
End Sub
```

Note The **vbCrLf** string constant is the same as **Chr(13)** & **Chr(10)**; this forces a carriage return–linefeed combination, which places any text that follows on the next line.

3. Test the application.

Exercise 2: Creating an Error-Handling Routine

In this exercise, you will trap errors in an event procedure by using an error-handling routine.

▶ **Create an event procedure**

1. Run the application, and in the main form, delete the value in the **Interest Rate** combo box.

2. Click on the **Monthly Payments** command button. This should produce a run-time error.

3. What is the run-time error number?

   For help in completing this exercise, see Hint 10.1 in Appendix B.

4. Click the **Debug** button. Notice the line of code in which the error occurred.

5. Click the **End** button.

▶ Create an error handler

1. Set an error trap by using the **On Error** statement in the **MonthlyPayment** function.

2. Create the error-handling routine.

   In the error-handling routine, add code to test for different errors that could be generated. To see an example of how your code should look, see Hint 10.2 in Appendix B.

3. Run and test the application. Does the error handler trap the error generated in the previous example?

For help in completing this exercise, see Hint 10.3 in Appendix B.

Exercise 3: Creating an Error-Handling Function

In this exercise, you will create a function for running applications. This function will return **True** if it was able to shell the application and **False** if it was not.

▶ Create a function procedure

1. In the **Click** event procedure for the **Other Application** button, add code that calls a function named **RunApp**, and test the return value of this function. If the result is false, display a message box that tells the user that the application was not found.

   Your code should look similar to the following example code:

   ```
   Private Sub cmdOtherApp_Click()
       Dim strAppName As String
       strAppName = InputBox("To run Calculator type 'Calc'. " & _
           "To run Notepad type 'NotePad'.")
       If RunApp(strAppName) = False Then
           MsgBox "Unable to find " & strAppName & vbCrLf & _
           "Error Number " & Err.Number
       End If

   End Sub
   ```

2. In the main form, create a form-level function procedure named **RunApp**. Make sure you do the following:

    a. Handle run-time errors, using either inline error handling or an error-handling routine.

    b. Return **True** if the **Shell** statement was successful, and return **False** if an error occurred.

       To see an example of how your code should look, see Hint 10.4 in Appendix B.

3. Test the procedures.

Self-Check Questions

See page 393 for answers.

1. If an error-handling routine is not enabled and a run-time error occurs:

A. The program continues execution but might provide unexpected results.

B. The program continues execution and passes the error code to the current form module's **Unload** event.

C. The program stops execution and displays the cause of the error.

D. The program stops execution without displaying the cause of the error.

2. If an error occurs in a procedure after the statement On Error GoTo 0:

A. The error-handling routine at the label 0 executes.

B. The generic Visual Basic error-handling routine processes the error, allowing continued execution.

C. Execution continues at the line following the error.

D. Execution stops and an error message appears.

3. When writing error-handling code for a procedure, which of the following statements causes execution to continue on the line following the error in the procedure?

A. Resume

B. Resume Next

C. Resume *line*

D. Resume After Error

Student Notes:

Chapter 11:
Enhancing the User Interface

Multimedia

Writing sound code and using forms effectively is only part of programming with Microsoft Visual Basic. In this chapter, you will learn how to give your application a more professional look through the use of menus, toolbars, and status bars.

Designing an easy-to-use interface is a critical part of building a Visual Basic solution and often the most challenging development task. Effective use of menus, toolbars, and status bars makes your application easy to use and can serve as an efficient system to deliver information to users. For example, through the use of menus, users can easily navigate through various commands organized in a fashion common to many Microsoft Windows applications. The use of menus is a great alternative to placing a large number of command buttons on your forms, which can clutter your interface. Through the use of a status bar, you can display useful information, such as the name of a file being edited or the status of a database connection.

Objectives

After completing this chapter, you will be able to:

- Create and edit custom menu bars, menus, submenus, and menu items by using the Menu Editor.
- Identify the menu properties that can be set in the **Menu Editor** dialog box.
- Create a pop-up menu by using the Menu Editor.
- Assign code to menu items that respond to the **Click** event.
- Create a status bar on a form that provides users with feedback.
- Create a toolbar by using the **Toolbar** control.

Menus

In this section, you will learn about creating menus for your Visual Basic applications. If you want your application to provide a set of commands for users, menus are a convenient and consistent way to group commands and an easy way for users to access them. In addition, hot keys and shortcut keys can make menu navigation easier for experienced users of your application.

Menu Terminology

A menu system typically consists of several related elements, some of which are more directly visible than others. Menu systems need not necessarily implement each of the elements.

The following illustration shows the menu-specific elements of the user interface.

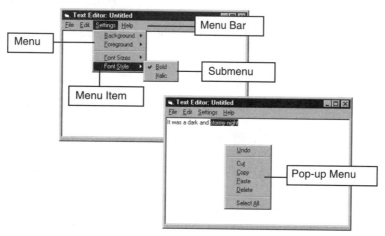

The following table describes the menu elements of a typical user interface, such as those used by Microsoft Windows applications.

Menu element	Description
Menu bar	The menu bar is a special toolbar at the top of the screen that contains menus such as **File**, **Edit**, and **View**. You can customize the menu bar the same way you customize any built-in toolbar; for example, you can quickly add and remove buttons and menus on the menu bar, but you can't hide the menu bar.

table continued on next page

Menu element	Description
Menu	The menu contains the list of commands that appear when you click a menu bar item. This list includes the menu title at the top.
Menu item	A menu item, also called a command, refers to one of the choices listed on a menu. According to standard user-interface design guidelines, every menu should contain at least one command.
Submenu	A submenu, or cascading menu, is a menu that branches off from a menu item. The command from which the cascading menu branches has an arrow next to it to indicate that a new menu will appear when the user points to that command.
Pop-up menu	A pop-up menu is a context-sensitive menu that typically appears when you right-click the mouse (or secondary mouse button) in your application — however, this can be controlled through your code. A pop-up menu contains commands that are commonly associated with the object that is clicked. For example, if a selection of text is clicked, the pop-up menu may contain **Cut, Copy, Paste,** and **Delete** commands.

To see the demonstration "Implementing Menus," see the accompanying CD-ROM.

Using the Menu Editor

Visual Basic provides a Menu Editor, which you can use to create menus that will help users operate your application easily and intuitively.

You can use the Menu Editor to:

◆ Create menu bars, menus with menu items and submenus, and pop-up menus.

◆ Assign properties to menu items, such as **Name, Caption, Checked, Enabled, Visible, NegotiatePosition, HelpContextID,** and **Index.**

◆ Assign a Help topic to a menu.

The following illustration shows an example of the Menu Editor being used to create a **Settings** menu for an application.

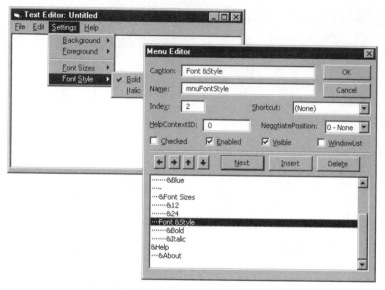

▶ **To open the Menu Editor**

◆ On the **Tools** menu, click **Menu Editor**.

  −or−

◆ On the toolbar, click the **Menu Editor** button.

Note Each menu bar, menu, submenu, pop-up menu, and menu item has events. You can write code in these events to manipulate the properties of the menus and take any appropriate action.

For more information about menus and the Menu Editor, search for "Menus Basics" in MSDN Help.

Adding Menu Items to a Form

Menus, menu items, submenus, and submenu items for a form are displayed in a hierarchical format in the Menu Editor. The items are indented to indicate their position. You can change the position of an item in the hierarchy by clicking the left or right arrow buttons.

The following illustration shows the **Menu Editor** dialog box with several menus defined.

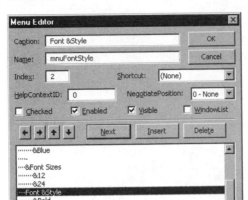

Note Up to four levels of submenus are allowed, for a total of five menu levels. For clarity, however, you should limit your menu hierarchy to two levels whenever possible.

▶ To add a menu item to a form

1. Activate the form that will contain the menus.

2. On the **Tools** menu, click **Menu Editor**.

   −or−

   On the standard toolbar, click the **Menu Editor** button.

3. In the **Caption** box, type a caption for your menu.

Note To create a separator bar in your menu, type a hyphen (-) in the **Caption** box. You can also designate an access key by typing an ampersand (&) before any letter in the caption (for example, &Save or Save &As).

4. In the **Name** box, type a name for your menu item object.

   You should use the prefix **mnu** for the menu item name.

Note You can make your code more efficient by creating a control array from the menu items. For example, make all of the commands on a menu members of the same control array, make all of the submenu items for a command members of another control array, and so on. For more information about control arrays, see "Using Control Arrays" on page 339 in Chapter 13, "More About Controls."

5. If you want to change the hierarchical position of the menu item, click the right arrow button.

Note Use the up and down arrow buttons to change the position of a menu item within the same menu level. To add a new menu item before the selected item, click the **Insert** button.

6. Change any of the properties in the **Menu Editor** dialog box.

7. Click **Next** to add your menu item to the menu bar.

8. Repeat steps 3 through 7 until you've completed your menu, and then click **OK**.

Adding Code to Menu Items

Menu items have a **Click** event procedure. You can write code to change the properties of menu bars, menus, menu items, and submenus, and to respond to the menu item **Click** event.

For example, you can:

♦ Use the **Enabled** property to enable or disable a menu item.

♦ Use the **Checked** property to place check marks next to menu items.

♦ Use the **Visible** property to show or hide menu content dynamically.

Note Only one menu bar is allowed for each form. You can simulate multiple menu bars by setting the **Visible** property for various menus to **True** or **False**, depending on when it is appropriate to display the menu.

In the following example, the **Bold** command on the **Font Style** menu runs the procedure **mnuFontStyleBold_Click**. The following procedure toggles the **Font.Bold** property of a text box and places a check mark next to the menu command.

```
Private Sub mnuFontStyleBold_Click()
    With mnuFontStyleBold
        .Checked = Not .Checked
        txtEdit.Font.Bold = .Checked
    End With
End Sub
```

Note When using this type of code, be aware of initial settings. In the previous example, the initial settings make the font in the text box bold.

Pop-Up Menus

A pop-up menu is a menu that is not visibly connected to the menu bar and, typically, appears when the user right-clicks the mouse. The following illustration shows a pop-up menu on a form.

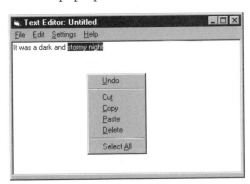

The appearance of a particular pop-up menu depends on the location of the mouse pointer when the user right-clicks the mouse. You should provide a pop-up menu that gives the user the most useful commands for the current location. For example, if the user right-clicks in a form, you should display a pop-up menu that includes commands that are commonly applied to a form.

Types of Pop-Up Menus

There are two types of pop-up menus that you can create with Visual Basic:

◆ System pop-up menu

The system pop-up menu is provided automatically with certain controls. For example, the system pop-up menu for a **TextBox** control contains commands that apply to text editing, such as **Undo, Cut, Copy, Paste, Delete,** and **Select All.** All commands on the system pop-up menus are fully functional; no additional code is required.

◆ Custom pop-up menu

A custom pop-up menu is a menu that you create that is specific to your application. You then write code to display the pop-up menu when needed.

Creating and Displaying a Custom Pop-Up Menu

To create a pop-up menu, use the Menu Editor as you do to create any other menu. However, set the **Visible** property to **False** so that the menu is not displayed automatically.

To display the pop-up menu, use the **PopupMenu** method. To call the **PopupMenu** method, use the following syntax:

object.*PopupMenu menuname,* flags, x, y, boldcommand

You typically call this method in the **MouseUp** event for the object that will serve as the context for the pop-up menu. The following example code displays a pop-up menu when the user right-clicks a form:

```
Private Sub Form_MouseUp(Button As Integer, _
    Shift As Integer, X As Single, Y As Single)
    If Button = vbRightButton Then
        frmCustomerInfo.PopupMenu mnuShortcut
    End If
End Sub
```

Note The secondary mouse button is either the right button for a right-handed mouse, or the left button for a left-handed mouse. The **MouseUp** event checks the current mouse setting in the Control Panel.

By default, an item on the pop-up menu will respond only to the left button. If you want to make it respond to either the left or right button, use the **vbPopupMenuRightButton** flag.

The following example code will cause the pop-up menu's items to respond to either mouse button:

```
frmCustomerInfo.PopupMenu mnuShortcut, vbPopupMenuRightButton
```

Status Bars

One of the simplest ways to provide feedback to users is to place a label that contains instructions or information on a form. By providing simple instructions, users often understand the procedures necessary to accomplish tasks in your applications. Sometimes, however, it can be difficult to include all of the instructions and documentation on the form itself. Instead, you may have to use other features in Visual Basic to build more complex feedback or to build Help into your application's user interface.

The **StatusBar** control is used to display various kinds of status data. Unlike a message box, a status bar displays its data in an unobtrusive manner, in an area usually located at the bottom of the form.

The status bar can display and update certain types of information automatically. Set the **Style** property of the **StatusBar** control to display the following:

◆ Keyboard status for the CAPS LOCK, NUM LOCK, INSERT, and SCROLL LOCK keys

◆ Time

◆ Date

The status bar can also contain text and bitmaps. You can display messages from the application in the status bar by using the **Text** property.

To see the demonstration "Implementing Status Bars," see the accompanying CD-ROM.

Note The StatusBar control is part of the Microsoft Windows Common Controls.

▶ **To add a StatusBar control to the project**

1. On the **Project** menu, click **Components**.

2. On the **Controls** tab, select **Microsoft Windows Common Controls 6.0** from the list of available controls, then click **OK**.

▶ **To display the Properties window for the Status Bar control**

1. Draw a **StatusBar** control on your form.

2. Point to the status bar and right-click. On the pop-up menu that appears, click **Properties**.

> **Note** Some custom controls have property pages associated with them. Property pages are usually tabbed dialog boxes that contain additional properties not listed in the Properties window. To access a control's property page, right-click the control and click **Properties** on the pop-up menu that appears, or click the (**Custom**) property from the Properties window.

Setting Status Bar Panel Text at Run Time

To change the text that appears in a status bar panel, set the **Text** property of one of the panels in the **StatusBar** control. The following example code displays the number of characters in an edit box while the user types:

```
'The Key property for the Panel is equal to "One"
sbrEditor.Panels("One").Text = "Number of Characters: " & _
  Len(txtEdit.Text)
```

If the status bar contains only one pane (the **Style** property is set to **sbrSimple**), you can display text by using the **SimpleText** property, as in the following example code:

```
sbrEditor.SimpleText = "Processing, please wait..."
```

For more information on the **StatusBar** control, search for "StatusBar Control" in MSDN Help.

Toolbars

In this section, you will learn how to create a toolbar and add code to respond to toolbar events. The toolbar has become a standard feature in many Windows-based applications. A toolbar typically contains buttons that correspond to items in an application's menu. A toolbar provides a graphical interface through which the user can access an application's most frequently used functions and commands.

Creating a Toolbar

Toolbars usually feature buttons that use icons to represent a function of the application. For example, an icon of a floppy disk is generally used to represent a **File Save** function. To get your toolbar to display such images, you must first associate an **ImageList** control with the **Toolbar** control, which can be done either at design time or at run time.

Note The **ImageList** and **Toolbar** controls are part of the Microsoft Windows Common Controls.

▶ **To add either an ImageList control or a Toolbar control to the toolbox**

1. On the **Project** menu, click **Components**.

2. On the **Controls** tab, select **Microsoft Windows Common Controls 6.0** from the list of available controls, and then click **OK**.

   A number of controls are added to the toolbox, including the **ImageList** control.

An **ImageList** control contains a **ListImages** collection that contains picture objects, each of which can be referred to by its index or key. The **ImageList** control is a convenient central repository that supplies images to other controls, such as a toolbar.

▶ **To build an image list**

1. Add an **ImageList** control to the form.

2. Display the **Properties** dialog box for the image list by right-clicking the control and clicking **Properties** on the pop-up menu that appears.

3. On the **General** tab, select an image size.

   The standard button size is 16 x 16 pixels.

4. On the **Images** tab, click **Insert Picture** to insert the desired number of pictures into the **ImageList** control, and then click **OK**.

Note To use the **ImageList** control at design time, the **ImageList** control must be on the same form as the controls using it. You can, however, reference the **ImageList** from another form by using code to conserve system resources.

▶ **To create a toolbar**

1. Add a **Toolbar** control to the form.

2. Display the **Properties** dialog box for the **Toolbar** control.

3. On the **General** tab, set the **ImageList** property to the **ImageList** control.

Note Selecting the **AllowCustomize** option on the **General** tab enables a built-in **Edit Toolbars** dialog box, which appears when the user double-clicks an empty area of the toolbar.

4. On the **Buttons** tab, insert buttons by using the **Insert Button** command and then setting properties.

5. Assign the properties described in the following table to each button, and then click **OK**.

Property	Description
Key	Returns or sets a string that uniquely identifies a member in a collection
ToolTipText	Returns or sets a tool tip
Image	Returns or sets a value that specifies which **ImageList** object in an **ImageList** control to use with another object

Creating Code for the ButtonClick Event

The **Toolbar** control contains a collection of **Button** objects. All buttons on a toolbar share a single **Click** event. You can determine which button was clicked by evaluating the **Key** property for the **Button** object within the **ButtonClick** event procedure.

Toolbar buttons are frequently used to provide easy access to other commands; most of the time you call other procedures, such as a corresponding menu command, from within each button's **Click** event.

After the toolbar is in place, you add code to the **ButtonClick** event of the **Toolbar** control.

The **ButtonClick** event contains the **Button** parameter, which is the button that the user clicked on the toolbar. The following example code determines which button was clicked and runs the corresponding menu item's **Click** event procedure:

```
Private Sub tbrStandard_ButtonClick(ByVal Button As Button)
    'Evaluate the Button object's Key property
    Select Case Button.Key
    Case "New"
        'call File, New menu item click event
        mnuFileNew_Click
    Case "Open"
        mnuFileOpen_Click
    Case "Save"
        mnuFileSave_Click
    End Select
End Sub
```

Lab 11: Adding Menus

In this lab, you will add functionality to the loan project that you started in Lab 2. You will add a menu and a status bar to the main form of the loan application. In an optional exercise, you can add a toolbar.

You can continue to work with the files that you have already created, or you can use the files that have been provided in the folder *<install folder>*\Labs\Lab11.

Estimated time to complete this lab: **60 minutes**

To see the demonstration "Lab 11 Solution," see the accompanying CD-ROM.

Objectives

After completing this lab, you will be able to:

♦ Add a menu to a form.

♦ Add a status bar to a form.

♦ Add a toolbar to a form.

To complete the exercises in this lab, you must have the required software. For detailed information about the labs and setup for the labs, see "Labs" in "About This Course."

The solution for this lab is located in the folder *<install folder>*\Labs\Lab11\Solution.

Prerequisites

Before working on this lab, you should be familiar with the following:

♦ Adding new procedures

Exercises

The following exercises provide practice in working with the concepts and techniques covered in this chapter:

♦ Exercise 1: Adding a Menu

In this exercise, you will delete the command buttons on frmMain and call their functions from menu items instead.

◆ Exercise 2: Adding a Status Bar

In this exercise, you will add a status bar to frmMain and post messages on the status bar instead of using message boxes.

◆ Exercise 3 (Optional): Adding a Toolbar

In this exercise, you will add a toolbar with two buttons to frmMain.

Exercise 1: Adding a Menu

In this exercise, you will delete the command buttons on frmMain and call their functions from menu items instead.

Like command buttons, a menu provides the user with a way to invoke actions in an application.

▶ **Open the loan project**

◆ Open the loan project on which you have been working, or open the loan project in the *<install folder>*\Labs\Lab011 folder.

▶ **Create a menu on frmMain**

1. With frmMain open, on the **Tools** menu, click **Menu Editor**.

2. Add the menu items described in the following table.

Caption	Name	Shortcut
&File	mnuFile	none
....E&xit	mnuFileExit	none
&Loan	mnuLoan	none
....&Monthly Payment	mnuLoanMonthly	CTRL+M
....&Total Paid	mnuLoanTotal	CTRL+T

3. After adding the menu items, click **OK**.

▶ **Create new Sub procedures**

1. Open the Code Editor window for frmMain.

2. Insert two new private **Sub** procedures: **ShowMonthly** and **ShowTotal**.

3. Copy the code from the **cmdMonthly_Click** event procedure to the new **ShowMonthly Sub** procedure.

4. Copy the code from the **cmdTotal_Click** event procedure to the new **ShowTotal Sub** procedure.

▶ **Add code to the menu item Click events**

1. Add code to the **Click** event procedure of the **Exit** menu item, **mnuFileExit**, which unloads frmMain.

2. Add code to the **Click** event procedure of the **Monthly Payment** menu item, **mnuLoanMonthly**, which calls the new **ShowMonthly** procedure.

3. Add code to the **Click** event procedure of the **Total Paid** menu item, **mnuLoanTotal**, which calls the new **ShowTotal** procedure.

▶ **Save and test your application**

1. Select each menu item.

2. Test the access keys.

3. Test the shortcut keys: CTRL+M and CTRL+T.

▶ **Delete the command buttons**

Now that there are menu items to invoke the functions previously called by the command buttons, you can delete the command buttons and their **Click** event procedures.

1. Delete the **Monthly Payment, Total Paid,** and **Done** command buttons on frmMain.

   The **Click** event procedures for the command buttons will move to the General Declarations section of the Code Editor window for the form.

2. Delete the **Click** event procedures **cmdMonthly_Click, cmdTotal_Click,** and **cmdDone_Click.**

Exercise 2: Adding a Status Bar

In this exercise, you will add a status bar to frmMain and post messages on the status bar instead of using message boxes.

Like message boxes, a status bar provides feedback to the user.

▶ **Add Microsoft Windows Common Controls to the project**

1. On the **Project** menu, click **Components**.

2. From the list of available controls, select **Microsoft Windows Common Controls 6.0**, and then click **OK**.

   Notice that the new controls are added to the Visual Basic Toolbox.

> **Note** If **Microsoft Windows Common Controls** does not appear in the list of available controls, ensure that the **Selected Items Only** option is not selected and that the **Controls** tab is selected in the **Components** dialog box.

▶ **Create a status bar**

1. From the toolbox, add a **StatusBar** control to the bottom of frmMain.

2. Set the **Name** property of the status bar to **sbrLoan**.

3. In the Properties window, select the **Custom** property of the status bar to open the **Property Pages** dialog box of the **Status Bar** control.

4. Select the **Panels** tab, and click the **Insert Panel** button to insert a second panel.

5. Set properties for the two panels as shown in the following table.

Panel index	Property	Desired setting
1	Key Style Autosize	msg 0 - sbrText 1 - sbrSpring
2	Key Alignment Style Autosize	time 1 - sbrCenter 5 - sbrTime 2 - sbrContents

> **Note** The Panel's **Key** property is case-sensitive.

6. Click **Apply** to observe the effects of the **Minimum Width** setting.

7. Click **OK** when the width is set to your satisfaction.

▶ **Post messages to the status bar**

1. In the **ShowMonthly** procedure:

    a. Replace the error message box with a message in the status bar:

```
sbrLoan.Panels("msg").Text = "Numeric value required."
```

    b. Replace the message box showing the results of the **MonthlyPayment** function with a message in the status bar:

```
sbrLoan.Panels("msg").Text = "Monthly payment: " & _
                Format(dblMonthly, "currency")
```

2. In the **ShowTotal** procedure, replace each message box with a message in the status bar.

3. Save and test your work.

Exercise 3 (Optional): Adding a Toolbar

In this exercise, you will add a toolbar with two buttons to frmMain.

▶ **Add an image list to frmMain**

1. From the toolbox, add an **ImageList** control to frmMain.

> **Note** The image list is invisible when the application runs, so don't worry about its placement.

2. In the Visual Basic Properties window, set the image list's **Name** property to **imlLoan**.

3. In the Properties window, select the **Custom** property of the status bar to open the **Property Pages** dialog box of the **Image List** control.

4. Click the **16 x 16** option button on the **General** tab.

5. Move to the **Images** tab and insert two pictures that have been provided on this CD-ROM in the following folders:

    <install folder>\Labs\Lab11\exit.bmp

    <install folder>\Labs\Lab11\month.bmp

6. After inserting the pictures, click **OK**.

> **Note** The image on a toolbar button should be 16 x 16 pixels. You can use the Visual Basic Image Editor to create these images. In a complete installation of Visual Basic, the Image Editor, Imagedit, is found in the COMMON\ TOOLS\VB\IMAGEDIT folder of the Visual Studio 98 CD-ROM.

▶ **Add a toolbar with two toolbar buttons to frmMain**

1. From the toolbox, add a **Toolbar** control to the top of frmMain.

2. In the Visual Basic Properties window, set the toolbar's **Name** property to **tlbLoan**.

3. In the Properties window, select the **Custom** property of the status bar to open **Property Pages** dialog box of the **Toolbar** control.

4. On the **General** tab:

    a. Set the **ImageList** property to the image list that you just created, imlLoan.

    b. Set the **Style** property to **1-tbrFlat**.

5. On the **Buttons** tab, insert two buttons with the properties described in the following table.

Button index	Property	Desired setting
1	Description Key ToolTip Text Image	Exit button exit Exit 1
2	Description Kcy ToolTip Text Image	Monthly Payment button month Monthly Payment 2

6. After inserting the buttons, click **OK**.

▶ **Respond to the toolbar ButtonClick event**

All buttons on a toolbar share the same **ButtonClick** event procedure. Therefore, you must determine which button invoked the event and call the appropriate function.

1. Open the Code Editor window for the **ButtonClick** event of the **tlbLoan** toolbar.

2. Add code that determines which button was selected and executes the appropriate procedure:

```
Select Case Button.Key
    Case "month"
        ShowMonthly
    Case "exit"
        Unload frmMain
End Select
```

3. Save and test your work.

Self-Check Questions

See page 395 for answers.

1. To display a custom pop-up menu:

    A. Modify a system pop-up menu.

    B. Add label controls to the form and set the **Menu** property to **True**.

    C. Use the form's **PopupMenu** method.

    D. Create a menu control array.

2. Which of the following code statements changes the contents of the simple status bar named "StatusBar" to read "Input error - press F1 for Help."?

    A. "Input error - press F1 for Help" = StatusBar.Text

    B. StatusBar.Caption = "Input error - press F1 for Help"

    C. StatusBar.SimpleText = "Input error - press F1 for Help"

    D. StatusBar.Panels(Single).Caption = "Input error - press F1 for Help"

3. Images for a toolbar's buttons are:

    A. Loaded dynamically from the toolbar .ocx file.

    B. Loaded dynamically from the toolbar .dll file.

    C. Automatically attached to the toolbar button based on function.

    D. Maintained in a separate **ImageList** control.

Student Notes:

Chapter 12:
Drag-and-Drop Operations

Multimedia

In this chapter, you will learn about the two ways that Microsoft Visual Basic supports implementing drag-and-drop operations. The first enables users to move controls on a form. The second, a more advanced option found in Visual Basic 5 or later, enables users to move objects between applications.

Objectives

After completing this chapter, you will be able to:

◆ Describe the role of mouse events in implementing drag-and-drop features.

◆ Perform the steps required to add drag-and-drop features to an application.

◆ Identify the source control and target form or control in a drag-and-drop operation.

◆ Implement OLE drag-and-drop features.

Overview of Drag-and-Drop Features

The action of holding a mouse button down and moving an object is called dragging, and the action of releasing the button is called dropping.

There are two types of drag-and-drop operations:

◆ Drag-and-drop operation within an application

An example of this can be found in Microsoft Excel when a range of cells is moved to a new location on the worksheet by dragging the selection.

◆ Drag-and-drop operation between two applications

This is a feature of the Microsoft Office products and other programs that support OLE, called OLE drag-and-drop features. Visual Basic 6.0 supports dragging data (text or graphics) to and from controls in other applications.

For example, you can drag a range of cells from an Excel worksheet and drop it into a Microsoft Word document; the range of cells becomes an embedded object in the Word document. Or, for another example, you can drag WordArt from Word and drop it into a Visual Basic **Picture** control.

Because some users find it difficult to perform the drag-and-drop operation, you should always provide an alternate method that uses the keyboard, a button, or a menu command to accomplish the same task.

To see the demonstration "Implementing Drag-and-Drop," see the accompanying CD-ROM.

Mouse Events

Understanding mouse events is the key to implementing drag-and-drop editing in your programs. There are three mouse events in Visual Basic:

◆ **MouseDown**

Occurs when the user clicks any mouse button

◆ **MouseUp**

Occurs when the user releases any mouse button

◆ **MouseMove**

Occurs when the user moves the mouse

Each of these events takes four parameters. For example, to code the **MouseDown** event procedure, use the following syntax:

Sub object_*MouseDown (*button *As Integer,* shift *As Integer,* x *As Single,* y *As Single)*

The following table explains the four parameters.

Parameter	Returns	Values
button	Which mouse button was pressed	VbLeftButton VbRightButton VbMiddleButton
shift	Which key or keys are held down	vbShiftMask = SHIFT vbCtrlMask = CTRL vbAltMask = ALT Combinations can be checked by adding the values together. For example, CTRL+SHIFT = 3 = 1 + 2.
x	Current X position (relative to upper-left of control receiving event)	Not applicable.
y	Current Y position	Not applicable.

For a complete list of the controls that support the mouse events, see "MouseUp," "MouseDown," and "MouseMove" in MSDN Help.

Drag-and-Drop Editing Basics

In this section, you will learn how to implement drag-and-drop editing in an application.

Dragging Controls

To enable the user to drag a control, you can:

◆ Set the control's **DragMode** property to vbAutomatic.

   –or–

◆ Set the control's **DragMode** property to vbManual (the default) and program-matically enable drag-and-drop editing by using the **Drag** method.

Automatic Drag-and-Drop Editing

The **DragMode** property can be set at design time or at run time. If you set **DragMode** to vbAutomatic, the user can drag the control at any time. Visual Basic displays an outline of the control as it is being dragged. The following example code sets the **DragMode** property for a **Picture** control to enable the user to drag the picture box:

```
picLogo.DragMode = vbAutomatic
```

Note When the **DragMode** property of a control is set to automatic, it does not receive mouse events, such as the **Click** event.

Manual Drag-and-Drop Editing

If you want more control over when dragging takes place, you can leave the **DragMode** property set to vbManual (the default) and establish dragging program-matically by using the **Drag** method. This is useful if you want to allow the user to drag the control at some times but not at others. The following example code begins a drag operation:

```
Sub picLogo_MouseDown()
  'Start dragging when mouse button is pressed
  picLogo.Drag vbBeginDrag
End Sub
```

Dropping Controls

If a user releases the mouse while dragging an object, dragging stops. You can also programmatically stop dragging, by passing the argument **vbEndDrag** to the **Drag** method, as shown in the following example code:

```
picLogo.Drag vbEndDrag          'Stop dragging
```

Note When the user releases the mouse button, the control does not automatically move to the new location. You must write code to move the control.

Setting the **DragMode** or calling the **Drag** method enables a control to be dragged. You determine what will happen to the control when it is dropped. One option is to move the control to the new location.

Before writing the code to move a control, you should first identify the source and target of the drag-and-drop procedure:

◆ Source

   The control that is being dragged by the user

◆ Target

   The form or control that will receive the control

The following illustration shows a picture box being dragged onto a form. The picture box is the source. The form is the target.

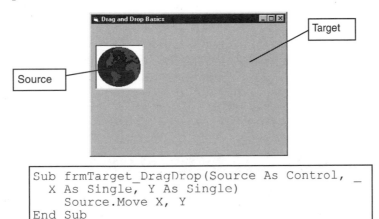

```
Sub frmTarget_DragDrop(Source As Control, _
  X As Single, Y As Single)
    Source.Move X, Y
End Sub
```

When the user drops the source control onto the target, the **DragDrop** event of the target occurs. You can place code in this event to perform any task that you want to occur when the user drops the control.

The **DragDrop** event provides three parameters: *source*, *x*, and *y*. The *source* parameter refers to the control that is dropped. The *x* and *y* parameters return the location at which the control is dropped. You can use the *x* and *y* parameters to reposition the source control, as in the following example code:

```
Sub frmTarget_DragDrop(Source As Control, _
  X As Single, Y As Single)
  'Position control with upper-left corner in X, Y location
  Source.Move X, Y
End Sub
```

If you want to position the control relative to the pointer, you need to save the *x, y* positions in the **MouseDown** event and use them as an offset in the **DragDrop** event, as in the following example code:

```
'In the Declarations section of the form:
Dim DragX As Single
Dim DragY As Single

Sub picSource_MouseDown(Button As Integer, _
  Shift As Integer, X As Single, Y As Single)
  DragX = X
  DragY = Y
  picSource.Drag  vbBeginDrag
End Sub

Sub frmTarget_DragDrop(Source As Control, _
  X As Single, Y As Single)

  Source.Move (X - DragX), (Y - DragY)
End Sub
```

Changing the Drag Image of the Source Control

By default, Visual Basic displays a white outline of the source control when a user drags a control. You can change the image used for dragging by setting the **DragIcon** property of the source control, as in the following example code:

```
picSource.DragIcon  = LoadPicture("PLANE.ICO")
```

The following illustration shows the **DragIcon** property for a **Picture** control set to an image of a plane. This can be done by using **LoadPicture** to load a graphic file, such as an .ico file. Another option is to set the **DragIcon** property to the **Picture** property of an **Image** or **Picture** control. Both techniques are shown in the following illustration.

```
picSource.DragIcon = LoadPicture("PLANE.ICO")
```

```
picSource.DragIcon = imgplane.Picture
```

It is important to set the Drag icon before the control is first dragged. Typically you set the Drag icon at design time or in the **Form_Load** event. If you set it in the **MouseDown** event for the source control, the Drag icon will reset each time you drag the control. The following example code sets the Drag icon in the **MouseDown** event for a **Picture** control:

```
Private Sub picSource_MouseDown(Button As Integer, _
  Shift As Integer, X As Single, Y As Single)

  picSource.DragIcon = LoadPicture("PLANE.ICO")
  picSource.Drag  vbBeginDrag
End Sub
```

Instead of using the **LoadPicture** function, you can save resources and make your program faster by adding an **Image** control for each Drag icon used by your program. Set the **Picture** property of the **Image** control to the icon or bitmap that you intend to use. Then set the **Visible** property of the **Image** control to **False**, so that the control is not visible to the user. You can quickly set the **DragIcon** property of the source control by making it equal to the **Picture** property of the **Image** control, as in the following example code:

```
picSource.DragIcon = imgPlane.Picture
```

Changing the Drag Icon During the Drag

You can add visual cues to your application to show users where controls can and cannot be dropped. The following illustration shows the Drag icon changing to a stop sign, indicating that the control cannot be dropped on the label.

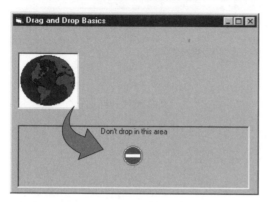

The **DragOver** event of an object occurs when a user drags a control over the object. The **DragOver** event provides a parameter, *state*, which indicates whether the source control is entering (*state* = vbEnter), leaving (*state* = vbLeave), or over (*state* = vbOver) the object, as shown in the following example code:

```
Sub frmTarget_DragOver(Source As Control, X As Single, _
  Y As Single, State As Integer)
Select Case State
  ' Entering frmTarget
  Case vbEnter
      ' Set the DragIcon to illustrate a valid
      ' drop zone.
      Source.DragIcon = imgPlane.Picture
  ' Leaving frmTarget
  Case vbLeave
      ' Set the DragIcon to illustrate an invalid
      ' drop zone.
      Source.DragIcon = imgStop.Picture
End Select
End Sub
```

Note Add code to change the **DragIcon** property in the **DragOver** event for both the source and target controls.

OLE Drag-and-Drop

You can add OLE drag-and-drop features to an application to support moving data (text or graphics) from one control to another within a form. Drag-and-drop editing also offers the ability to move data from one application to another. For example, you can drag a graphic from WordArt in Word into a Visual Basic picture box.

Automatic OLE Drag and Drop

Most Visual Basic controls, including standard and ActiveX controls, support some degree of OLE drag and drop. There are two kinds of support for OLE drag and drop: automatic and manual. However, not all controls support both automatic and manual OLE drag and drop. To find out the type of OLE drag and drop support for a particular control, select the control in design mode and examine its **OLEDragMode** and **OLEDropMode** properties in the Properties window. If either of these properties has a setting for automatic, you can add automatic support for OLE drag and drop to the control. When **OLEDragMode** or **OLEDropMode** is set to automatic, you do not need to write any additional code to implement these features.

Note To support OLE drag and drop, you must set the **DragMode** property of a control to manual. If a control's **DragMode** property is set to automatic, the control itself rather than the contents of the control is dragged when the user drags the control.

To see the demonstration, "Implementing Drag and Drop Within a Form," see the accompanying CD-ROM.

By default, a control will move the data from the source control to the target. To copy the data, the user must hold down CTRL during the drag-and-drop operation.

Manual OLE Drag-and-Drop Editing

Not all controls have an automatic setting for the **OLEDragMode** and **OLEDropMode** properties. If a control does not have an automatic setting, you can implement the OLE drag-and-drop functionality by using various properties, methods, and events. For example, if the control supports manual but not automatic OLE drag, the control's **OLEDragMode** property will have settings for only manual or none. However, the control will support the **OLEDrag** method and the OLE drag-and-drop events to accomplish OLE drag operations.

Implementing OLE drag-and-drop functionality for controls that do not support automatic drag-and-drop editing is beyond the scope of this course.

Moving Data Between Applications

Drag-and-drop functionality offers the ability to move data from one application to another.
For example, you can drag a graphic from WordArt in Word into a Visual Basic picture box.

To add this drag-and-drop feature to your application, set the **OLEDragMode** and **OLEDropMode** properties of a control to automatic.

Not all controls automatically support the **OLEDragMode** and **OLEDropMode** properties. If a control does not support these properties, you can implement the functionality by using various properties and events.

The following table lists the various OLE drag-and-drop properties, methods, and events.

Category	Name	Description
Property	OLEDragMode	Enables automatic or manual dragging of a control. If the control supports manual but not automatic OLE drag, the control will not have the **OLEDragMode** property, but it will support the **OLEDrag** method and the OLE drag-and-drop events.
Property	OLEDropMode	Specifies whether the object can act as an OLE drop target.
Event	OLEDragDrop	Occurs when a source object is dropped onto the control.
Event	OLEDragOver	Occurs when a source object is dragged over a control.
Event	OLEGiveFeedback	Occurs after every **OLEDragOver** event. You can use this event to provide visual feedback to the user, such as changing the mouse cursor to indicate what will happen if the user drops the object.

table continued on next page

Category	Name	Description
Event	**OLEStartDrag**	Specifies which data formats and which drop effects (copy, move, or refuse data) the source supports when dragging is initiated.
Event	**OLESetData**	Provides data when the source object is dropped.
Event	**OLECompleteDrag**	Informs the source of the action that was performed when the object was dropped into the target.
Method	**OLEDrag**	Starts manual dragging.

Implementing OLE drag-and-drop functionality for controls that do not support automatic drag-and-drop editing is beyond the scope of this course.

Lab 12: Adding Drag-and-Drop

In this lab, you will create a file viewer application that uses drag-and-drop functionality between two list boxes.

To see the demonstration "Lab 12 Solution," see the accompanying CD-ROM.

Estimated time to complete this lab: **40 minutes**

Objectives

After completing this lab, you will be able to:

♦ Implement drag-and-drop functionality in your application.

♦ Identify both a target control and a source control.

♦ Implement code in an object's **DragDrop** event.

♦ Implement code in an object's **DragOver** event.

To complete the exercises in this lab, you must have the required software. For detailed information about the labs and setup for the labs, see "Labs" in "About This Course."

The solution for this lab is located in the folder *<install folder>*\Labs\Lab12\Solution.

Prerequisites

There are no prerequisites for this lab.

Exercises

The following exercises provide practice in working with the concepts covered in this chapter.

♦ Exercise 1: Creating the Interface

In this exercise, you will create the user interface for a file viewer application.

♦ Exercise 2: Adding Drag-and-Drop Functionality

In this exercise, you will implement drag-and-drop functionality between the file list box and the simple list box.

♦ Exercise 3 (Optional): Adding a Path

In this optional exercise, you will add the full path to the target list box, instead of only the file name.

Exercise 1: Creating the Interface

In this exercise, you will create the user interface for a file viewer application.

▶ **Start a new project**

◆ On the **File** menu, click **New Project,** and select **Standard EXE.**

▶ **Add controls to the form**

1. On the toolbox, add controls to the default form so that it looks like the form shown in the following illustration.

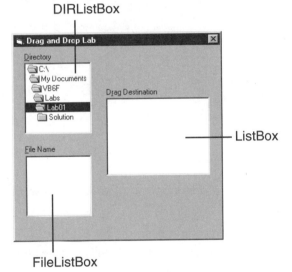

2. Set the control property values to correspond with those in the following table.

Control	Property	Value
DirListBox	Name	dirDirectories
FileListBox	Name	filSource
ListBox	Name	lstTarget

▶ **Programmatically connect the directory and file list boxes**

◆ Edit the **Change** event procedure for the directory list box, and add the following line of code:

```
filSource.Path = dirDirectories.Path
```

▶ **Save and test your work**

1. Name the form frmFileDrag, and the project DragProject.

2. Save your project in the *<install folder>*\Labs\Lab12 folder.

3. Run your application. Double-click entries in the directory list box to move between folders.

4. Close the running application.

Exercise 2: Adding Drag-and-Drop Functionality

In this exercise, you will implement drag-and-drop functionality between the file list box and the simple list box.

▶ **Implement the source of the drag operation**

The file list box is the source of the drag operation for this application. Start the drag operation on the **MouseDown** event.

◆ Edit the **MouseDown** event procedure for the file list box. If the value of the **FileName** property is not a zero-length string, call the **Drag** method of the file list box with the parameter vbBeginDrag:

```
If filSource.FileName <> "" Then
    filSource.Drag vbBeginDrag
End If
```

Note Checking the value of the **FileName** property prevents empty folders from being dragged to the list box.

▶ **Set DragIcon property**

   ◆ Set the **DragIcon** property for the source control as shown in the following table.

Control	Property	Setting
filSource	DragIcon	*<install folder>*\Labs\Lab12\Drag1pg

▶ **Add drag-and-drop Image controls**

   ◆ Add two **Image** controls and set properties, as listed in the following table.

Control	Property	Setting
Image1	Name	imgValid
	Picture	*<install folder>*\Labs\Lab12\Drag1pg
	Visible	False
Image2	Name	imgInvalid
	Picture	*<install folder>*\Labs\Lab12\trffc14
	Visible	False

▶ **Implement the target of the drag operation**

1. Edit the **DragDrop** event procedure of the target list box. Add the file name selected in the source file list box to the target list box:

```
lstTarget.AddItem filSource.Filename
```

2. Save and test your work.

> **Note** The simple list box is the target of the drag operation for this application. When **lstTarget** receives a **DragDrop** event, it will add the selected file name in the file list box to the items already in **lstTarget**.

▶ **Handle the DragOver event**

To provide the user visual feedback, you will change the Drag icon to indicate what is a valid drop zone and what isn't.

1. Code the **DragOver** event procedure for the target control, **lstTarget**.

   a. When the State parameter is equal to vbEnter, set the **DragIcon** property of the source control to the **Picture** property of **imgValid**.

   b. When the State parameter is equal to vbLeave, set the **DragIcon** property of the source control to the **Picture** property of **imgInvalid**.

2. Code the **DragOver** event procedure for the source control, **filSource**.

   a. When the State parameter is equal to vbEnter, set the **DragIcon** property of the source control to the **Picture** property of **imgValid**.

   b. When the State parameter is equal to vbLeave, set the **DragIcon** property of the source control to the **Picture** property of **imgInvalid**.

To see an example of how your code should look, see Hint 12.1 in Appendix B.

▶ **Save and test your work**

1. Save your project.

2. Run your application. Select a file name in the file list box and drag it to the target list box. What happens?

   For help in completing this exercise, see Hint 12.2 in Appendix B.

3. Close the running application.

Exercise 3 (Optional): Adding a Path

In this optional exercise, you will add the full path to the target list box, instead of only the file name.

▶ **Add the full path of the file name to lstTarget**

1. Edit the **DragDrop** event of the target control, **lstTarget**.

2. Concatenate the path selected in the directory list box with the file name selected in the file list box, and add the following code to the target list box, **lstTarget**:

```
lstTarget.AddItem _
    dirDirectories.Path & "\" & filSource.Filename
```

▶ Check for the root directory

1. Edit the **DragDrop** event of the target control, **lstTarget.**

2. Before adding a new item to the list box, check the last character of the currently selected path in the directory list box.

    a. If the last character is the backslash character (\), don't add "\" to the string before adding the string to the target list box.

    b. If the last character isn't the backslash character, then add "\" to the string before adding the string to the target list box.

To see an example of how your code should look, see Hint 12.3 in Appendix B.

Self-Check Questions

See page 397 for answers.

1. A control with its DragMode property set to vbAutomatic can be dragged:

A. Whenever one of the control's procedures is executing.

B. Whenever one of the control's procedures is not executing.

C. Anytime.

D. Never.

2. To drop a control programmatically:

A. Use the **vbEndDrag** constant with the control's **Drag** method.

B. Set the control's **Stop** property to **True**.

C. Set the control's **Drop** property to **True**.

D. Set the control's **DragMode** property to vbAutomatic.

3. In an application, dragging a PictureBox control appears to work except that when the mouse is released, the PictureBox control remains at its original position. What is wrong?

A. **PictureBox** controls cannot be moved by using the drag-and-drop feature with Visual Basic.

B. There is no code in the application to move the control.

C. The **DragMode** property is not set to vbAutomatic.

D. The **DragDrop** source control is hanging.

Chapter 13:
More About Controls

Multimedia

Lab 13 Solution 346

In this chapter, you will learn how to create an array of controls and how to work with object variables and collections, building on the understanding of custom controls developed in Chapter 7, "Working with Controls."

Objectives

After completing this chapter, you will be able to:

◆ Define and describe the use of control arrays.

◆ Create an array of controls.

◆ Build an application for Microsoft Visual Basic that adds and deletes controls dynamically.

◆ Use the Visual Basic **Controls** collection.

◆ Create and use object variables.

Collections

In this section, you will learn about collections. A collection is an ordered set of items that can be referred to as a unit. Unlike arrays, collections are objects themselves. The **Collection** object provides a convenient way to refer to a related group of items as a single object. The items, or members, in a collection need only be related by the fact that they exist in the collection. In other words, members of a collection don't have to share the same data type.

The Collection Object

In Visual Basic, a collection is a way of grouping related objects. There are many types of collections in Visual Basic.

Some collections are created automatically by Visual Basic when you load forms or controls into your application. Other collections are created as a result of using a custom control or by creating a **Collection** object.

A custom control can also contain a collection of items. For example, the **TreeView** control has a collection of **Node** objects, the **ListView** control has a collection of **ListItem** objects, and the **ImageList** control has a collection of **ListImage** objects. You can create your own collection by using the **Collection** object.

The items in your collection are stored as **Variants**. This allows you to store many types of data in your collections. The same collection, for example, could contain string data as well as a reference to an object, such as a control in your application.

The **Collection** object has the properties and methods described in the following table.

Property or method	Description
Add method	Adds items to the collection
Count property	Returns the number of items in the collection—read-only
Item method	Returns an item, by index or by key
Remove method	Deletes an item from the collection, by index or by key

When you add, delete, and retrieve objects from a collection, you work with keys and indexes.

A key is **String** value. It can be a name, a driver's license number, a social security number, or simply an **Integer** converted to a **String**. You use the **Add** method to associate a key with an item.

An index is a **Long** value between one and the number of items in the collection. You can control the initial value of an item's index by using the before and after named parameters, but the value may change as other items are added and deleted.

The following example code adds two different types of data to a collection:

```
Dim txtMessage As TextBox
Dim colSomeItems As New Collection

'Add a string and a textbox control to the collection
colSomeItems.Add "Hello World!"
colSomeItems.Add txtMessage
```

A **Collection** object is similar to a user-defined type array, as discussed in "User-Defined Data Types" on page 107 in Chapter 4, "Variables and Procedures." A major difference between a collection and a user-defined type array is that, when removing items from a collection array, the element numbers are automatically updated (a normal array requires your "delete" code to reorder the elements based on the one that was removed). Because the element numbers can change, your code should not rely on these for reference to a particular item; use the key instead.

Working with Collections

A collection can be used as a way of grouping a set of related objects. Visual Basic has a number of predefined collection objects including the **Printers, Forms,** and **Controls** collections, which are created automatically.

The Controls Collection

When you put two command buttons on a form, they are separate objects with distinct **Name** property settings, but they are both **CommandButton** objects. They also share the characteristics that they are on the same form, and that they are both controls. All controls have common characteristics that make them different from forms and other objects in the Visual Basic environment.

Visual Basic provides an object that contains all controls on a form. This object is known as the **Controls** collection. The **Controls** collection is useful for performing an action on a group of controls.

There are two primary ways to enumerate a collection. You can use the **For To...Next** statement, counting from the base of the collection through its **Count** property. A more efficient method is to use the **For Each...Next** statement. The **For Each...Next** statement uses an object called an enumerator. An enumerator keeps track of current position in a collection, and returns the next item when it's needed.

The following example code iterates through the **Controls** collection and sets the font size of all text boxes to a value of 12:

```
Private Sub cmdModifyFont_Click()
    Dim ctl As Control

    'Loop through the controls collection
    For Each ctl In Me.Controls
        'Test to see if the current control
        'is a textbox control
        If TypeOf ctl Is TextBox Then
            ctl.FontSize = 12
        End If
    Next
End Sub
```

You can also use the **Count** property of the **Controls** collection to evaluate the number of controls on a form, as shown in the following example code:

```
Private Sub cmdCountControls_Click()
    MsgBox "There are " & Controls.Count & " controls on this
    form."
End Sub
```

Working with Object Variables

Visual Basic allows you to create and work with many types of objects. Almost everything in Visual Basic is an object, so it is important to know how to use them. One way to do this is by creating object variables. There are many types of object variables that you can declare in Visual Basic. You can declare variables as controls, types of controls, forms, menus, and generic objects.

Control and Form Data Types

Although you can create objects such as forms, controls, and menus in the Visual Basic integrated development environment (IDE), you can also create objects by declaring and setting object variables, as in the following example code:

```
Dim frmNewForm As Form
Dim ctlGenericControl As Control
Dim txtNewTextBox As TextBox
Dim lblNewLabel As Label
```

> **Note** You should declare object variables as explicit types whenever possible. In other words, it would be more efficient to declare a variable as a **TextBox** rather than a **Control**, if you can do so.

You associate an object variable with a particular control by using the **Set** statement, as shown in the following example code:

```
Dim txtMyText As TextBox
Set txtMyText = frmData.txtName
```

After the assignment has been made, you can use the variable as an alias for the control name. By using the alias, rather than the complete control name, you can shorten your code.

For example, in the following example code, the object variable refers to a control:

```
txtMyText.Text = "Hello World!"
```

Using the Object Data Type

You can also use a generic object variable, which can assume the value of any type of object, as in the following example code:

```
Private Sub cmdSetObject_Click()
    Dim objGeneric As Object

    'Set the object equal to a textbox on the form
    Set objGeneric = txtName
    objGeneric.Text = "John"
```

code continued on next page

code continued from previous page

```
    'Set the object equal to a new instance of a form
    Set objGeneric = New frmData
    objGeneric.Show

    'Destroy the object
    Set objGeneric = Nothing
End Sub
```

The advantage of a generic object variable is that it can refer to an object of any type. However, using a generic object is less efficient than using a specific object variable, so you should declare object variables as specific types of objects whenever possible. Also, there is a greater chance of errors when a generic object variable is used to refer to a method or property that is not available with the current object.

Working with Object Arrays

Object arrays provide a way to work with multiple controls on a form. For example, a form contains four command buttons, and you want a simple method of disabling all four controls. You could use four separate statements to disable the controls. However, it is easier to use an array of command button object variables that refer to the command buttons. You can then use a **For** loop to disable all four command buttons.

▶ **To use an array of object variables to disable controls**

1. In the Declarations section of the form, create the array:

```
Dim cmd(4) As CommandButton
```

2. In the **FormLoad** event, initialize the array:

```
Set cmd(1) = cmdNext
Set cmd(2) = cmdPrevious
Set cmd(3) = cmdFirst
Set cmd(4) = cmdLast
```

3. Whenever you need to do something to all four command buttons, use a **For** loop:

```
Dim i As Integer

For i = 1 to 4
    cmd(i).Enabled = False
Next i
```

Using Control Arrays

In this section, you will learn how to use control arrays in Visual Basic. Sometimes it is necessary to add controls to a form at run time. For example, you might add a slider control to adjust volume settings for a number of speakers; if the number of speakers was set at run time, you would have to add slider controls at run time, based on the number of speakers. This can be done with control arrays.

Creating a Control Array

A control array is a group of controls that share the same name, type, and event procedures. Each control, however, is physically separate from the others and has its own property settings.

The new dynamic control addition feature of Visual Basic 6.0 allows you to add controls to or remove them from a form programmatically without having to use a control array. Although this feature can provide flexibility in your applications, handling events for these controls can be difficult. For more information about creating controls at run time, search for "Add Method Controls Collection" in MSDN Help.

Advantages of Using Control Arrays

Control arrays offer three advantages. First, using a control array to add new controls at run time uses fewer resources than adding multiple controls to a form at design time. Second, control arrays are better managed when several controls can share code. For example, if your form has several text boxes and each receives a date value, a control array can be set up so that all of the text boxes share the same validation code. The third, and perhaps most significant advantage, is that control arrays allow you to add new controls at run time. Control arrays are especially useful when you do not know how many controls you will need at run time. Each new element that you add to a control array inherits the common event procedures of the array. After a control array is established, you can dynamically add controls at run time by using the **Load** statement. As a result, controls added at run time are often referred to as dynamic controls.

The following illustration shows a control array of text box controls.

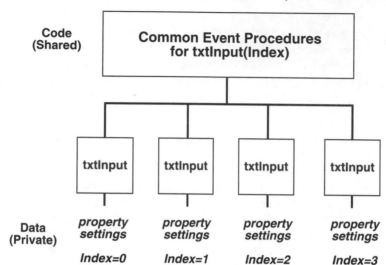

Each control is referred to with the syntax *controlname(index)*. You specify the index of a control when you create it. For example, when the control **txtInput(2)** recognizes the **Click** event, Visual Basic invokes the **txtInput_Click** event procedure and passes the index value 2 as an argument.

Creating a Control Array at Design Time

You can create control arrays at design time in three ways:

◆ Give two controls the same name. (They must be the same type of control.) Visual Basic automatically creates a control array and gives these controls the indexes 0 and 1.

◆ Copy and paste a control.

◆ Set the **Index** property by using the Properties window.

▶ **To create a control array at design time**

1. Draw the first control and set the initial properties that are to be shared by all controls in the control array.

2. Set the **Name** property for the control.

3. Do either of the following:

    a. Select the first control and copy it. When the control is pasted back on the form, Visual Basic asks if a control array should be created. Choose **Yes** to create a control array.

    b. Draw the next control. Set the **Name** property to the name selected for
       the first control. Visual Basic asks if a control array should be created.

4. Repeat step 3 until all controls have been added to the form.

Creating an Event Procedure for a Control Array

One advantage of creating a control array is that it allows several controls to share
event procedures. However, for your application to respond to the **Click** event for a
control in a control array, it must determine which control in the array received the
event. You can do this by using the **Index** argument in the event procedure as
shown in the following syntax example:

   Sub ControlArrayObjectName_*Click(Index As Integer)*

   [statement block]

   End Sub

The **Index** argument is an integer that uniquely identifies the control calling the
event procedure. You can use the **Index** argument a number of different ways to
refer to the control. The following example code sets the **Caption** property of the
control that invoked the **Click** event:

```
MsgBox optReports(Index).Caption & " was selected."
```

The following illustration shows a control array of option buttons and their corresponding indexes.

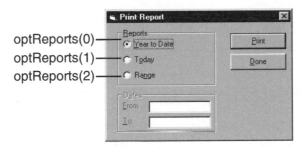

optReports(0)

optReports(1)

optReports(2)

The following sample code is for the option buttons in the previous illustration. To copy this code for use in your own projects, see "Option Buttons" on the accompanying CD-ROM.

```
Private Sub optReports_Click(Index As Integer)
    Select Case Index
        Case 0, 1
            fraDates.Enabled = False
            txtTo.Enabled = False
            txtFrom.Enabled = False
            lblTo.Enabled = False
            lblFrom.Enabled = False
        Case 2
            frmDates.Enabled = True
            txtTo.Enabled = True
            txtFrom.Enabled = True
            lblTo.Enabled = True
            lblFrom.Enabled = True
    End Select
    MsgBox optReports(Index).Caption & " was selected."
End Sub
```

The sample code sets the **Enabled** property for the **txtTo, txtFrom, frmDates, lblTo,** and **lblFrom** text boxes to **True** or **False,** based on the option button selected. The user can enter dates in these text boxes only if the **Range report** option is selected (Index = 2). When **Year to Date** or **Today** options are selected (Index = 0 or 1), the date range text boxes are disabled.

Note Setting an object variable equal to the control that was selected makes it easier to refer to that control later in the procedure.

Creating Controls Dynamically

After a control array is established, you can add controls dynamically at run time by using the **Load** statement.

The following illustration shows controls loaded and unloaded from a control array.

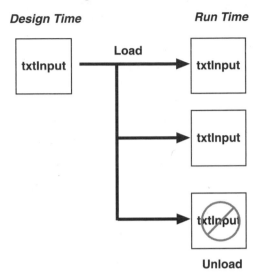

The **Load** statement copies all the property settings except **Visible, Index,** and **TabIndex** from the lowest existing element in the array. When you want to display the control, set the **Visible** property to **True.**

If you try to load a control that already exists, a run-time error will occur.

The following sample code creates a new text box every time the user clicks a command button. To copy this code for use in your own projects, see "Using a Control Array to Add Controls Dynamically" on the accompanying CD-ROM.

```
Sub cmdCreateNewTextBox_Click()
    Static intCount As Integer
    'Get the next array index number (new controls index)
    intCount = intCount + 1
    'Create the new control dynamically
    Load txtInput(intCount)
    'Set the position for upper-left corner of new control so
    'it won't fall on top of previous dynamically created
    'controls
    txtInput(intCount).Top = txtInput(intCount - 1).Top + 495
    txtInput(intCount).Left = txtInput(intCount - 1).Left
    'Now, display the new control
    txtInput(intCount).Visible = True
End Sub
```

Use the **Unload** statement to remove a control. If you try to unload a control that was created at design time or that is already unloaded, a run-time error will occur.

The following example code unloads a text box from a control array:

```
Sub cmdUnloadControl_Click
  Unload txtInput(3)
End Sub
```

Editing the Active Control

If you build an application that adds and removes controls at run time, you may also need to change the properties of the control or the form that contains the control.

Editing Text in a Control

The **Clipboard** object is used to manipulate text and graphics on the Windows Clipboard. You can use this object to enable a user to copy, cut, and paste text or graphics in your application. For example, you can copy text to the Clipboard from a control, then copy the text from the Clipboard to another control. For more information about how to cut, copy, and paste data, search for "Clipboard Object" in MSDN Help.

The following sample code copies text from one text box to another text box serving as a local buffer. To copy this code for use in your own projects, see "Editing Text in a Control" on the accompanying CD-ROM.

Note In the code sample that follows, the Screen.ActiveControl statement refers to the control that has the focus.

```
Sub mnuEditCut_Click()
  'Cut text to the Windows clipboard.
  If TypeOf Screen.ActiveControl Is TextBox Then
    Clipboard.SetText Screen.ActiveControl.SelText
    Screen.ActiveControl.SelText = ""
  End If
End Sub

Sub mnuEditCopy_Click()
  'Copy text to the Windows clipboard.
  If TypeOf Screen.ActiveControl Is TextBox Then
    Clipboard.SetText Screen.ActiveControl.SelText
  End If
End Sub

Sub mnuEditPaste_Click()
  'Paste text from the Windows clipboard.
  If TypeOf Screen.ActiveControl Is TextBox Then
    Screen.ActiveControl.SelText = Clipboard.GetText(vbCFText)
  End If
End Sub
```

Resizing a Form

The following example code makes room in a form for new controls:

```
'Increase width and height of form by 500 twips
Me.Width = Me.Width + 500
Me.Height = Me.Height + 500
```

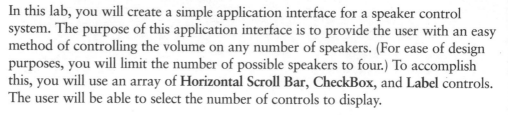

Lab 13: Using Control Arrays

In this lab, you will create a simple application interface for a speaker control system. The purpose of this application interface is to provide the user with an easy method of controlling the volume on any number of speakers. (For ease of design purposes, you will limit the number of possible speakers to four.) To accomplish this, you will use an array of **Horizontal Scroll Bar, CheckBox**, and **Label** controls. The user will be able to select the number of controls to display.

To see the demonstration "Lab 13 Solution," see the accompanying CD-ROM.

Estimated time to complete this lab: **30 minutes**

Objectives

After completing this lab, you will be able to:

◆ Create control arrays.

◆ Add controls dynamically based on user input.

◆ Enable and disable controls dynamically based on user input.

To complete the exercises in this lab, you must have the required software. For detailed information about the labs and setup for the labs, see "Labs" in "About This Course."

The solution for this lab is located in the folder *<install folder>*\Labs\Lab13\Solution.

Prerequisites

There are no prerequisites for this lab.

Exercises

The following exercises provide practice in working with the concepts and techniques covered in this chapter.

◆ Exercise 1: Creating the User Interface

In this exercise, you will create the basic user interface for the speaker control application.

◆ Exercise 2: Writing Code for the Form_Load Event

In this exercise, you will declare a module level variable that will be used to store the number of controls to be added to the form. Then, you will accept and validate the number of speaker controls to be displayed. Finally, you will write code to dynamically load, position, and display the controls.

◆ Exercise 3: Setting the Volume Control Options

In this exercise, you will enable or disable the horizontal scroll bars, based on the status of the **Mute** check boxes. Additionally, you will use the labels for each of the scroll bars to indicate the volume level.

Exercise 1: Creating the User Interface

In this exercise, you will create the basic user interface for the speaker control application.

▶ **Start a new project**

◆ On the **File** menu, click **New Project**, and select **Standard EXE**.

▶ **Add controls to the main form**

1. Add controls to the form so that it looks like the form shown in the following illustration.

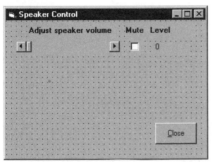

2. Change the default names of the form and controls, as shown in the following table.

User interface element	New name
Project	SpeakerProject
Form	frmSpeaker
Horizontal scroll bar	hsbVolume
Check box	chkMute
LabellblAdjustVolume	lblMute lblLevel

3. Set the **Index** property of the horizontal scroll bar, the check box, and the **Level** label to 0.

4. Set the **Min** and **Max** properties of the horizontal scroll bar to 0 and **100**, respectively.

5. Write code that unloads the form if the **Close** button is clicked.

```
Private Sub cmdClose_Click()
    Unload Me
End Sub
```

6. Save and test the application.

Exercise 2: Writing Code for the Form_Load Event

In this exercise, you will declare a module level variable that will be used to store the number of controls to be added to the form. Then, you will accept and validate the number of speaker controls to be displayed. Finally, you will write code to dynamically load, position, and display the controls.

▶ **Dimension public variables**

◆ Declare a variable named mintMaxSpeakers in the Declarations section. This will be an integer.

```
Private mintMaxSpeakers As Integer
```

▶ **Prompt for and validate the number of controls**

1. In the **Form_Load** event, use the **InputBox** function to set the MaxSpeakers variable to a value entered by the user.

```
mintMaxSpeakers = 0
mintMaxSpeakers = InputBox("Control how many speakers?")
```

2. Create an **If... Then** statement to validate the user's input. If the input value is greater than 4, display a message box explaining the limitation and set MaxSpeakers to **4**.

```
If mintMaxSpeakers > 4 Then
    MsgBox "Sorry, 4 speakers only"
    mintMaxSpeakers = 4
End If
```

▶ **Create and display the dynamic controls**

1. In the **Form_Load** event, create a **For... Next** loop that:

   a. Uses the mintMaxSpeakers value to load the correct number of controls (one for each speaker).

   b. Positions each of the controls 400 twips below the previous control.

   c. Set each control's **Visible** property to **True**.

   To see an example of how your code should look, see Hint 13.1 in Appendix B.

2. Save and test the application.

Exercise 3: Setting the Volume Control Options

In this exercise, you will enable or disable the horizontal scroll bars, based on the status of the **Mute** check boxes. Additionally, you will use the labels for each of the scroll bars to indicate the volume level.

▶ **Set the level caption to indicate the volume**

◆ Write code that changes the **Level** label control to indicate the value of its respective horizontal scroll bar.

```
Private Sub hsbVolume_Change(Index As Integer)
    lblLevel(Index).Caption = hsbVolume(Index).Value
End Sub
```

▶ **Enable/Disable the volume controls by using the Mute check boxes**

1. In the **chkMute_Click** event, create an **If... Then** statement that enables or disables a horizontal scroll bar when its check box status changes.

   a. When a check box is checked (vbChecked), set the **Enabled** property of its control to **False**.

   b. When the check box is unchecked, set the **Enabled** property to **True**.

2. Set the **Caption** property of the respective **Volume** label to indicate 0 if the scroll bar is disabled or its current value when it is enabled.

   To see an example of how your code should look, see Hint 13.2 in Appendix B.

3. Save and test your work.

Self-Check Questions

See page 399 for answers.

1. To create a control array:

A. Set the **Index** property for the control(s) by using the Properties window.

B. Give two controls of the same type the same name.

C. Copy and paste a control.

D. Do all of the above.

2. A statement in your program loads a new control in an array, but when the program runs the control does not appear. What is the most probable cause?

A. Dynamically loaded controls are invisible by default. Set the control's **Visible** property to **True**.

B. Controls in an array must load before the **Form_Load** event. Change the code to load the controls in the **Form_Initialize** event.

C. Dynamically loaded controls must be declared in the General Declarations code.

D. Visual Basic 6.0 no longer supports dynamically loaded controls.

3. What does the following code segment do?

```
Dim ctl As Control

For Each ctl In Me.Controls
    If TypeOf ctl Is CommandButton Then
        ctl.Enabled = False
    End If
Next
```

A. Disables all command buttons on the current form

B. Disables all but the last command button on the current form

C. Disables all command buttons in the project

D. Disables all but the last command button in the project

Chapter 14:
Finishing Touches

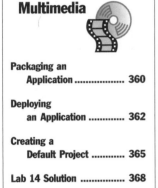

Multimedia

This chapter provides ideas for adding finishing touches to your application. For example, you will learn some principles of user interface design. You will also learn how to create a Setup program and how to create a project template that can be used as the basis for new applications.

Objectives

After completing this chapter, you will be able to:

◆ Create applications that incorporate basic principles of user interface design.

◆ Create a Setup program for an application by using the Package and Deployment Wizard.

◆ Create custom projects.

User Interface Design Principles

In this section, you will learn about designing an effective user interface. If an application has a well-designed user interface, a novice user can become productive quickly. The user interface should minimize user errors and provide visual cues to help a user discover how to complete a task.

User Control

An important principle of user interface design is that the user should always feel in control of the software, rather than feeling controlled by the software. This principle has a number of implications.

The first implication is the operational assumption that the user initiates actions, not the computer or software—the user plays an active, rather than reactive, role. You can use techniques to automate tasks, but implement them in a way that allows the user to choose or control the automation.

The second implication is that users, because of their widely varying skills and preferences, must be able to personalize aspects of the interface. The system software provides user access to many of these aspects. Your software should reflect user settings for different system properties, such as color, fonts, or other options.

The final implication is that your software should be as interactive and responsive as possible. Avoid modes whenever possible. A mode is a state that excludes general interaction or otherwise limits the user to specific interactions. If a mode is the only or the best design alternative—for example, for selecting a particular tool in a drawing program—make certain that the mode is obvious, visible, the result of an explicit user choice, and easy to cancel.

Minimal Modal Interactions

Design your software to give the user maximum control by minimizing modal interactions.

Modal interaction is when a user must complete one task before continuing on with a different task.

Modeless interactions allow the user to move freely between one task and another without fully completing one of them.

As a general rule, your applications should minimize modal interactions, but each type of interaction can be effective in certain situations. Long processes should run in the background, keeping the foreground interactive. For example, when something is printing, it should be possible to minimize the window even if the document cannot be altered.

Modal interaction is effective at focusing the user's attention to submitting some information, but it takes control away from the user and restricts him or her from using the rest of the application at the same time. However, limiting the amount of user control sometimes benefits the user.

Modeless interaction gives control back to the user. The **Spelling and Grammar** (spell checker) dialog box in Microsoft Word 97 is a good example of a modeless dialog box. The spell checker allows the user to work in the document without closing the dialog box.

Personalization Support

Users of your application will have different working styles and different levels of experience in working with the application. Therefore, try to accommodate as many levels and styles as possible. For example, do not hard-code colors in your applications. Program your application to use the system colors selected by the user.

SaveSetting Statement

You can use the **SaveSetting** statement to save a new value for a registry key stored in your application's registry location. For example, you could add code to the **Form_Unload** event in the application's main form in order to preserve settings at shutdown, or you could add code to the **Form_Unload** event in an options dialog box to update user preferences.

To use the **SaveSetting** statement, use the following syntax:

SaveSetting appname, section, key, value

The following example code saves new values for the "Top" and "Left" keys in the Startup section of the registry for an application named "MyApp." If an entry for the MyApp application, any sections, or any keys do not exist in the Software/ Microsoft section in the registry, the following code will create it:

```
Private Sub Form_Unload(Cancel As Integer)
    SaveSetting appname:="MyApp", section:="Startup", _
        Key:="Top", setting:=75
    SaveSetting appname:="MyApp", section:="Startup", _
        Key:="Left", setting:=50
End Sub
```

Direct User Manipulation

Design your software so that users can directly manipulate software representations of information.

To implement directness:

◆ Use clear object metaphors so the user can directly manipulate objects.

Metaphors support user recognition rather than recollection. Users remember a meaning associated with a familiar object more easily than they remember the name of a particular command. For example, a folder on the Windows desktop can be used to organize a variety of objects such as printers, calculators, and other folders.

◆ Define "verbs" for the objects of your interface that can be invoked when an object is selected. Add the actions to a pop-up menu and display the menu when the user right-clicks an object. The user selects an object and then selects an action to perform on the object.

For example, when you right-click a .wav file in Windows, the verb "Play" is accessible on the pop-up menu.

◆ Incorporate the concept of affordance into your design. Affordance refers to the way an object communicates its use to the user. For example, use ToolTips to assist the user in learning the purpose of controls.

Consistency

Consistency allows users to transfer existing knowledge to new tasks, learn new things more quickly, and focus more on their work without the need to spend time trying to remember the differences in interaction. By providing a sense of stability, consistency makes the interface familiar and predictable.

Consistency is important through all aspects of the interface, including names of commands, visual presentation of information, and operational behavior. To design consistency into software, you must consider several aspects:

◆ Consistency within a product

Present common functions by using a consistent set of commands and interfaces. For example, avoid implementing a copy command that immediately carries out an operation in one situation but in another presents a dialog box that requires a user to type in a destination. As a corollary to this example, use the same command to carry out functions that seem similar to the user.

◆ Consistency within the operating environment

By maintaining a high level of consistency between the interaction and interface conventions provided by Microsoft Windows, your software benefits from users' ability to apply interaction skills that they have already learned.

◆ Consistency with metaphors

If a particular behavior is more characteristic of a different object than its metaphor implies, the user may have difficulty learning to associate that behavior with an object. For example, for the recoverability of objects placed in it, an incinerator communicates a different model than a wastebasket.

Simplicity

An interface should be simple (not simplistic), easy to learn, and easy to use. It must also provide access to all functionality provided by an application. Maximizing functionality and maintaining simplicity work against each other in the interface, but an effective design balances these objectives.

One way to support simplicity is to limit the presentation of information to a minimum. Display only information that is required to communicate adequately. For example, avoid wordy descriptions for command names or messages. Irrelevant or verbose phrases clutter your design, making it difficult for users to easily extract essential information.

You can also help users manage complexity by using progressive disclosure. Progressive disclosure involves careful organization of information so that it is shown only at the appropriate time. By doing this, you reduce the amount of information to process. For example, clicking a menu displays its choices; the use of dialog boxes can reduce the number of menu options.

The following is a list of key rules that you should follow to help make your application simple to use:

◆ Eliminate visual clutter.

◆ Eliminate ambiguity.

◆ Avoid jargon.

◆ Use progressive disclosure.

Forgiveness

Users like to explore an interface and often learn by trial and error. An effective interface allows for interactive discovery. It provides only appropriate sets of choices and warns users about potential situations in which they may damage the system or data, or better, makes actions reversible or recoverable.

Even within the best-designed interface, users can make mistakes. These mistakes can be both physical (accidentally pointing to the wrong command or data) or mental (making a wrong decision about which command or data to select). An effective design avoids situations that are likely to result in errors. It also accommodates potential user errors and makes it easy for the user to recover.

To implement forgiveness in your application:

◆ Minimize the opportunity for errors.

◆ Give the user an escape route.

◆ Handle errors gracefully.

◆ Supply reasonable default values.

Feedback

Always provide feedback for a user's actions. Visual and audio cues can be presented with user interaction to confirm that the software is responding to the user's input and to communicate details that distinguish the nature of the action.

Effective feedback is timely and is presented as close to the point of the user's interaction as possible. Even when the computer is processing a particular task, provide the user with information regarding the state of the process and how to cancel that process (if that is an option). Nothing is more disconcerting than a "dead" screen that is unresponsive to input. A typical user will tolerate only a few seconds of an unresponsive interface.

Visual Design

Effective visual design serves a greater purpose than decoration; it is an important tool for communication. How you organize information on the screen can make the difference between a design that communicates a message and one that leaves a user feeling puzzled or overwhelmed.

Even the best product functionality can suffer if its visual presentation does not communicate effectively. If you are not trained in visual or information design, it is a good idea to work with a designer who has education and experience in this field and include that person as a member of the design team early in the development process. Good graphic designers provide a perspective on how to take the best advantage of the screen and how to use effectively the concepts of shape, color, contrast, focus, and composition. Moreover, graphic designers understand how to design and organize information, and how fonts and color affect perception.

User Assistance

Online user assistance is an important part of a product's design and can be supported in a variety of ways, from automatic display of information based on context to commands that require explicit user selection. User assistance content can be composed of contextual, procedural, explanatory, reference, or tutorial information. But user assistance should always be simple, efficient, and relevant so that a user can obtain it without becoming lost in the interface.

Contextual User Assistance

A contextual form of user assistance provides information about a particular object and its context. It answers questions such as "What is this?" and "Why would I use it?"

Task-Oriented Help

Task-oriented Help provides the steps for carrying out a task. It can involve a number of procedures. You present task-oriented Help in task Help topic windows. Task Help topic windows are displayed as primary windows. The user can size this window like any other primary window.

Reference Help

Reference Help is a form of Help information that serves more as online documentation. Use reference Help to document the features of a product or use it as a user's guide to a product. Often the use determines the balance of text and graphics used in the Help file. Reference-oriented documentation typically includes more text and follows a consistent presentation of information. User's guide documentation typically organizes information by specific tasks and may include more illustrations.

The Help Topics Browser

The **Help Topics** browser dialog box provides user access to Help information. To open this window, include a **Help Topics** menu item on the **Help** drop-down menu. Alternatively, you can include menu commands that open the window to a particular tabbed page—for example, **Contents, Index,** and **Find Topic** tabs.

In addition, provide a **Help Topics** button in the toolbar of a task or reference Help topic window. When the user chooses this button, display the Help Topics browser window with the last page that the user accessed. If you prefer, provide **Contents, Index,** and **Find Topic** buttons for direct access to a specific page. For example, by default, reference Help windows include **Contents** and **Index** button access to the Help Topics browser.

Wizards

A wizard is a special form of user assistance that automates a task through a dialog with the user. Wizards help the user accomplish tasks that can be complex and require experience. Wizards can automate almost any task, including creating new objects and formatting the presentation of a set of objects, such as a table or paragraph. They are especially useful for complex or infrequent tasks that the user may have difficulty learning or doing.

Distributing an Application

When you distribute your application, you should provide users with a Setup program to perform some or all of the following tasks:

- Copy the necessary files to the user's computer.
- Place the files in the appropriate folders.
- Register files.
- Create a **Start** menu item or group.
- Create an icon on the user's desktop.

In this section, you will learn how to use the Package and Deployment Wizard provided by Visual Basic to create a Setup program that can be used to install and distribute your application.

Overview of the Deployment Process

After you create a Visual Basic application, you may want to distribute it to others. You can freely distribute any application that you create with Visual Basic to anyone who uses Windows. You can distribute your applications on disk, on CDs, across networks, or over the Internet or an intranet.

Steps for Distributing an Application

When you distribute an application, you must follow a two-step process:

1. Packaging

   You must package your application files into one or more .cab files that can be deployed to the location that you choose, and you must create Setup programs for certain types of packages. A .cab file is a compressed file that is well suited to distribution either on disks or over the Internet.

2. Deployment

   You must move your packaged application to a location from which users can install it. This may mean copying the package to floppy disks or to a local or network drive, or dispersing the package to a Web site.

Tools for Packaging and Distribution

You can use two tools provided with your Visual Basic installation to package and distribute your applications: the Package and Deployment Wizard (formerly the Setup Wizard) or the Setup Toolkit. The Package and Deployment Wizard automates many of the steps involved in distributing applications by presenting you with choices about how you want to configure your .cab files. The Setup Toolkit lets you customize some of what happens during the installation process.

Using the Package and Deployment Wizard

There are three ways you can start the Package and Deployment Wizard:

1. Run it from within Visual Basic as an add-in.

2. Run it as a stand-alone component from outside the development environment.

3. Run it in silent mode by launching it from a command prompt.

This course describes using the Package and Deployment Wizard from within Visual Basic as an add-in.

Installing the Package and Deployment Wizard

To use the Package and Deployment Wizard from within Visual Basic, you may first need to load it from the Add-In Manager.

▶ **To load the Package and Deployment Wizard as an add-in**

1. On the **Add-ins** menu, click **Add-In Manager**.

2. In the Available Add-Ins list, select **Package & Deployment Wizard**.

3. Select the **Loaded/Unloaded** option and click **OK**.

Packaging an Application

Application packaging is the act of creating a package that can install your application onto the user's computer. A package consists of the .cab file or files that contain your compressed project files and any other necessary files that the user needs to install and run your application. These files may include Setup programs, secondary .cab files, or other necessary files. The additional files vary based on the type of package you create.

You can create two kinds of packages—standard packages or Internet packages. If you plan to distribute your application on disk, floppy, or via a network share, you should create a standard package for your application. If you plan to distribute your application via an intranet or Internet site, you should create an Internet package.

In most cases, you will package your applications by using the Package and Deployment Wizard, which is provided with Visual Basic. You can package applications manually, but the wizard provides valuable shortcuts and automates some of the tasks that you would have to perform yourself in a manual packaging session.

To see the demonstration "Packaging an Application," see the accompanying CD-ROM.

▶ **To create a standard package**

1. Open the project that you want to package or deploy by using the wizard.

Note You should save and compile a project before running the Package and Deployment Wizard. If you are working in a project group or have multiple projects loaded, make sure before starting the wizard that the project that you want to package or deploy is the current project.

2. On the **Add-Ins** menu, select **Package & Deployment Wizard** to start the wizard.

3. On the main screen, click **Package**.

4. Select **Standard Setup Package** as the package type and click **Next**.

   Alternatively, you can select **Dependency File** to create a file that lists information about the run-time components required by your application.

5. Choose a folder location where your package will be assembled, and then click **Next**.

   At this point, you can create a new folder to avoid the possibility of overwriting existing files or subfolders

6. In the list of files to include as part of your application, select or clear the check box to the left of the file name, and then click **Next**.

   Setup.exe, Setup1.exe, St6unst.exe, and Vb6stkit.dll are required for a standard setup package and cannot be removed. You can also add additional files by clicking the **Add** button.

7. Choose either **Single cab** or **Multiple cabs** and click **Next**.

   If you intend to distribute your application on floppy disks, you must create multiple cabs and specify a cab size no larger than the disks that you plan to use.

8. Enter the title to be displayed when the Setup program is run, and click **Next**.

9. Choose the **Start** menu groups and items that will be created by the installation process, and click **Next**.

   There are several options in this screen of the wizard. You can create groups and items for your application in one of two locations: on the main level of the **Start** menu or within the Programs subfolder of the **Start** menu. In addition, you can edit the properties for an existing item, or you can remove groups and items.

10. Modify any file location and subfolder information for each of the files listed, if desired, and click **Next**.

11. Check any files that you want to install as shared, and then click **Next**.

Shared files may be used by more than one program. If any other applications that use the file still exist on the computer, such a file will not be removed when the end user uninstalls your application.

12. In the **Script name** field, enter a name under which to save settings for the current session, and then click **Finish** to create the package.

The wizard creates a packaging report, which you can save for later use.

Deploying an Application

Application deployment is the process of moving your packaged application to either the distribution media that you have chosen or to a Web site from which it can be downloaded. There are two ways that you can deploy your Visual Basic application:

1. You can use the Deployment portion of the Package and Deployment Wizard to deploy your application to floppy disks, a local or network drive, or to a Web site.

2. You can manually copy files to disks or shares, or you can manually publish files to the appropriate Web location.

To see the demonstration "Deploying an Application," see the accompanying CD-ROM.

▶ **To deploy a package by using the Package and Deployment Wizard**

1. On the main screen of the Package and Deployment Wizard, click **Deploy**.

2. Select the package that you want to deploy, and click **Next**.

3. Select either **Folder** or **Web Publishing** as the deployment method, and click **Next**.

Depending on the option that you choose, the wizard will display slightly different screens. If you choose to deploy the package to a Web-publishing site, you will continue running the wizard as follows:

a. In the list of items to deploy, select or clear the check box to the left of the file name, and then click **Next**.

b. Check any additional project files and folders that you want to deploy, and then click **Next**.

c. Enter a destination URL, select the desired Web-publishing protocol, and click **Next**.

Alternatively, if you choose to deploy the package to a local or a network folder, you will continue running the wizard as follows:

- Choose a folder location, and then click **Next**.

At this point, you can create a new folder to avoid the possibility of overwriting existing files or subfolders.

4. In the Script Name field, enter a name under which to save settings for the current session, and then click **Finish** to deploy the package.

   The wizard creates a packaging report, which you can save for later use.

   Depending on the deployment option selected, the default name in the Script Name field will appear as either Web Deployment 1 or Folder Deployment 1.

5. Close the Package and Deployment Wizard.

Understanding Setup Files

The Package and Deployment Wizard creates all of the files necessary to install your application on a user's computer.

The following list describes some of the necessary files:

◆ Cabinet file (.cab file)

The Package and Deployment Wizard compresses your application files into one or more .cab files for distribution. The Setup program then extracts application files from this .cab file and copies them to the appropriate locations on a user's computer.

◆ Setup.exe

The Package and Deployment Wizard copies Setup.exe from a Visual Basic folder to your application's distribution site. The user runs Setup.exe to install your application.

Setup.exe copies the bootstrap files and then executes the main Setup program (usually named Setup1.exe) listed in Setup.lst.

◆ Setup.lst

The Package and Deployment Wizard creates the Setup.lst file. This file contains the list of files required by your application and general information such as default folders and the required disk space.

The following example code illustrates what a sample Setup.lst file might contain:

```
[Bootstrap]
File1=1,,setup1.ex_,setup1.exe,$(WinPath),...
..
[Files]
File1=1,,GRID32.OC_,GRID32.OCX,$(WinSysPath),,$(Shared)..
..
[Setup]
Title=LoanSheet
DefaultDir=$(ProgramFiles)\Loan
```

◆ Setup1.exe

The Package and Deployment Wizard includes Setup1.exe, the main Setup program, in the .cab file that contains your application files. Setup1.exe copies and registers application files, and creates startup icons. Setup1.exe also increments the reference count for shared files in the registry.

◆ St6Unst.log

The Setup program creates an application log file (St6Unst.log) that is copied to the application folder, and includes the following information:

- Folders that were created.
- Files that were installed. The log indicates if a file was not copied because a newer version of the file was already found on the disk.
- Registry entries that were created.
- **Start** menu entries that were created.
- DLLs, .exe files, or .ocx files that were self-registered.

◆ St6Unst.exe

The Setup program also copies an application-removal utility (St6Unst.exe) to the Windows folder. The application-removal utility removes the application files and icons or groups, and it decrements the reference count for shared components. If a reference count is zero, the utility prompts the user to remove the shared component.

Note The application-removal utility depends on an accurate log file and an accurate registry entry to perform its function.

If your application uses a shared component that you know is already on the user's system, you should still include the component with your Setup program. This ensures that the reference count for the component is incremented when the user installs your application.

To remove an application with either Microsoft Windows NT or Windows 98, click the **Add/Remove Programs** icon in the Control Panel.

Creating a Default Project

Visual Basic provides you with several templates for creating a new project. These are listed in the **New Project** dialog box when Visual Basic first starts. This list is also presented if you create a new project from within Visual Basic.

In addition to the templates provided, you can create your own default projects to be used as templates.

All files associated with a template project are saved in the Projects folder located under the VB98\Template folder. To create your own custom template project, create a new project, and then add the specific forms and controls that will comprise the new template. Then, save the project in the Projects folder. When you save the project, the name that you provide will be used in the **New Project** dialog box. Projects that are created from this template will automatically include any forms and controls that you added in the original project.

To see the demonstration "Creating a Default Project," see the accompanying CD-ROM.

Review: Steps to Creating a Visual Basic Program

There are eight basic steps to creating a Visual Basic application:

1. Create a design plan.

   The design plan should be the road map that you use when creating an application. Take time before writing any code to design the application that you will be building. Although Visual Basic provides tools to help you quickly develop a solution, having a clear understanding of the user needs and initial feature set will help you be more efficient in your development efforts. This will also help you save time by minimizing the potential for recoding due to a poor or nonexistent design plan.

2. Create the user interface.

You create an interface by drawing controls and objects on a form. To make your code easier to read and debug, you then assign names to the objects by using standard naming conventions. You can look at other applications such as Excel or Word for interface ideas.

3. Set the properties of the interface objects.

After adding objects to a form, you set the object properties. You can either set initial values by using the Properties window at design time, or you can use code to modify the properties at run time.

4. Write code for events.

After setting initial properties for the form and each object, you add code that executes in response to events. Events occur when different actions happen on a control or object. For example, **Click** is one event that can occur for a command button.

5. Save the project.

When you create the project, make sure you give it a name by using the **Save Project As** command on the **File** menu. Save your project frequently as you add code. Saving a project will also save each form and code module in the project.

6. Test and debug the application.

While you add code to the project, you can use the **Run** tool on the toolbar to start the application and view its behavior. You can also use the debug tools to check for errors and to modify code.

7. Make an executable file.

Upon completion of your project, create an executable file by using the **Make <Project>.exe** command on the **File** menu.

8. Create a Setup program.

Because your executable file depends on other files, such as any custom control files used in the project, you should create a Setup program by using the Package and Deployment Wizard, which ensures that the user of your program has all the required files.

Development Resources

A variety of resources exists to help you in developing applications. These resources provide essential reference material for developers and can be used to help you develop solutions that implement Microsoft technology.

The Microsoft Developer Network (MSDN)

The Microsoft Developer Network (MSDN) CD-ROM is a collection of current documentation, technical articles, and the Microsoft Knowledge Base created for developers. MSDN features full-text searches to quickly locate all documents that relate to your area of interest.

In addition, MSDN is now used as the online Help facility integrated within Visual Basic.

Microsoft Technical Information Network (TechNet)

The TechNet is an information service created for support personnel, database and network administrators, and business solution providers. TechNet members receive monthly CDs that contain the Microsoft Knowledge Base (a tool containing thousands of articles developed and used by Microsoft Product Support Services to answer users' support questions), resource kits, migration information, product facts and features, education materials, conference notes, and related material. To join TechNet in the United States, call (800) 344-2121.

Microsoft Web Site on the Internet

The Microsoft Web site is a dynamic and informative source of information for developers. The Microsoft site is located at www.microsoft.com.

To go to the Visual Basic home page, visit the Microsoft Web site at http://www.microsoft.com/VBASIC.

To go to the Mastering Series home page, visit the Mastering Series Web site at http://www.microsoft.com/mastering/.

Lab 14: Using the Package and Deployment Wizard

When you have finished an application, you will want to package it for shipping to customers. The Package and Deployment Wizard automates the process of compressing and copying files onto floppy disks or into a distribution folder. In this lab, you will create a Setup program for the loan payment estimate application.

You can work with the files provided in the folder *<install folder>*\Labs\Lab14.

To see the demonstration "Lab 14 Solution," see the accompanying CD-ROM.

Estimated time to complete this lab: **20 minutes**

Objectives

After completing this lab, you will be able to:

◆ Use the Package and Deployment Wizard to create a Setup program.

◆ Install your application.

◆ Remove your application.

To complete the exercises in this lab, you must have the required software. For detailed information about the labs and setup for the labs, see "Labs" in "About This Course."

The solution for this lab is located in the folder *<install folder>*\Labs\Lab14\Solution.

Prerequisites

There are no prerequisites for this lab.

Exercises

The following exercises provide practice in working with the concepts covered in this chapter.

◆ Exercise 1: Creating a Setup Program

In this exercise, you will use the Package and Deployment Wizard to create a Setup program for distributing your application.

◆ Exercise 2: Installing an Application

In this exercise, you will run the Setup program for your application that you created in the previous exercise.

◆ Exercise 3: Removing an Application

In this exercise, you will remove the application that you installed in the previous exercise.

Exercise 1: Creating a Setup Program

In this exercise, you will use the Package and Deployment Wizard to create a Setup program for distributing your application.

▶ **Open the loan project**

1. If Visual Basic isn't running, start it from the **Start** menu.

2. Open the project provided for you in the *<install folder>*\Labs\Lab14 folder.

▶ **Add the final touches to the application**

1. Set the **Icon** property of the startup form, frmMain, to the House icon in *<install folder>*\Labs\Lab14 folder.

2. On the **Project** menu, click **Components**, and remove all unused controls from the project.

> **Note** Visual Basic will not allow you to remove a control or reference that is being used by the project.

3. On the **Project** menu, click **References**, and remove all unused references from the project.

4. Save all changes to your project.

5. Define the application title and create an executable file.

   The application title is the default text displayed in the title bar of message boxes and input boxes when a specific string is not supplied.

   a. On the **File** menu, click **Make Loan.exe.**

   b. Click the **Options** button.

   c. Set the **Application Title** to **Loan Payment Estimate.**

   d. Select **frmMain** as the icon to be displayed, and click **OK.**

   e. Click **OK** to create the .exe file.

6. Save and exit Visual Basic. Test your application by double-clicking the .exe file just created.

▶ **Create a Setup program**

1. On the **Start** menu, click **Microsoft Visual Basic 6.0.** Click **Microsoft Visual Basic 6.0 Tools,** and then click **Package & Deployment Wizard.**

2. In the Package and Deployment Wizard, click the **Browse** button and **Open** the Loan project provided in the folder *<install folder>*\Labs\Lab14, and then click the **Package** button.

   Because you saved the project files after compiling the executable file, the Package and Deployment Wizard will detect a difference and prompt you to recompile. Click **No** to use the executable file that you created in the previous procedure.

Note If you have previously run the Package and Deployment Wizard, the Packaging Script screen will be presented. This screen lists previously saved scripts for the current project and (None) if you do not want to use an existing script. The default is the last script that was run for the current project.

3. On the Package Type screen, select **Standard Setup Package** as the Package Type, and then click **Next.**

4. On the Package Folder screen, select the folder *<install folder>*\Labs\Lab14\Setup for the location of the distribution files, and then click **Next.**

5. On the Included Files screen, browse through the list of included files, and then click the **Add** button. Locate the file Readme.txt in folder *<install folder>*\Labs\Lab14, click **Open,** and then click **Next.**

Note If there are any files that Visual Basic did not include, use the **Find** utility on the **Start** menu to locate the files. There should be only one control dependency, MSCOMCTL.OCX. If there are any more file dependencies than this one, clear their check boxes.

6. On the Cab Options screen, select **Single Cab** from the Cab options, and then click **Next.**

7. On the Installation Title screen, leave the default title, and then click **Next.**

8. On the Start Menu Items screen, note the default menu location. Click **Next.**

9. On the Install Locations screen, notice that you can modify the install location for each of the files listed. Without making changes, click **Next.**

10. On the Shared Files screen, click **Next.**

11. On the Finished! screen, name the script **Loan Setup Package 1**, and then click **Finish**.

    The Setup Wizard creates the Setup program for your application. Click the **Close** button in the **Report** dialog box.

12. When the Package and Deployment Wizard is finished, click **Close**.

Exercise 2: Installing an Application

In this exercise, you will run the Setup program for the application that you created in the previous exercise.

▶ **Run the Setup program**

1. Start Windows Explorer.

2. Open the Setup folder (\Labs\Lab14\Setup).

3. Run the Setup program by double-clicking it, and follow the directions.

▶ **Run your application**

   ◆ After Setup is complete, run your application from the Programs group on the **Start** menu.

Exercise 3: Removing an Application

In this exercise, you will remove the application that you installed in the previous exercise.

▶ **Remove the application**

1. On the **Start** menu, point to **Settings**, and click **Control Panel**.

2. Run the Add/Remove Programs application, and click the **Install/Uninstall** tab.

3. Select the application that you installed in the previous exercise, and click **Add/Remove**.

4. If prompted to remove shared files, choose not to remove them.

▶ **Try to run your application**

1. Check the **Programs** group on the **Start** menu. Has your application been removed?

2. Look for the folder that was created by the Setup program. Has it been removed?

To see the answers to these questions, see Hint 14.1 in Appendix B.

Self-Check Questions

See page 402 for answers.

1. Which of the following statements best describes how forms should be used to interact with users?

A. Modal interactions provide flexibility to the user and should be used more often than modeless interactions.

B. Modal interactions provide flexibility to the user and should be used just as often as modeless interactions.

C. Modeless interactions provide flexibility to the user and should be used more often than modal interactions.

D. Modeless interactions provide flexibility to the user and should be used just as often as modal interactions.

2. Which of the following is not a valid way to start the Package and Deployment Wizard?

A. On the **File** menu in Visual Basic, click **Package & Deployment Wizard**.

B. Run it as a stand-alone component from outside the development environment.

C. Run it from within Visual Basic as an add-in.

D. Run it in silent mode by launching it from a command prompt.

3. The easiest way to distribute your application is to:

A. Copy all of the files in the project folder to a floppy disk.

B. Compile your application and copy the .exe file to a floppy disk.

C. Create an installation program by using the Package and Deployment Wizard.

D. Create a separate executable file in Visual Basic that installs your project folder.

Appendix A:
Self-Check Answers

Chapter 1

1. Visual Basic is the basis for a common programming language known as:

   A. C++.

      Incorrect

      Visual Basic is not based on C++. The C++ programming language is based on the C programming language.

   B. QuickBasic.

      Incorrect

      Visual Basic is not based on QuickBasic.

   C. PC Basic.

      Incorrect

      Visual Basic is not based on PC Basic.

   D. Visual Basic for Applications.

      Correct

      The common programming language for all Microsoft Office applications is now Visual Basic for Applications. This language has also been licensed to other vendors for a variety of applications.

For more information, see *Features of Visual Basic*, page 2.

2. **A small business plans to create applications that share an Access database and create custom data reports. The business owners do not require any remote database access tools. Which edition of Visual Basic is best suited for their purposes?**

A. Learning

Incorrect

Although the Learning Edition supports simple data access, it does not offer the capabilities of data reporting as the other editions of Visual Basic. In addition, the other limitations of the Learning Edition may not make it the best choice for future needs of a small business.

B. Professional

Correct

Because the Learning Edition does not contain the reporting tools necessary, the Professional Edition is required. Since no remote database connectivity tools are necessary, it is hard to justify the additional expense of the Enterprise Edition (unless the remote connectivity tools might be required in the near future).

C. Enterprise

Incorrect

Since no remote database connectivity tools are necessary, it is hard to justify the additional expense of the Enterprise Edition (unless the remote connectivity tools might be required in the near future).

D. None of these

Incorrect

This answer is incorrect because one of the listed versions of Visual Basic includes the features needed to solve the business problem.

For more information, see *Editions of Visual Basic*, page 3.

3. **The actions an object can perform are called _____, while those recognized by an object are _____ .**

A. events, methods.

Incorrect

Events are actions recognized by Visual Basic for which you can write code to respond.

B. methods, events.

Correct

The actions an object can perform are called methods (cmdCommandButton.Move). Objects respond to events triggered by the user, operating system, or other objects in the application.

C. properties, methods

Incorrect

A property is a named attribute of an object that is used to a characteristic of an object, such as name, size, enabled, and visible.

D. procedures, events

Incorrect

A procedure is a set of instructions that work as a unit either as a function or subroutine. There are various types of procedures, such as an event procedure. Procedures are discussed in Chapter 4.

For more information, see *Visual Basic Terminology*, page 5.

4. To distribute an application, you first create a single executable file containing all the forms and code modules for a project. To do this, you:

A. Create a test project.

Incorrect

Creating a test project does not enable you to distribute an application.

B. Zip the project.

Incorrect

You can create a Zip file that will compress all project files into a single file; however, this will not enable you to distribute your program.

C. Compile the project.

Correct

When you are finished with an application, you can compile it into an executable file. This creates a single executable file that contains all of the forms and code modules specific to the project.

D. Assemble the project.

Incorrect

Assembly language projects can be assembled using an application such as Microsoft Macro Assembler (MSAM). This process does not apply to Visual Basic applications.

For more information, see *Project and Executable Files*, page 15.

Chapter 2

1. **In the following line of code, frmEdit is the _____, Caption is the _____, and Edit is the _____.**

```
frmEdit.Caption = "Edit"
```

A. object, property, value

Correct

In the line of code - frmEdit.Caption = "Edit" - the literal string "Edit" is assigned to frmEdit's **Caption** property.

B. object, method, value

Incorrect

A value is not assigned to a method.

C. method, event, property

Incorrect

An event procedure is a subroutine for which you can write code to respond. The example code does not contain the correct syntax for an event procedure. In the example code - frmEdit - is not a method, and Edit is not a property.

D. method, object, value

Incorrect

In the line of code - .Caption - is not an object, and frmEdit is not a method.

For more information, see *Properties, Methods, and Events*, page 29.

2. **You are writing a program and need to place the contents of the txtFirstName text box into a variable called CustomerName. Which of the following lines of code does this correctly?**

A. txtFirstName.Value = CustomerName

   Incorrect

   A textbox control does not have a **Value** property. This answer shows a property value being set to a variable's value.

B. CustomerName = txtFirstName.Value

   Incorrect

   A textbox does not have a **Value** property.

C. CustomerName = txtFirstName.Text

   Correct

   The proper syntax for obtaining the value of a property is *Variable = Object.Property*. In this example, TempVariable is the variable, while Check1.Value is the object and property queried.

D. CustomerName = txtFirstName.Caption

   Incorrect

   A label control has a **Caption** property, a textbox control does not.

For more information, see *Returning Property Values*, page 31.

3. **An error occurs when you enter the following code segment. What is causing the error?**

```
With txtName
    FontBold = True
    FontSize = 24
    Text = "Hello, World!"
End With
```

A. Only two properties can be set by using a **With** statement.

   Incorrect

   You may perform several actions on the same object using the **With...End With** statement. The number of properties you can set is not limited to two.

B. The equal sign (=) is missing after txtName.

   Incorrect

   An equals sign is not required after TxtName.

C. Both "True" and "24" need to be enclosed in quotations.

Incorrect

Neither a Boolean value, such as **True** or **False**, nor a numeric value, such as 24 is enclosed in quotations.

D. A period (.) is missing before each of the properties.

Correct

The name of the object is placed on the With line and is followed by any number of subsequent lines of code written without the object qualifier. The period (.) that separates the object from its property or method must still be included.

For more information, see *Setting Control Properties*, page 42.

Chapter 3

1. You are writing several Sub procedures that will be accessed from several forms. What type of module should be used?

A. Form

Incorrect

Although you can use a form module to create public functions and sub procedures, it is not the preferred solution.

B. Standard

Correct

When an application contains code that is shared by several forms, store the shared code in a standard module. Standard modules can contain public or module-level declarations of variables, constants, types, external procedures, and global procedures. The code in Standard modules is public by default making it easily sharable with other code modules, such as a form module.

C. Class

Incorrect

You should not use a class module to store pubic functions and sub procedures.

D. Project

Incorrect

A project is not a module itself. It can contain objects such as form, standard, and class modules.

For more information, see *Understanding Modules*, page 56.

2. **Which of the following lines of code displays a message box titled "Invalid File Name" and a message indicating that the chosen filename was not valid?**

A. intReturnValue = MsgBox ("The selected file name was not valid", vbOKOnly, "Invalid File Name")

Correct

The proper syntax for the **MsgBox** function is: MsgBox(prompt[, buttons] [, title] [, helpfile, context]). In this case, helpfile and context are not used and do not need to be included.

B. intReturnValue = MsgBox (vbOKOnly, "The selected file name was not valid", "Invalid File Name")

Incorrect

This answer is incorrect because the first two arguments have invalid values.

C. intReturnValue = MsgBox ("The selected file name was not valid", "Invalid File Name", vbOKOnly)

Incorrect

This answer is incorrect because the last two arguments have invalid values.

D. intReturnValue = MsgBox ("Invalid File Name", "The selected file name was not valid", vbOKOnly)

Incorrect

This answer is incorrect because all three arguments are arranged improperly within the MsgBox function.

For more information, see *Using the MsgBox Function*, page 72.

3. A form's Load event occurs:

A. As the result of the use of a **Load** statement.

Incorrect

One of the ways in which the **Load** event occurs is as a result of using the **Load** statement. There are also other ways that will cause the **Load** event to occur.

B. The first time that a form's **Show** method is used.

Incorrect

This answer could be true depending on whether or not the form is already loaded. If the form is already loaded when the **Show** method is used, the **Load** event will not occur.

C. The first time that the form is referenced, if it isn't loaded.

Incorrect

Any reference to a form automatically causes the **Load** event to occur if the form is not already loaded.

D. When each of the above occurs.

Correct

The **Load** event occurs when the form is loaded into memory. This results from the use of the **Load** statement, or by invoking the **Show** method (if the form is not already loaded into memory). Any reference to a form automatically loads the form if it is not already loaded.

For more information, see *Displaying Forms*, page 78.

4. The End statement terminates:

A. Only the form that contains it.

Incorrect

The **End** statement immediately terminates any code executing. Placing the **End** statement anywhere in a procedure ends code execution, closes any files opened and clears all variables.

B. All of the forms in a module.

Incorrect

The End statement will unload more than the form that contains the statement.

C. The last form opened.

Incorrect

The **End** statement will unload more than the last open form.

D. All forms and modules.

Correct

The End statement will terminate the entire application causing all objects (including forms and modules) to be unloaded.

For more information, see *Ending an Application*, page 82.

Chapter 4

1. **What is the scope of the variable intImageCount if it is declared by using the following syntax within the General Declarations section of frmProcImage?**

```
Dim intImageCount As Integer
```

A. Only in procedures within the frmProcImage form

Correct

When a variable is declared using the **Dim** statement within the General Declarations section of a module, it is private to the module.

B. Only the Declarations section of frmProcImage

Incorrect

It would not be accurate to state that a variable only has scope in the General Declarations section of a module. The scope of a variable may be limited to a single procedure, all procedures within a single module, or all procedures within an application.

C. All forms in the project

Incorrect

It is not possible to limit the scope of a variable to a particular type of module. Using the **Public** keyword, you can give a variable scope throughout an entire project.

D. All modules in the project

Incorrect

In this case the variable would not have scope throughout the project. To give a variable scope throughout your application, declare it as **Public**.

For more information, see *Scope of Variables*, page 99.

2. **Your program is supposed to add the contents of two text boxes. Testing the application shows that instead of the expected value of 78, the program returns 3,543. How can you solve this problem?**

A. Use an '&' to combine the strings.

Incorrect

In this case you would not want to combine two strings, but instead add the numeric values of the strings.

B. Create a separate variable to hold the result.

Incorrect

Creating another variable to hold the result will not solve the problem. Instead, you want to perform a mathematical calculation using the numeric values of the two strings.

C. Use conversion functions to convert the strings to integers.

Correct

In this example, although the two text boxes contain what appears to be numbers, they actually contain strings. When two strings are added together, Visual Basic concatenates the strings regardless of their contents. So "35" + "43" = "3543." To correct this, simply use the conversion functions to convert the string values to a numeric value before adding them together.

D. Have the values entered into labels instead of text boxes.

Incorrect

Both the **Caption** property for a label and the **Text** property for a textbox contain string values. Changing controls will not solve the problem. Instead, you want to perform a mathematical calculation using the numeric values of the two strings.

For more information, see *Converting Data Types*, page 109.

3. **Which of the following code statements calls the CheckPassword function and passes the contents of the txtPassword textbox?**

   A. blnValid = CheckPassword.Text(txtPassword)

   Incorrect

   A function does not have properties. In this answer, the function is displayed as having a text property, which makes this answer incorrect.

   B. TxtPassword.Text(CheckPassword)

   Incorrect

   The function name should be to the left of the parentheses and any arguments should be within the parantheses.

   C. CheckPassword() = txtPassword.Text

   Incorrect

   The equals sign should be positioned to the left of the function name that you are calling. The return value should be to the left of the equals sign. This is because the variable is set by the return value of the function, the function is not set by the variable.

   D. blnValid = CheckPassword(txtPassword.Text)

   Correct

   The correct syntax for passing a single argument to a function or procedure is: *Procedure(argument)*.

   For more information, see *Passing Arguments to Procedures*, page 121.

Chapter 5

1. **The value of a variable can contain one of five different STRING values. Which of the following statements should be used to evaluate the variable?**

   A. If...Then...ElseIf

   Incorrect

   While using an **If...Then...ElseIf** statement can be used to evaluate a variable with multiple possible values, it is not the most efficient. In addition, in the case of more than three possible values, this statement can be difficult to maintain.

   For more information, see *If...Then...ElseIf Statements*, page 147.

B. **Select Case**

Correct

Since the variable can contain one of many values, using the **Select Case** statement is the most efficient and easy to maintain.

For more information, see *Using Select Case Statements*, page 148.

C. **If...Then**

Incorrect

Using an **If...Then** statement is most efficient when a variable can only be one of two values, such as **True** or **False**. You should consider using a different conditional statement when a variable can have one of many different values.

For more information, see *If...Then Statements*, page 145.

D. **For...Next**

Incorrect

The **For...Next** statement is used for looping, not testing, values of variables. Consider the **If...Then** or **Select...Case** conditional statements for this operation.

For more information, see *For...Next Statement*, page 151.

2. **In the statement, "If X < Y Then blnCheck = True" and X=5 and Y=3, what is the value of blnCheck?**

A. blnCheck is set to **True**.

Incorrect

Because the value of X is not less than Y, the value of blnCheck will not be set to **True**.

B. blnCheck is set to **False**.

Incorrect

Regardless of the outcome of this statement, blnCheck will not be set to **False**. It can only potentially be set to **True**.

C. The value of blnCheck remains unchanged.

Correct

Since the value of X is not less than Y, the value of blnCheck will remain unchanged.

D. The value of blnCheck is unknown.

Incorrect

Based on the **If...Then** statement, the value of blnCheck will be set to **True**, **False**, or remain unchanged.

For more information, see *Comparison and Logical Operators*, page 142.

3. When it is known how many times a set of statements should be executed, use the:

A. **Do...Loop** structure.

Incorrect

Consider using a Do...Loop when the number of times a statement should be executed is unknown.

B. **Loop Until** structure.

Incorrect

The **Loop Until** statement should be used when the number of times a statement should be executed is unknown.

C. **For...Next** structure.

Correct

When the number of times to execute a loop is known (or can be calculated), use the **For...Next** statement. The other looping structures use a conditional statement to determine whether to execute or not and can loop indeterminately until a set condition is reached.

D. **While...Wend** structure.

Incorrect

The **While...Wend** statement should be used when the number of times a statement should be executed is unknown.

For more information, see *Using Do...Loop Structures*, page 152.

Chapter 6

1. **To cause a Visual Basic program to enter Break mode when a value changes, use:**

   A. A **Stop** statement.

   Incorrect

   A **Stop** statement is used to enter break mode regardless of the current state of any variable or object.

   For more information, see *Using a Stop Statement*, page 169.

   B. A breakpoint.

   Incorrect

   Setting a break point is a good way to stop an application at a particular line of code or statement. However, when a break point is reached, your program will stop executing regardless of any condition.

   For more information, see *Setting Breakpoints*, page 169.

   C. A **Debug.Break** statement.

   Incorrect

   Although you can use a **Debug.Assert** statement to cause your application to enter Break mode when an expression evaluates to **False,** the Debug.Break statement does not exist in Visual Basic.

   For more information, see *Break Mode*, page 167.

   D. A watch expression.

   Correct

   The easiest way to enter Break mode when a certain variable changes is by setting a watch expression for the variable. Breakpoints cannot be set so they are conditional on a value changing.

   For more information, see *Overview of the Watch Window*, page 172.

2. **The scope of the Immediate window is:**

   A. Limited to the current procedure.

   Correct

   The scope of the Immediate window is limited to the current procedure only. This includes any local variables declared within the current procedure, module variables declared within the current code module, and global variables. Any variables or properties out of this scope are not displayed.

B. Limited to the current module.

Incorrect

The scope of the Immediate window is actually limited to a lower level than the current module. This means that the scope is actually *smaller* than a form, code, or class module.

C. Limited to the current form.

Incorrect

It would not be accurate to say that the scope of the Immediate window is limited to the current form. The immediate window can be used in modules other than form modules, which also makes this answer incorrect.

D. Global.

Incorrect

The scope of the Immediate Window is not global. Its scope is actually limited to a much lower level.

For more information, see *Using the Immediate Window*, page 176.

3. The output of a Debug.Print statement is sent to:

A. The default printer.

Incorrect

The **Printer** object's **Print** method sends output to the default printer. However, the this is not true when using the **Debug.Print** statement.

B. The Immediate window.

Correct

The **Debug** object's **Print** method sends output to the Immediate window so that tracking of variable values can be accomplished during run-time.

C. The Call Stack.

Incorrect

The Call Stack feature creates a list of procedures that trace the flow of code through multiple active procedure calls. However, this has nothing to do with using the **Debug.Print** Statement.

D. The txtDebug variable.

Incorrect

The **Debug.Print** statement will not assign a value to a variable.

For more information, see *Using the Debug.Print Statement*, page 179.

Chapter 7

1. Which of the following returns the value of the selected item in a combo box?

A. strSelection = cboCustomer.Text

Correct

The proper syntax for returning a string from a combo box is: *stringvariable = combobox*.Text. (This is sometimes confused with returning a string from a listbox - *stringvariable = simplelistbox*.List(*simplelistbox*.ListIndex).)

B. strSelection = cboCustomer.IndexItem

Incorrect

A combo box control does not have an **IndexItem** property.

C. cboCustomer.ListIndex = strSelection

Incorrect

If you set the **ListIndex** property to a string value, a type mismatch run-time error will occur. The **ListIndex** property will return or sets the index of the currently selected item in the control, but will not return the text value for the currently selected item.

D. cboCustomer.strSelection

Incorrect

cboCustomer.strSelection is not a valid statement. In addition, a combo box control does not have a strSelection property or method.

For more information, see *Setting or Returning the Current Selection*, page 199.

2. In the following example, what happens if no item is selected in the list?

```
lstRegions.RemoveItem  lstRegions.ListIndex
```

A. The first item is removed.

Incorrect

The first item in a list will remain if no item is selected when the **RemoveItem** method is invoked.

B. The last item is removed.

Incorrect

The last item in a list will not be removed if no item is selected when the **RemoveItem** method is invoked.

C. The last item added to the list is removed.

Incorrect

If no item is selected in a list when the **RemoveItem** method is invoked, the last item added to the list will not be removed.

D. None of the above.

Correct

If no item is selected, an error occurs and no items are removed from the list. Before using the **RemoveItem** method, check to ensure at least one item is selected.

For more information, see *Removing Items from a List*, page 200.

3. When several option buttons are grouped into a container:

A. Only one can be selected at a time.

Correct

OptionButton controls grouped within a container (form, **Frame** control, or **PictureBox** control) allow the user to select one option from the group. When an option is clicked, all other option buttons within the group are cleared.

B. Multiple options can be selected at a time.

Incorrect

Multiple items can be selected when using grouped **CheckBox** controls, however this is not true when using **OptionButton** controls.

C. The value property of the container is **True** when an option is selected.

Incorrect

Property values of the container control do not effect whether or not **OptionButton** controls are mutually exclusive.

D. None of the above.

Incorrect

One of the above answers is correct.

For more information, see *Using OptionButton and Frame Controls*, page 203.

Chapter 8

1. Rows are often referred to as _____, and columns are referred to as _____.

A. primary keys, foreign keys

Incorrect

A primary key is used to identify a specific record in a table. A foreign key is used to identify a record in a related table.

B. tables, keys

Incorrect

A table consists of rows and columns. There are two types of keys: primary and foreign. A primary key is used to identify a specific record within a table. A foreign key is used to identify a record in a related table.

C. fields, records

Incorrect

A record consists of one or more fields. For example, an employee record might contain a first name, last name, and social security field.

D. records, fields

Correct

Each row in a table is considered a record which contains one or more columns. Each column or field contains a specific attribute for each record or row.

For more information, see *Relational Database Concepts*, page 226.

2. When using the ADO Data control, changes to a record are updated when:

A. A different record is accessed.

Correct

Moving off a record updates the database with any changes made, similar to the **Update** function.

B. The **AddNew** method is used.

Incorrect

The **AddNew** method will create a new, initialized record. After the **AddNew** method is used, the **Update** method must be used in order to save the new record.

C. The **Refresh** method for the **ADO Data** control must be invoked.

Incorrect

The **Refresh** method of the **ADO Data** control will cause the control to be repainted on the form, but will not cause the current record to be updated.

D. The **RecordSource** property is changed.

Incorrect

The **RecordSource** property is a table name or SQL query that defines the records included in a recordset. This property is not used to update a record.

For more information, see *Modifying and Updating Records*, page 239.

3. What does the following code statement do?

```
adcEmployees.Recordset.Bookmark = varCurrentRecord
```

A. Moves the record pointer to the record position stored in the varCurrentRecord variable

Correct

Using the **Bookmark** property, you can save the current position in a database. By setting the record position equal to a saved bookmark, the record pointer can be restored to a previous position.

B. Makes the current record equal to the value of the varCurrentRecord variable

Incorrect

In order to use the Bookmark property effectively, you must first save the value of the **Bookmark** property. You do not assign the value of a variable to a record in a recordset.

C. Sets a bookmark at the current record

Incorrect

To save the current record location, you assign the **Bookmark** property value to a variable.

D. None of the above

Incorrect

Using the Bookmark property, you can save the current position in a database. By setting the record position equal to a saved bookmark, the record pointer can be restored to a previous position.

For more information, see *Searching for Records*, page 241.

Chapter 9

1. How do you make a text box read-only?

A. Set the **MaxLength** property to 0.

Incorrect

The **MaxLength** property of a text box is set to zero by default. This setting does not impose a limit to the number of characters a user can enter into a text box.

B. Set the **Cancel** property to **True**.

Incorrect

A text box control does not have a **Cancel** property. The **Cancel** property is used to invoke a command button's click event when the user presses the ESC key.

C. Set the **Locked** property to **True**.

Correct

The **Locked** property determines if users can modify the data in a text box. If **Locked** is set to **True**, users can view data in the text box, but they cannot edit it.

D. Set the **Enabled** property to **True**.

Incorrect

Setting the **Enabled** property to **True** will allow the user to move to the field. Setting **Enabled** to **False** is one way to make the control read-only.

For more information, see *Using Text Box Properties to Restrict Data Entry*, page 259.

2. What occurs if a user enters an invalid character in a Masked Edit control?

A. The invalid character is not accepted and the program continues.

Incorrect

An event occurs if the user types an invalid character in a control. This can be used to provide some feedback to the user to indicate the problem.

For more information, see *Using the Masked Edit Control*, page 259.

B. The invalid character is not accepted and a **ValidationError** event occurs.

Correct

A **ValidationError** event occurs if the user types an invalid character in a control. This can be used to provide some feedback to the user to indicate the problem.

For more information, see *The ValidationError Event*, page 262.

C. The invalid character is accepted, but the program ends.

Incorrect

A program will not end as a result of a user typing an invalid character into a **Masked Edit** control.

For more information, see *Using the Masked Edit Control*, page 259.

D. The invalid character is accepted and a **ValidationError** event occurs.

Incorrect

An invalid character will not be accepted in a **Masked Edit** control.

For more information, see *Using the Masked Edit Control*, page 259.

3. Setting the KeyPreview property to True allows:

A. The key to be displayed but not used in a mask.

Incorrect

The **KeyPreview** property does not have anything to do with an input mask.

B. The form to receive keyboard events before the active control.

Correct

If the **KeyPreview** property is set to **True**, the form receives the keyboard event before the event occurs on the control. If the **KeyPreview** property of a form is set to **False**, the form does not receive keyboard events unless there are no enabled controls on a form.

C. The key press to be trapped by the control before it is displayed.
Incorrect

If the **KeyPreview** property is set to **True**, a **KeyPress** event procedure will not run for the control before the form's **KeyPress** event procedure.

D. None of the above.
Incorrect

One of the above answers is correct.

For more information, see *A Form-Level Keyboard Handler*, page 263.

Chapter 10

1. If an error-handling routine is not enabled and a run-time error occurs:

A. The program continues execution but might provide unexpected results.
Incorrect

Program execution will not continue if an unhandled run-time error occurs.

B. The program continues execution and passes the error code to the current form module's **Unload** event.
Incorrect

The unload event will not occur as a result of a run-time error. In addition, a run-time error will stop program execution.

C. The program stops execution and displays the cause of the error.
Correct

If an error occurs that is not trapped by an error-handling routine, program execution stops and an error message displays.

D. The program stops execution without displaying the cause of the error.
Incorrect

If a run-time error occurs in your application, an error message will be displayed containing information including the error description and error number.

For more information, see *Overview of the Error Handling Process*, page 274.

2. If an error occurs in a procedure after the statement On Error GoTo 0:

A. The error handling routine at the label 0 executes.

Incorrect

The **On Error GoTo 0** statement disables the current error trap, and does not force execution to a label.

B. The generic Visual Basic error handling routine processes the error, allowing continued execution.

Incorrect

Visual Basic does not have a generic error handling routine. In order to handle run-time errors, you must implement error traps.

C. Execution continues at the line following the error.

Incorrect

The **On Error Resume Next** statement will allow your application to continue processing at the line of code following the line that caused a run-time error. The **On Error GoTo 0** statement is used for a different purpose.

D. Execution stops and an error message appears.

Correct

The **On Error GoTo 0** statement disables the current error trap. This means any error occurring stops the program execution and displays an error message.

For more information, see *Implementing an Error Trap*, page 276.

3. When writing error handling code for a procedure, which of the following statements causes execution to continue on the line following the error in the procedure?

A. Resume

Incorrect

The **Resume** statement returns to the statement that caused the error, allowing an operation to be repeated after correcting the error.

B. Resume Next

Correct

The **Resume Next** statement returns to the statement immediately following the one that caused the error. The **Resume** statement returns to the statement that caused the error, allowing an operation to be repeated after correcting the error.

C. Resume *line*

Incorrect

When you use **Resume** *line*, execution resumes at line specified in the required line argument. The line argument is a line label or line number and must be in the same procedure as the error handler.

D. Resume After Error

Incorrect

The **Resume After Error** statement does not exist in Visual Basic.

For more information, see *Introduction to Error Handling*, page 274.

Chapter 11

1. To display a custom pop-up menu:

A. Modify a system pop-up menu.

Incorrect

Although you could modify a system pop-up menu using the Windows API, this would not be the same as creating a custom pop-up menu in Visual Basic.

B. Add label controls to the form and set the **Menu** property to **True**.

Incorrect

Placing controls on a form has nothing to do with creating a custom pop-up menu. In addition, a label control does not have a **Menu** property.

C. Use the form's **PopupMenu** method.

Correct

Popup menus are created using the Menu Editor. Once the menu is created, call the form's **PopupMenu** method to display it. You may set the Menu's **Visible** property to **False** to prevent the pop-up menu from being displayed on the menu bar.

D. Create a menu control array.

Incorrect

It is not possible to create an array of menus or menu control array in Visual Basic.

For more information, see *Pop-Up Menus*, page 299.

2. Which of the following code statements changes the contents of the simple status bar named "StatusBar" to read "Input error - press F1 for Help."?

   A. "Input error - press F1 for Help" = StatusBar.Text

      Incorrect

      A status bar control does not have a **Text** property. In addition, you can assign literal values to a property, but you cannot set a literal value equal to a property value.

   B. StatusBar.Caption = "Input error - press F1 for Help"

      Incorrect

      A status bar control does not have a **Caption** property.

   C. StatusBar.SimpleText = "Input error - press F1 for Help"

      Correct

      When the status bar contains only one pane (the **Style** property is set to sbrSimple), the text can be set using the **SimpleText** property: *StatusBar*.SimpleText = "*Text string*".

   D. StatusBar.Panels(Single).Caption = "Input error - press F1 for Help"

      Incorrect

      A **Panel** object in the **Panels** collection for a status bar control does not have a **Caption** property.

For more information, see *Status Bars*, page 301.

3. Images for a toolbar's buttons are:

   A. Loaded dynamically from the toolbar .ocx file.

      Incorrect

      The Mscomctl.ocx file does not contain images for the **Toolbar** control.

   B. Loaded dynamically from the toolbar .dll file.

      Incorrect

      There are no .dll files associated with the **Toolbar** control that contain button images.

   C. Automatically attached to the toolbar button based on function.

      Incorrect

      Images are not automatically assigned to buttons on a **Toolbar** control by Visual Basic.

D. Maintained in a separate **ImageList** control.

Correct

The **Toolbar** control contains a collection of **Button** objects. The picture for each button is stored in a separate **ImageList** control. The **ImageList** control contains a collection of **ListImage** objects, or pictures, which can be referred to by their **Index** or **Key** properties.

For more information, see *Toolbars*, page 303.

Chapter 12

1. A control with its DragMode property set to vbAutomatic can be dragged:

A. Whenever one of the control's procedures is executing.

Incorrect

If **DragMode** is set to vbAutomatic, the control can be dragged when one of the control's event procedures is executing. However, the ability for a control to be dragged is not exclusive to when an event procedure for the control is executing.

B. Whenever one of the control's procedures is not executing.

Incorrect

If **DragMode** is set to vbAutomatic, the control can be dragged when one of the control's event procedures is not executing. However, the ability for a control to be dragged is not exclusive to whether or not an event procedure is executing.

C. Anytime.

Correct

If **DragMode** is set to vbAutomatic, the user can drag the control at any time and Visual Basic displays an outline of the control as it is being dragged.

D. Never.

Incorrect

Setting the control's **DragMode** property to vbAutomatic allows the control to be dragged and dropped.

For more information, see *Dragging Controls*, page 317.

2. To drop a control programmatically:

A. Use the **vbEndDrag** constant with the control's **Drag** method.

Correct

Releasing the mouse button always stops dragging. Programmatically, a control is dropped by using: Object.Drag vbEndDrag.

B. Set the control's **Stop** property to True.

Incorrect

There is no **Stop** property associated with drag-and-drop operations.

C. Set the control's **Drop** property to True.

Incorrect

There is no **Drop** property associated with drag-and-drop operations.

D. Set the control's **DragMode** property to vbAutomatic.

Incorrect

Setting the **DragMode** property to vbAutomatic allows manual drag-and-drop operations using the mouse. This does not programmatically cause a drop.

For more information, see *Dropping Controls*, page 318.

3. In an application, dragging a PictureBox control appears to work except that when the mouse is released, the PictureBox control remains at its original position. What is wrong?

A. **PictureBox** controls cannot be moved by using the drag-and-drop feature with Visual Basic.

Incorrect

PictureBox controls can be dragged and dropped in Visual Basic.

B. There is no code in the application to move the control.

Correct

When the user drops the source control onto the target, the **DragDrop** event occurs. There are no default actions for the **DragDrop** event, so you must place code in this event to move the control to its new position.

C. The **DragMode** property is not set to vbAutomatic.

Incorrect

Setting the **DragMode** property does not affect whether the control is actually moved when a drop operation is performed.

D. The **DragDrop** source control is hanging.

Incorrect

The source control must have code associated with it to move the control when it is dropped.

For more information, see *Dropping Controls*, page 318.

Chapter 13

1. To create a control array:

A. Set the **Index** property for the control(s) by using the Properties window.

Incorrect

Although you can set the **Index** property by using the Properties window to create a control array, this is not the best answer.

B. Give two controls of the same type the same name.

Incorrect

You can create a control array by giving two controls the same name. (They must have the same type.) Visual Basic automatically creates a control array and gives these controls the indexes 0 and 1. However, this is not the best answer, and is not the only way to create a control array.

C. Copy and paste a control.

Incorrect

If you copy and paste a control on a form, Visual Basic will ask you if you want to create a control array. This is the easiest way to create a control array, however it is not the best answer.

D. Do all of the above.

Correct

Control arrays are created at design time in three ways:

- Set the **Index** property by using the Properties window.

- Give two controls the same name. (They must have the same type.) Visual Basic automatically creates a control array and gives these controls the indexes 0 and 1.

- Copy and paste a control.

For more information, see *Creating a Control Array*, page 339.

2. A statement in your program loads a new control in an array, but when the program runs the control does not appear. What is the most probable cause?

A. Dynamically loaded controls are invisible by default. Set the control's **Visible** property to **True**.

Correct

When loading controls in a control array, the **Load** statement copies all the property settings from the lowest existing element in the array except for the **Visible, Index,** and **TabIndex** properties. The **Visible** property defaults to **False**. To display a control in a control array, set the **Visible** property to **True**.

B. Controls in an array must load before the **Form_Load** event. Change the code to load the controls in the **Form_Initialize** event.

Incorrect

Controls cannot be loaded in a form's **Initialize** event, but can be loaded in the form's **Load** event.

C. Dynamically loaded controls must be declared in the General Declarations code.

Incorrect

Control variables do not have to be declared in the General Declarations section of a module.

D. Visual Basic 6.0 no longer supports dynamically loaded controls.

Incorrect

Visual Basic 6.0 not only supports control arrays to add controls at run time, but also includes the new dynamic control addition feature to programmatically add or remove controls to or from a form.

For more information, see *Creating Controls Dynamically*, page 342.

3. What does the following code segment do?

```
Dim ctl As Control

For Each ctl In Me.Controls
    If TypeOf ctl Is CommandButton Then
        ctl.Enabled = False
    End If
Next
```

A. Disables all command buttons on the current form

Correct

This code sample determines the number of controls on the current form using the **For Each...Next** loop structure, which repeats a group of statements for each element in a collection. It then uses the **TypeOf** keyword to determine whether the current control is a command button. If it is, the command button is disabled. This process is continued until all of the command buttons on the current form are disabled.

B. Disables all but the last command button on the current form

Incorrect

The last command button on the form will be disabled within the loop structure, however it will not be the only control disabled.

C. Disables all command buttons in the project

Incorrect

Although the code will disable command buttons, it will not cause each command button in the project to become disabled.

D. Disables all but the last command button in the project

Incorrect

Each command button that is in the specified collection will be disabled, however this does not include controls outside of that collection.

For more information, see *Working with Collections*, page 335.

Chapter 14

1. Which of the following statements best describes how forms should be used to interact with users?

A. Modal interactions provide flexibility to the user and should be used more often than modeless interactions.

Incorrect

Modal interactions require the user to complete one task before continuing on with a different task. This type of interaction does not provide flexibility to the user because the user cannot switch between various forms.

B. Modal interactions provide flexibility to the user and should be used just as often as modeless interactions.

Incorrect

Modal interactions require the user to complete one task before continuing on with a different task. This type of interaction does not provide flexibility to the user because the user cannot switch between various forms. Modal interactions should not be used as frequently as modeless interactions.

C. Modeless interactions provide flexibility to the user and should be used more often than modal interactions.

Correct

Modal interactions require the user to complete one task before continuing on with a different task. Modeless interactions allow the user to move freely between one task and another without fully completing one of them. As a general rule, your applications should minimize modal interactions, but each type of interaction can be effective in certain situations.

D. Modeless interactions provide flexibility to the user and should be used just as often as modal interactions.

Incorrect

Modal interactions should not be used as frequently as modeless interactions because they require the user to complete one task before continuing on with a different task.

For more information, see *User Interface Design Principles*, page 352.

2. Which of the following is not a valid way to start the Package and Deployment Wizard?

A. On the **File** menu in Visual Basic, click **Package and Deployment Wizard**.

Correct

There are three ways you can start the Package and Deployment Wizard:

1. Run from within Visual Basic as an add-in.

2. Run it as a stand-alone component from outside the development environment.

3. Run it in silent mode by launching it from a command prompt.

B. Run it as a stand-alone component from outside the development environment.

Incorrect

It is possible to run the Package and Deployment Wizard from outside the development environment.

C. Run it from within Visual Basic as an add-in.

Incorrect

You can use the Package and Deployment Wizard from within Visual Basic, however you may first need to load it from the Add-In Manager.

D. Run it in silent mode by launching it from a command prompt.

Incorrect

You may package and deploy your project files in silent mode by running the PDCmdLn.exe from an MS-DOS prompt. In silent mode, the wizard runs without your having to attend it to make choices and move through screens. For more information about starting the Package and Deployment Wizard in silent mode, search for "Running the Wizard in Silent Mode" in MSDN Help.

For more information, see *Distributing an Application*, page 358.

3. The easiest way to distribute your application is to:

A. Copy all of the files in the project folder to a floppy disk.

Incorrect

In order to properly install your application, some files have to be registered with Windows. Therefore, copying the program files to a floppy disk is not a solution.

B. Compile your application and copy the .exe file to a floppy disk.

Incorrect

Most applications require more than the .exe file in order to run. Typically there are run-time DLLs and custom controls that must be installed along with the .exe, and they must be registered in Windows.

C. Create an installation program by using the Package and Deployment Wizard.

   Correct

   The easiest way to distribute your application is to use the Package and Deployment Wizard provided with Visual Basic. The Package and Deployment Wizard examines your application for all of the necessary files (including the run-time .dll and .ocx files in other folders), compiles the project, and creates the distribution files and Setup program.

D. Create a separate executable file in Visual Basic that installs your project folder.

   Incorrect

   Installing the application's .exe file and copying the application's project folder does not allow you to distribute your application.

For more information, see *Deploying an Application*, page 362.

Appendix B:
Lab Hints

Lab Hint 1.1

This code draws a circle with a random fill color and fill style as the user moves the mouse pointer across the form.

Lab Hint 2.1

When the **OK** button is clicked, a message box displays the values entered into the **User Name** and **Password** textboxes.

Pressing the Enter key triggers the **OK** button's **Click** event. This occurs because the **OK** button's **Default** property is set to **True**.

Lab Hint 2.2

When the **Cancel** button is clicked, the message "This is the Cancel button." appears.

Pressing the Esc key triggers the **Cancel** button's **Click** event. This occurs because the **Cancel** button's **Cancel** property is set to **True**.

Lab Hint 2.3

The **OK** button should remain disabled until text is entered into both the **User Name** and **Password** text boxes.

Lab Hint 2.4

When the application starts, the graphic that was selected in the **Picture** property of the **Image** control at design time is displayed.

Clicking the **Image** control calls the **LoadPicture** function and changes the picture in the **Image** control.

Lab Hint 3.1

```
Private Sub Form_Load()
      frmLogon.Show vbModal
End Sub
```

Lab Hint 3.2

A message box appears, but the Logon form remains open. The code that will remove the Logon form has not been added to the **Click** event of the **OK** button.

Lab Hint 3.3

A message box appears showing the user name and password. When the message box is closed the Main form appears. When the **Done** button is clicked, the Main form is unloaded and the application ends.

Lab Hint 4.1

```
'Constant below is declared in the
'general declaration section of the form
Private Const CONV_PERIOD As Integer = 12

Public Function MonthlyPayment() As Double
  Dim dblMonthRate As Double
  Dim intNumPayments As Integer
  Dim dblLoanAmt As Double

  dblLoanAmt = CDbl(txtPurchase.Text)
  intNumPayments = 30 * CONV_PERIOD
  dblMonthRate = 0.065/CONV_PERIOD

  MonthlyPayment = Pmt(Rate:=dblMonthRate, NPer:=intNumPayments,
PV:=-dblLoanAmt)
End Function
```

Lab Hint 5.1

```
Private Sub Form_Load()
Static sintLogonAttempts As Integer
frmLogon.Show vbModal
Do Until frmLogon.txtPassword.TEXT = PASSWORD
sintLogonAttempts = sintLogonAttempts + 1
MsgBox prompt:="You have typed an invalid password.", _
       buttons:=vbOKOnly + vbInformation
frmLogon.txtPassword.Text = ""
frmLogon.Show vbModal
Loop
End Sub
```

Lab Hint 5.2

The Logon form reappears if an invalid password is entered. After entering the correct password, the Main form appears.

Lab Hint 6.1

Four procedures should be displayed.

Lab Hint 6.2

Use breakpoints and add a watch expression to find the error.

Lab Hint 7.1

It is a good habit to initialize the controls on a form in the **Form_Load** event. This centralizes the initialization code and is often easier than trying to set all the appropriate properties at design time.

Lab Hint 7.2

The finished code segment should look something like this:

```
txtPurchase.Text = "0.0"
cboRate.Text = "4.25"
optLength(0).Value = True
optLength_Click 0
```

Lab Hint 9.1

```
Private Sub cmdMonthly_Click()
    Dim dblMonthly As Double
    If IsNumeric(txtPurchase.Text) Then
        'Calculate the monthly payment
        dblMonthly = MonthlyPayment()
        MsgBox "Your monthly payments will be: " & _
            Format(dblMonthly, "currency")
    Else
        MsgBox "The purchase price must be a numeric value."
        With txtPurchase
            .SetFocus
            .SelStart = 0
            .SelLength = Len(.Text)
        End With
    End If
End SubLab Hint 10.1
```

The error number is Runtime Error '13'. The description of this error is Type
mismatch. The value in the calculation isn't of the correct type. For example, if a
calculation requires a double value, it can't accept a string value unless the whole
string can be recognized as a double.

Lab Hint 10.2

```
Public Function MonthlyPayment() As Double
On Error GoTo Err_MonthlyPayment
   Dim dblRate As Double
   Dim dblMonthRate As Double
   Dim intNumPayments As Integer
   Dim dblLoanAmt As Double

   'convert the purchase price to a Double value
   dblLoanAmt = CDbl(txtPurchase.Text)

   'retrieve the interest rate and convert to a
   'double percentage
   dblRate = CDbl(cboRate.Text) / 100

   'Calculate the number of payments and the
   'monthly interest rate
   intNumPayments = mintLength * CONV_PERIOD
   dblMonthRate = dblRate / CONV_PERIOD

   'calculate monthly payment
   MonthlyPayment = Pmt(Rate:=dblMonthRate, NPer:=intNumPayments,
PV:=-dblLoanAmt)

   Exit Function

Err_MonthlyPayment:
   Select Case Err.Number
     Case 13
         MsgBox "Not all data was entered. " & _
             "The values shown will be incorrect. " & _
             vbCrLf & "Fill in all the fields and try again."
     Case Else
         MsgBox "Unknown error. Number : " & Err.Number & vbCrLf & _
             Err.Description
   End Select

End Function
```

Lab Hint 10.3

If no interest rate is selected, a message box is displayed advising the user, "Not all data was entered. The values shown will be incorrect. Fill in all the fields and try again." The application will continue to run.

Lab Hint 10.4

```
Private Function RunApp(App As String) As Boolean
On Error Resume Next
  Shell App, vbNormalFocus
  If Err.Number <> 0 Then
    RunApp = False
  Else
    RunApp = True
  End If
End Function
```

Lab Hint 12.1

```
Select Case State
    Case vbEnter
        Source.DragIcon = imgValid.Picture
    Case vbLeave
        Source.DragIcon = imgInvalid.Picture
End Select
```

Lab Hint 12.2

The file name selected from the file list is added to the list box.

Lab Hint 12.3

```
Dim strDir As String

If TypeOf Source Is FileListBox Then
  strDir = dirDirectories.Path
  If Right(strDir, 1) = "\" Then
      lstTarget.AddItem strDir & Source.FileName
  Else
      lstTarget.AddItem strDir & "\" & Source.FileName
  End If
End If
```

Lab Hint 13.1

```
Dim intIndex As Integer
For intIndex = 1 To (mintMaxSpeakers - 1)
Load hsbVolume(intIndex)
Load chkMute(intIndex)
Load lblLevel(intIndex)
hsbVolume(intIndex).Top = hsbVolume(intIndex - 1).Top + 400
chkMute(intIndex).Top = chkMute(intIndex - 1).Top + 400
lblLevel(intIndex).Top = lblLevel(intIndex - 1).Top + 400
hsbVolume(intIndex).Visible = True
chkMute(intIndex).Visible = True
lblLevel(intIndex).Visible = True
Next intIndex
```

Lab Hint 13.2

```
Private Sub chkMute_Click(Index As Integer)
    If chkMute(Index).Value = vbChecked Then
        hsbVolume(Index).Enabled = False
        lblLevel(Index).Caption = "0"
    Else
        hsbVolume(Index).Enabled = True
        lblLevel(Index).Caption = hsbVolume(Index).Value
    End If
End Sub
```

Lab Hint 14.1

Question 1: The application has been removed from the menu.

Question 2: The folder for the program has been removed.

Glossary

action query

A query that copies or changes data. Action queries include append, delete, make-table, and update. Delete and update queries change existing data; append and make-table queries move existing data. In contrast, select queries return data records. An SQL pass-through query may also be an action query.

ActiveX

The Microsoft brand name for the technologies that enable interoperability by using the Component Object Model (COM).

ActiveX component

The physical file (for example, .exe, .dll, .ocx) that contains classes, which are definitions of objects. You can use these objects in your Visual Basic application.

ActiveX control

An object that you place on a form to enable or enhance a user's interaction with an application. ActiveX controls have events and can be incorporated into other controls. These controls have a .ocx file name extension.

ActiveX document

A Visual Basic application that can be viewed in another container provided by an application, such as Microsoft Internet Explorer version 3.0 or later or Microsoft Office Binder. Forms created with Visual Basic can be easily converted into ActiveX documents by using the Visual Basic ActiveX Document Migration Wizard.

ActiveX scripting

A Microsoft technology for hosting scripts in Microsoft Internet Explorer and other browsers. The technology uses COM to connect third party scripts to Internet Explorer without regard to language and other elements of implementation.

add-in

A customized tool that adds capabilities to the Visual Basic development environment. You select available add-ins by using the **Add-In Manager** dialog box, which is accessible from the **Add-Ins** menu.

application programming interface (API)

The set of commands that an application uses to request and carry out lower-level services performed by a computer's operating system.

application project

A Visual Basic project that will be made into a .exe file.

asynchronous call

A function call where the caller does not wait for the reply.

asynchronous processing

A type of I/O in which some file I/O functions return immediately, even though an I/O request is still pending. This enables an application to continue with other processing and wait for the I/O to finish at a later time.

In asynchronous mode, the client issues a request but continues processing until a response is returned. The client may issue multiple requests and can field them in whatever order they return. Asynchronous communications are network independent, and clients can issue requests even if the network or remote system is down.

asynchronous query

A type of query in which SQL queries return immediately, even though the results are still pending. This enables an application to continue with other processing while the query is pending completion.

bind

To associate two pieces of information with one another, most often used in terms of binding a symbol (such as the name of a variable) with some descriptive information (such as a memory address, a data type, or an actual value).

binding

The process of putting an object into a running state so that operations (such as edit or play) supplied by the object's application can be invoked. The type of binding determines the speed by which an object's methods are accessed by using the object variable. See also *early bound*, *late bound*.

bound control

A data-aware control that can provide access to a specific column or columns in a data source. A data-aware control can be bound to a data source through its **DataSource, DataMember** and **DataField** properties. When a data source moves from one row to the next, all bound controls connected to the data source change to display data from columns in the current row.

browse

To walk through data a record or row at a time.

browse back

A button, which looks like <<.

browse forward

A button, which looks like >>.

browse sequence

The order in which topics are displayed when user clicks the >> button (forward) or the << button (backward).

browser

Software that interprets HTML, formats it into Web pages, and displays it to the user. Some browsers can also contain ActiveX components, and make it possible to play sound or video files.

by reference

A way of passing the address of an argument to a procedure instead of passing the value. This allows the procedure to access the actual variable. As a result, the variable's actual value can be changed by the procedure to which it is passed. Unless otherwise specified, arguments are passed by reference.

by value

A way of passing the value, rather than the address, of an argument to a procedure. This allows the procedure to access a copy of the variable. As a result, the variable's actual value can't be changed by the procedure to which it is passed.

calling convention

The coding convention used to make a function call.

class

The formal definition of an object. The class acts as the template from which an instance of an object is created at run time. The class defines the properties of the object and the methods used to control the object's behavior.

class factory

An object that implements the **IClassFactory** interface, which allows it to create other objects of a specific class.

class factory table

A list of registered class factory objects for specific class identifiers (CLSID), where a server for each CLSID is currently running.

class identifier (CLSID)

A unique identifier (UUID) that identifies an object. An object registers its CLSID in the system registration database so that it can be loaded and programmed by other applications.

class name

Defines the type of an object. Applications that support Automation fully qualify class names using either of the following syntaxes: application.objecttype.version or objecttype.version, where application is the name of the application that supplies the object, objecttype is the object's name as defined in the object library, and version is the version number of the object or application that supplies the object, e.g., Excel.Sheet.5.

class of an object
The class or type of an Automation object (for example, **Application**, **WorkSheet**, **Toolbar**).

client
Any application or component that accesses or otherwise makes use of services provided by components.

client batch cursor library
A library that provides client-side cursor support for database applications. This library supports all four types of cursors (keyset, static, dynamic, and forward-only) and provides a number of other features including the ability to dissociate connections and perform optimistic batch updates.

client/server
A term generally applied to a software architecture in which processing functions are segmented into independent collections of services and requesters on a single machine or segmented among several machines. One or more processing servers provide a set of services to other clients on the same or across multiple platforms. A server completely encapsulates its processing and presents a well-defined interface for clients.

code component
A .exe or .dll file that provides objects created from one of the classes that the component provides. Formerly server and Automation server.

code module
A module containing public code that can be shared among all modules in a project. A code module is referred to as a standard module in later versions of Visual Basic.

code signing
A means to certify that code downloaded over the Internet has not been tampered with. Also known as digital signing.

collection
An object that contains a set of related objects. For example, a collection named **Tax Preparation Objects** might contain the names of objects such as **EndOfYear**, **RoyaltyCalc**, and **ExemptionCalc**. An object's position in the collection can change whenever a change occurs in the collection; therefore, the position of any specific object in the collection may vary.

collection object
A grouping of exposed objects. You create collection objects when you want to address multiple occurrences of an object as a unit, such as when you want to draw a set of points.

column
The visual representation of a field in a grid. A column defines the data type, size, and other attributes of one field of a row (record) of data. All columns taken as a set define a row (record) in the database. An individual column contains data related in type and purpose throughout the table; that is, a column's definition doesn't change from row to row.

COM

See *Component Object Model.*

component

Any software that supports Automation, meaning it can be used programmatically in a custom solution. This includes **ActiveX** controls (.ocx files), ActiveX documents, and ActiveX code components.

Component Object Model (COM)

An industry-standard architecture for object-oriented development. The Component Object Model defines interfaces on which ActiveX components are built.

connection string

A string used to define the source of data for a database.

consistent

The state of a multiple-table **Recordset** object that allows you to only perform updates that result in a consistent view of the data. For example, in a **Recordset** that is a join of two or more tables (a one-to-many relationship), a consistent query would not allow you to set the many-side key to a value that isn't in the one-side table.

control

A file in a Visual Basic project with an .ocx file name extension that is associated with a visible interface. **Grid** and **CommonDialog** are examples of controls.

control array

A group of controls that share a common name, type, and event procedures. Each control in an array has a unique index number that can be used to determine which control recognizes an event.

create an instance

To create an instance of a class (instantiate), allocating and initializing an object's data structures in memory.

cursor

This keeps track of the driver's position in the result set. The cursor is so named because it indicates the current position in the result set, just as the cursor on a CRT screen indicates current position. Cursors let the user scroll through and update a result set with fewer restrictions than browse mode.

data access object (DAO)

An object that is defined by the Microsoft Jet database engine. You use data access objects, such as the **Database**, **TableDef**, **Recordset** and **QueryDef** objects, to represent objects that are used to organize and manipulate data in code.

Data control

A built-in Visual Basic control used to connect a Visual Basic application with a selected data source. Bound controls require use of the **Data** control as a source of data.

Data Definition Language (DDL)

The language used to describe attributes of a database, especially tables, fields, indexes and storage strategy.

data services

These support the lowest visible level of abstraction used for the manipulation of data within an application. This support implies the ability to define, maintain, access, and update data. Data services manage and satisfy requests for data generated by business services.

data source

The data the user wants to access and its associated operating system, DBMS, and network platform (if any).

data source name (DSN)

The name of a registered data source.

data type

Visual Basic supports 12 different variable data types. When a variable is used in a Visual Basic program, they can be declared as a specific data type, such as a STRING for better performance.

data-aware

This describes an application or control that is able to connect to a database.

data-definition query

An SQL-specific query that can create, alter, or delete a table, or create or delete an index in a database.

database

A set of data related to a particular topic or purpose. A database contains tables and can also contain queries and indexes as well as table relationships, table and field validation criteria and linkages to external data sources.

Database object

A **Database** object is a logical representation of a physical database. A database is a set of data related to a specific topic or purpose. A database contains tables and can also contain queries and indexes as well as table relationships, table and field validation criteria and linkages to external data sources.

deadlock

An incident when one user has locked a data page and tries to lock another page that is locked by a second user who, in turn, is trying to lock the page that is locked by the first user. While such occurrences are rare, the longer that a record (or file) is locked the greater the chance of a deadly embrace.

declaration

Variables in Visual Basic should be declared before they are used. When a variable is declared it can be assigned a specific data type for better performance.

dependent object

Dependent objects can only be accessed by using a method of a higher-level object. For example, the **Cells** method of the **Microsoft Excel Worksheet** object returns a **Range** object.

early bound

Also called early binding. This is a form of binding where object variables are declared as variables of a specific class. Object references that use early-bound variables usually run faster than those that use late-bound variables. See also *late bound*.

Error statement

A keyword used in **Error Function, Error Statement, On Error Statement. Error** is also a Variant subtype indicating a variable is an error value.

error-handling routine

User-written code that deals with some kinds of errors at run time.

event

An action recognized by an object, such as clicking the mouse or pressing a key, for which you can write code to respond. Events can occur as a result of a user action or program code, or they can be triggered by the system.

event procedure

A procedure automatically invoked in response to an event initiated by the user, program code, or system. Event procedures are private by default.

event-driven

This describes an application that responds to actions initiated by the user or program code, or that are triggered by the system.

exception handling

A server's ability to inform their client in some uniform way that an exception was raised or encountered.

executable code

Code that Visual Basic translates into a specific action at run time, such as carrying out a command or returning a value. In contrast, non-executable code defines variables and constants.

executable file

A Windows-based application that can run outside the development environment. An executable file has a .exe file name extension.

executable statement

A statement that Visual Basic translates into a specific action at run time. Most Visual Basic statements are executable. The main exceptions are declarations, constant definitions, comments, and user-defined type definitions.

explicit declaration

A declaration in which a variable is explicitly declared using **DIM, STATIC, PUBLIC,** or **PRIVATE** statements.

expose

To make available to other applications by using Automation. An exposed object can be a document, a paragraph, a sentence, a graph, and so on.

external database

Either an ODBC database such as SQL Server that resides on a remote server, or one of the external databases such as Btrieve, Paradox, dBase, FoxPro, Microsoft Excel or Microsoft Access.

foreign table

A database table used to contain foreign keys. Generally, you use a foreign table to establish or enforce referential integrity. The foreign table is usually on the many side of a one-to-many relationship. An example of a foreign table is a table of state codes or customer orders.

form code

All the procedures and declarations saved in the same file as a form and its controls.

form module

A file in a Visual Basic project with a .frm file name extension that can contain graphical descriptions of a form; its controls and their property settings; form-level declarations of constants, variables, and external procedures; and event and general procedures.

form-level variable

A variable recognized by all procedures attached to a form.

function pointer

A stored memory location of a function's address.

Function procedure

A procedure that performs a specific task within a Visual Basic program and returns a value. A **Function** procedure begins with a **Function** statement and ends with an **End Function** statement.

general declaration

All modules contain a general code area that allows for variables to be declared and general procedures (functions or subs) to be created. To locate the General Declarations of a module, open the code window for that module and use the **Object** list and **Procedure** list to find General Declarations.

general procedure

A procedure that must be explicitly called by another procedure. In contrast, an event procedure is invoked automatically in response to a user or system action.

GUID

Globally unique identifier used to identify objects and interfaces precisely.

handle

A unique integer value defined by the operating environment and used by a program to identify and access an object, such as a form or control.

IID

See *interface identifier*.

implicit declaration

A declaration that occurs when a variable is used in a procedure without previously declaring its name and type.

incremental rendering

When an image file is delivered over a network, especially the Internet, the performance of the delivery is affected by bandwidth. Incremental rendering is a process whereby the image is shown immediately to the user, but is blurry. As the data arrives over the network, the image continually gets clearer until its final state is presented.

inner join

A join in which records from two tables are combined and added to a Recordset only if the values of the joined fields meet a specified condition. For instance, an equi-join is an inner join in which the values of the joined fields must be equal. See also *join*.

installable ISAM

A driver you can specify, which allows access to external database formats such as Btrieve, Microsoft Excel, and Paradox. ISAM is an acronym for Indexed Sequential Access Method. The Microsoft Jet database engine installs (loads) these ISAM drivers when referenced by your application. The location of these drivers is maintained in the Microsoft Windows registration database.

instance

Any one of a set of objects sharing the same class. For example, multiple instances of a **Form** class share the same code and are loaded with the same controls with which the **Form** class was designed. During run time, the individual properties of controls on each instance can be set to different values.

instantiate

See *create an instance*.

interface

A set of related functions (methods) used to manipulate data.

interface identifier (IID)

Unique identifier tag associated with each interface; applications use the IID to reference the interface in function calls.

interface negotiation

The process by which an object or container can query another object about a specified interface and have the object return a pointer to that interface if it is supported.

intrinsic constant

A constant provided by an application. Visual Basic constants are listed in the Visual Basic object library and can be viewed using the Object Browser.

ISAM

Indexed sequential access method.

IUnknown

A base interface that describes the group of functions all objects must support.

join

A database operation that combines some or all records from two or more tables, such as an equi-join, outer join, or self-join. Generally, a join refers to an association between a field in one table and a field of the same data type in another table. You create a join with an SQL statement.

When you define a relationship between two tables, you create a join by specifying the primary and foreign table fields. When you add a table to a query, you need to create a join between appropriate fields in the SQL statement that defines the query.

key

The Windows Registry stores data in a hierarchically structured tree. Each node in the tree is called a key. Each key can contain both sub-keys and data entries called values.

In a database, a key is a column used as a component of an index.

late bound

Object references are late-bound if they use object variables declared as variables of the generic Object class. Late-bound binding is the slowest form of binding, because Visual Basic must determine at run time whether or not that object will actually have the properties and methods you used in your code. See also *early bound*.

locked

The condition of a data page, **Recordset** object, or **Database** object that makes it read-only to all users except the one who is currently entering data in it.

locking

A system of ensuring that two processes do not affect the same record in a database at the same time.

MDI

See *multiple-document interface*.

MDI child

A form contained within an MDI form in a multiple-document interface (MDI) application. To create a child form, set its **MDIChild** property to **True**.

MDI form

A window that makes up the background of a multiple-document interface (MDI) application. The MDI form is the container for any MDI child forms in the application.

member

A constituent element of a collection, object, or user-defined type.

member function

One of a group of related functions that make up an interface.

method

A member function of an exposed object that performs some action on the object.

modal

Describes a window or dialog box that requires the user to take some action before the focus can switch to another form or dialog box.

modeless

A window or dialog box that does not require user action before the focus can be switched to another form or dialog box.

module

A set of declarations and procedures.

module level

Code in the declarations section of a module. Any code outside a procedure is referred to as module-level code. Declarations must be listed first, followed by procedures. For example:

```
Dim X As Integer       'This is a module-level variable declaration
Const RO = "Readonly" 'This is a module-level constant declaration
Type MyType 'This is a module-level user-defined type declaration
   MyString As String
   MyAge As Integer
End Type
```

module variable

A variable declared outside of **Function**, **Sub**, or **Property** procedure code. Module variables must be declared outside any procedures in the module. They exist while the module is loaded, and are visible in all procedures in the module.

multiple-document interface (MDI)

Interface that allows you to create an application that maintains multiple forms within a single container form. Microsoft Excel and Word for Windows are examples of applications that have a MDI.

multiple-document interface (MDI) application

An application that can support multiple documents from one application instance. MDI object applications can simultaneously service a user and one or more embedding containers.

multiple-object application

An application that is capable of supporting more than one class of object; for example, a spreadsheet program might support charts, spreadsheets, and macros. See also *single-object application*.

named argument

An argument that has a name that is predefined in the object library. Instead of providing values for arguments in the order expected by the syntax, you can use named arguments to assign values in any order. For example, suppose a method accepts three arguments:

```
DoSomeThing namedarg1, namedarg2, namedarg3
```

By assigning values to named arguments, you can use the following statement:

```
DoSomething namedarg3:=4,namedarg2:=5,namedarg1:=20
```

Note that the arguments need not be in their normal position order.

Null

A value indicating that a variable contains no valid data. Null is the result of:

◆ An explicit assignment of Null to a variable.

◆ Any operation between expressions that contain Null.

◆ A field in a database that has never contained information.

Some database fields, such as those defined as containing the primary key, can't contain null values.

null field

A field containing no characters or values. A null field isn't the same as a zero-length string (" ") or a field with a value of 0. A field is set to null when the content of the field is unknown. For example, a Date Completed field in a task table would be left null until a task is completed.

object

A combination of code and data that can be treated as a unit, for example a control, form, or application. Each object is defined by a class.

An object is an instance of a class that combines data with procedures.

Object Browser

A dialog box that lets you examine the contents of an object library to get information about the objects provided.

object class

A type of object that is registered in the registration database and serviced by a particular server.

object data type

Object variables are stored as 32-bit (4-byte) addresses that refer to objects. Using the **Set** statement, a variable declared as an **Object** can have any object reference assigned to it.

object expression

An expression that specifies a particular object. This expression may include any of the object's containers. For example, if your application has an **Application** object that contains a **Document** object that contains a **Text** object, the following are valid object expressions:

◆ Application.Document.Text

◆ Application.Text

◆ Documention.Text

◆ Text

object library

Data stored in a .olb file or within an executable (.exe, .dll, or .ocx) that provides information used by Automation controllers (such as Visual Basic) about available **Automation** objects. You can use the Object Browser to examine the contents of an object library to get information about the objects provided.

object model

See *Component Object Model.*

object type

A type of object exposed by an application through **Automation**; for example, **Application**, **File**, **Range**, and **Sheet**. Refer to an application's documentation (Microsoft Excel, Microsoft Project, Microsoft Word, and so on) for a complete listing of available objects.

object variable

A variable that contains a reference to an object.

ODBC data source

A term used to refer to a database or database server used as a source of data. ODBC data sources are referred to by their Data Source Name. Data sources can be created using the Windows control panel or the **RegisterDatabase** method.

OLE DB

OLE DB is a set of COM interfaces that provide applications with uniform access to data stored in diverse information sources, both relational and nonrelational. These interfaces support the amount of DBMS functionality appropriate to the data source, enabling it to share its data. ADO is the way that programmers access OLE DB. All the new data bound controls, the Data Environment, and the Data Report designer are OLE DB-aware.

Open Database Connectivity (ODBC)

A standard protocol that permits applications to connect to a variety of external database servers or files. ODBC drivers used by the Microsoft Jet database engine permit access to Microsoft SQL Server and several other external databases.

The ODBC applications programming interface (API) may also be used to access ODBC drivers and the databases they connect to without using the Jet engine.

out of scope

When a variable loses focus. Scope is defined as the visibility of a variable, procedure, or object. For example, a variable declared as Public is visible to all procedures in all modules in a directly referencing project (unless Option Private Module is in effect). Variables declared in procedures are visible only within the procedure and lose their value between calls unless they are declared Static.

pointer

In programming, a variable that contains the memory location of data rather than the data itself.

primary key

One or more fields whose value or values uniquely identify each record in a table. Each table can have only one primary key. An Employees table, for example, could use the social security number for the primary key.

primary table

A database table used to contain primary keys. Generally, a primary key table is used to establish or enforce referential integrity. The primary table is usually on the one side of a one-to-many relationship with a foreign table.

Private

Private variables are available only to the module in which they are declared.

procedure

A named sequence of statements executed as a unit. For example, **Function**, **Property**, and **Sub** are types of procedures.

Procedure box

A list box at the upper-right of the Code and Debug windows that displays the procedures recognized for the object displayed in the **Object** box.

procedure call

A statement in code that tells Visual Basic to execute a procedure.

procedure level

Describes statements located within a **Function, Property,** or **Sub** procedure. Declarations are usually listed first, followed by assignments and other executable code. For example:

```
Sub MySub() ' This statement declares a sub procedure block.
  Dim A' This statement starts the procedure block.
  A = "My variable"    ' Procedure-level code.
  Debug.Print A  ' Procedure-level code.
End Sub' This statement ends a sub procedure block.
```

In contrast, module-level code resides outside any procedure blocks.

procedure stepping

A debugging technique that allows you to trace code execution one statement at a time. Unlike single stepping, procedure stepping does not step into procedure calls; instead, the called procedure is executed as a unit.

procedure template

The beginning and ending statements that are automatically inserted in the Code window when you specify a **Sub, Function,** or **Property** procedure in the Insert **Procedure** dialog box.

programmability

The ability of a server to define a set of properties and methods and make them accessible to Automation controllers.

programmable

Capable of accepting instructions for performing a task or operation. A programmable object (**Automation** object) can be manipulated programmatically with its methods and properties.

project

A group of related files, typically all the files required to develop a software component. Files can be grouped within a project to create subprojects. Projects can be defined in any way meaningful to the user(s) — as one project per version, or one project per language, for example. In general use, projects tend to be organized in the same way file directories are.

project file

A file with a .vbp file name extension that keeps track of the files, objects, project options, environment options, exe options, and references associated with a project.

Project window

A window that displays a list of the form, class, and standard modules; the resource file; and references in your project. Files with .ocx and .vbx file name extensions don't appear in this window.

Properties window

A window used to display or change properties of a selected form or control at design time. Some custom controls have customized Properties windows.

property

A named attribute of an object. Properties define object characteristics such as size, color, and screen location, or the state of an object, such as enabled or disabled.

A property is a data member of an exposed object. Properties are set or returned by means of get and let accessor functions. See *Property procedure*.

Property list

A two-column list in the Properties window that shows all the properties and their current settings for the selected object.

Property procedure

A procedure that creates and manipulates properties for a class module. A Property procedure begins with a **Property Let**, **Property Get**, or **Property Set** statement and ends with an **End Property** statement.

property setting

The value of a property.

Public

Variables declared using the **Public** statement are available to all procedures in all modules in all applications unless Option Private Module is in effect; in which case, the variables are public only within the project in which they reside.

query

A formalized instruction to a database to either return a set of records or perform a specified action on a set of records as specified in the query. For example, the following SQL query statement returns records:

```
® SELECT [Company Name] FROM Publishers WHERE State = 'NY'
```

You can create and run select, action, crosstab, parameter, and SQL-specific queries.

Recordset

A logical set of records.

reference count

The number of instances of an object loaded. This number is incremented each time an instance is loaded and decremented each time an instance is unloaded. Ensures an object is not destroyed before all references to it are released.

referential integrity

Rules that you set to establish and preserve relationships between tables when you add, change, or delete records. Enforcing referential integrity prohibits users from adding records to a related table for which there is no primary key, changing values in a primary table that would result in orphaned records in a related table, and deleting records from a primary table when there are matching related records.

If you select the **Cascade Update Related Fields** or **Cascade Delete Related Records** option for a relationship, the Microsoft Jet database engine allows changes and deletions but changes or deletes related records to ensure that the rules are still enforced.

registration

The process of adding a class, container, or object to the registration database.

registration database

A database that provides a system-wide repository of information for containers and servers that support Automation.

remote procedure call (RPC)

A mechanism through which applications can invoke procedures and object methods remotely across a network. Using RPC, an application on one machine can call a routine or invoke a method belonging to an application running on another machine.

reusable code

Software code written so that it can be used in more than one place.

row

A set of related columns or fields used to hold data. A row is synonymous with a record in the Microsoft Jet database engine. A table is composed of zero or more rows of data.

run time

The time when code is running. During run time, you interact with the code as a user would.

run-time error

An error that occurs when code is running. A run-time error results when a statement attempts an invalid operation.

scope

Defines the visibility of a variable, procedure, or object. For example, a variable declared as Public is visible to all procedures in all modules in a directly referencing project (unless Option Private Module is in effect). Variables declared in procedures are visible only within the procedure and lose their value between calls unless they are declared Static.

select query

A query that asks a question about the data stored in your tables and returns a **Recordset** object without changing the data. Once the **Recordset** data is retrieved, you can examine and make changes to the data in the underlying tables. In contrast, action queries can make changes to your data, but they don't return data records.

sequential access

A type of file access that allows you to access records in text files and variable-length record files sequentially; that is, one after another.

server

An application or DLL that provides its objects to other applications. You can use any of these objects in your Visual Basic application.

set

To assign a value to a property.

single-object application

A server that exposes only one class of object.

SQL database

A database that can be accessed through use of Open Database Connectivity (ODBC) data sources.

SQL Server

A relational database engine running on a network-accessible server. SQL Servers are responsible for comprehensive management of one or more relational databases residing on the server. They are controlled by and information is passed to and from these servers by way of Structured Query Language (SQL) statements. There are two types of SQL Server: Microsoft SQL Server and Sybase SQL Server.

SQL statement/string

1. An expression that defines a Structured Query Language (SQL) command, such as **SELECT**, **UPDATE**, or **DELETE**, and includes clauses such as **WHERE** and **ORDER BY**. SQL strings and statements are typically used in queries, **Recordset** objects, and aggregate functions but can also be used to create or modify a database structure.

2. A set of commands written using a dialect of Structured Query Language used to retrieve or pass information to a relational database. SQL statement syntax is determined by the SQL Server or other relational database engine it is intended to execute on.

stack

A fixed amount of memory used by Visual Basic to preserve local variables and arguments during procedure calls.

Static

A Visual Basic keyword you can use to preserve the value of a local variable.

static cursor

Neither the cursor owner nor any other user can change the results set while the cursor is open. Values, membership, and order remain fixed until the cursor is closed. You can either take a 'snapshot' (temporary table) of the results set, or you can lock the entire results set to prevent updates. When you take a snapshot of the results set, the results set diverges increasingly from the snapshot as updates are made.

Structured Query Language (SQL)

A language used in querying, updating, and managing relational databases. SQL can be used to retrieve, sort and filter specific data to be extracted from the database.

You can use SQL **SELECT** statements anywhere a table name, query name, or field name is accepted.

Sub procedure

A procedure that performs a specific task within a program, but returns no explicit value. A **Sub** procedure begins with a **Sub** statement and ends with an **End Sub** statement.

subroutine

A section of code that can be invoked (executed) within a program.

synchronous call

A function call in which the caller waits for the reply before continuing. Most interface methods are synchronous calls. An operation that completes synchronously performs all of its processing in the function call made by the application. The function returns different values depending on its success or failure.

synchronous processing

When the data interface blocks until an operation is complete or at least until the first row of the results is ready. Opposite of asynchronous processing.

table

The basic unit of data storage in a relational database. A table stores data in records (rows) and fields (columns) and is usually about a particular category of things, such as employees or parts. Also called a base table.

three-tiered architecture

An application model in which the feature set of the business application is expressed conceptually as three layers, each of which supplies services to the adjacent layers: user presentation, core business, and data management. Note that this is a conceptual architecture; while all business applications can be expressed conceptually in terms of these three layers, the implementation architecture may not be three layers.

trigger

Record-level event code that runs after an insert, update, or delete. Different actions can be attached to the different events. Triggers run last, after rules, and don't run during buffered updates. They are most often used for cross-table integrity.

validation

The process of checking whether entered data meets certain conditions or limitations.

validation properties

Properties used to set conditions on table fields and records. Validation properties include **ValidationRule**, **Required** and **AllowZeroLength**.

validation rule

A rule that sets limits or conditions on what can be entered in one or more fields. Validation rules can be set for a Field or a Table. Validation rules are checked when you update a record containing fields requiring validation. If the rule is violated, a trappable error results.

VBSQL

Visual Basic library for SQL Server.

Windows API

The Windows API (Application Programming Interface) consists of the functions, messages, data structures, data types, and statements you can use in creating applications that run under Microsoft Windows. The parts of the API you use most are code elements included for calling API functions from Windows. These include procedure declarations (for the Windows functions), user-defined type definitions (for data structures passed to those functions), and constant declarations (for values passed to and returned from those functions).

Index

MICROSOFT LICENSE AGREEMENT
Book Companion CD

IMPORTANT—READ CAREFULLY: This Microsoft End-User License Agreement ("EULA") is a legal agreement between you (either an individual or an entity) and Microsoft Corporation for the Microsoft product identified above, which includes computer software and may include associated media, printed materials, and "online" or electronic documentation ("SOFTWARE PROD-UCT"). Any component included within the SOFTWARE PRODUCT that is accompanied by a separate End-User License Agreement shall be governed by such agreement and not the terms set forth below. By installing, copying, or otherwise using the SOFTWARE PRODUCT, you agree to be bound by the terms of this EULA. If you do not agree to the terms of this EULA, you are not authorized to install, copy, or otherwise use the SOFTWARE PRODUCT; you may, however, return the SOFTWARE PROD-UCT, along with all printed materials and other items that form a part of the Microsoft product that includes the SOFTWARE PRODUCT, to the place you obtained them for a full refund.

SOFTWARE PRODUCT LICENSE

The SOFTWARE PRODUCT is protected by United States copyright laws and international copyright treaties, as well as other intellectual property laws and treaties. The SOFTWARE PRODUCT is licensed, not sold.

1. **GRANT OF LICENSE.** This EULA grants you the following rights:

    a. **Software Product.** You may install and use one copy of the SOFTWARE PRODUCT on a single computer. The primary user of the computer on which the SOFTWARE PRODUCT is installed may make a second copy for his or her exclusive use on a portable computer.

    b. **Storage/Network Use.** You may also store or install a copy of the SOFTWARE PRODUCT on a storage device, such as a network server, used only to install or run the SOFTWARE PRODUCT on your other computers over an internal network; however, you must acquire and dedicate a license for each separate computer on which the SOFTWARE PRODUCT is installed or run from the storage device. A license for the SOFTWARE PRODUCT may not be shared or used concurrently on different computers.

    c. **License Pak.** If you have acquired this EULA in a Microsoft License Pak, you may make the number of additional copies of the computer software portion of the SOFTWARE PRODUCT authorized on the printed copy of this EULA, and you may use each copy in the manner specified above. You are also entitled to make a corresponding number of secondary copies for portable computer use as specified above.

    d. **Sample Code.** Solely with respect to portions, if any, of the SOFTWARE PRODUCT that are identified within the SOFT-WARE PRODUCT as sample code (the "SAMPLE CODE"):

        i. **Use and Modification.** Microsoft grants you the right to use and modify the source code version of the SAMPLE CODE, *provided* you comply with subsection (d)(iii) below. You may not distribute the SAMPLE CODE, or any modified version of the SAMPLE CODE, in source code form.

        ii. **Redistributable Files.** Provided you comply with subsection (d)(iii) below, Microsoft grants you a nonexclusive, royalty-free right to reproduce and distribute the object code version of the SAMPLE CODE and of any modified SAMPLE CODE, other than SAMPLE CODE, or any modified version thereof, designated as not redistributable in the Readme file that forms a part of the SOFTWARE PRODUCT (the "Non-Redistributable Sample Code"). All SAMPLE CODE other than the Non-Redistributable Sample Code is collectively referred to as the "REDISTRIBUTABLES."

        iii. **Redistribution Requirements.** If you redistribute the REDISTRIBUTABLES, you agree to: (i) distribute the REDISTRIBUTABLES in object code form only in conjunction with and as a part of your software application product; (ii) not use Microsoft's name, logo, or trademarks to market your software application product; (iii) include a valid copyright notice on your software application product; (iv) indemnify, hold harmless, and defend Microsoft from and against any claims or lawsuits, including attorney's fees, that arise or result from the use or distribution of your software application product; and (v) not permit further distribution of the REDISTRIBUTABLES by your end user. Contact Microsoft for the applicable royalties due and other licensing terms for all other uses and/or distribution of the REDISTRIBUTABLES.

2. **DESCRIPTION OF OTHER RIGHTS AND LIMITATIONS.**

    - **Limitations on Reverse Engineering, Decompilation, and Disassembly.** You may not reverse engineer, decompile, or disassemble the SOFTWARE PRODUCT, except and only to the extent that such activity is expressly permitted by applicable law notwithstanding this limitation.

    - **Separation of Components.** The SOFTWARE PRODUCT is licensed as a single product. Its component parts may not be separated for use on more than one computer.

    - **Rental.** You may not rent, lease, or lend the SOFTWARE PRODUCT.

    - **Support Services.** Microsoft may, but is not obligated to, provide you with support services related to the SOFTWARE PRODUCT ("Support Services"). Use of Support Services is governed by the Microsoft policies and programs described in the user manual, in "online" documentation, and/or in other Microsoft-provided materials. Any supplemental software code provided to you as part of the Support Services shall be considered part of the SOFTWARE PRODUCT and subject to the terms and conditions of this EULA. With respect to technical information you provide to Microsoft as part of the Support Services, Microsoft may use such information for its business purposes, including for product support and development. Microsoft will not utilize such technical information in a form that personally identifies you.

- **Software Transfer.** You may permanently transfer all of your rights under this EULA, provided you retain no copies, you transfer all of the SOFTWARE PRODUCT (including all component parts, the media and printed materials, any upgrades, this EULA, and, if applicable, the Certificate of Authenticity), **and** the recipient agrees to the terms of this EULA.

- **Termination.** Without prejudice to any other rights, Microsoft may terminate this EULA if you fail to comply with the terms and conditions of this EULA. In such event, you must destroy all copies of the SOFTWARE PRODUCT and all of its component parts.

3. **COPYRIGHT.** All title and copyrights in and to the SOFTWARE PRODUCT (including but not limited to any images, photographs, animations, video, audio, music, text, SAMPLE CODE, REDISTRIBUTABLES, and "applets" incorporated into the SOFTWARE PRODUCT) and any copies of the SOFTWARE PRODUCT are owned by Microsoft or its suppliers. The SOFTWARE PRODUCT is protected by copyright laws and international treaty provisions. Therefore, you must treat the SOFTWARE PRODUCT like any other copyrighted material **except** that you may install the SOFTWARE PRODUCT on a single computer provided you keep the original solely for backup or archival purposes. You may not copy the printed materials accompanying the SOFTWARE PRODUCT.

4. **U.S. GOVERNMENT RESTRICTED RIGHTS.** The SOFTWARE PRODUCT and documentation are provided with RESTRICTED RIGHTS. Use, duplication, or disclosure by the Government is subject to restrictions as set forth in subparagraph (c)(1)(ii) of the Rights in Technical Data and Computer Software clause at DFARS 252.227-7013 or subparagraphs (c)(1) and (2) of the Commercial Computer Software—Restricted Rights at 48 CFR 52.227-19, as applicable. Manufacturer is Microsoft Corporation/One Microsoft Way/Redmond, WA 98052-6399.

5. **EXPORT RESTRICTIONS.** You agree that you will not export or re-export the SOFTWARE PRODUCT, any part thereof, or any process or service that is the direct product of the SOFTWARE PRODUCT (the foregoing collectively referred to as the "Restricted Components"), to any country, person, entity, or end user subject to U.S. export restrictions. You specifically agree not to export or re-export any of the Restricted Components (i) to any country to which the U.S. has embargoed or restricted the export of goods or services, which currently include, but are not necessarily limited to, Cuba, Iran, Iraq, Libya, North Korea, Sudan, and Syria, or to any national of any such country, wherever located, who intends to transmit or transport the Restricted Components back to such country; (ii) to any end user who you know or have reason to know will utilize the Restricted Components in the design, development, or production of nuclear, chemical, or biological weapons; or (iii) to any end user who has been prohibited from participating in U.S. export transactions by any federal agency of the U.S. government. You warrant and represent that neither the BXA nor any other U.S. federal agency has suspended, revoked, or denied your export privileges.

DISCLAIMER OF WARRANTY

NO WARRANTIES OR CONDITIONS. MICROSOFT EXPRESSLY DISCLAIMS ANY WARRANTY OR CONDITION FOR THE SOFTWARE PRODUCT. THE SOFTWARE PRODUCT AND ANY RELATED DOCUMENTATION ARE PROVIDED "AS IS" WITHOUT WARRANTY OR CONDITION OF ANY KIND, EITHER EXPRESS OR IMPLIED, INCLUDING, WITHOUT LIMITATION, THE IMPLIED WARRANTIES OF MERCHANTABILITY, FITNESS FOR A PARTICULAR PURPOSE, OR NONINFRINGEMENT. THE ENTIRE RISK ARISING OUT OF USE OR PERFORMANCE OF THE SOFTWARE PRODUCT REMAINS WITH YOU.

LIMITATION OF LIABILITY. TO THE MAXIMUM EXTENT PERMITTED BY APPLICABLE LAW, IN NO EVENT SHALL MICROSOFT OR ITS SUPPLIERS BE LIABLE FOR ANY SPECIAL, INCIDENTAL, INDIRECT, OR CONSEQUENTIAL DAMAGES WHATSOEVER (INCLUDING, WITHOUT LIMITATION, DAMAGES FOR LOSS OF BUSINESS PROFITS, BUSINESS INTERRUPTION, LOSS OF BUSINESS INFORMATION, OR ANY OTHER PECUNIARY LOSS) ARISING OUT OF THE USE OF OR INABILITY TO USE THE SOFTWARE PRODUCT OR THE PROVISION OF OR FAILURE TO PROVIDE SUPPORT SERVICES, EVEN IF MICROSOFT HAS BEEN ADVISED OF THE POSSIBILITY OF SUCH DAMAGES. IN ANY CASE, MICROSOFT'S ENTIRE LIABILITY UNDER ANY PROVISION OF THIS EULA SHALL BE LIMITED TO THE GREATER OF THE AMOUNT ACTUALLY PAID BY YOU FOR THE SOFTWARE PRODUCT OR US$5.00; PROVIDED, HOWEVER, IF YOU HAVE ENTERED INTO A MICROSOFT SUPPORT SERVICES AGREEMENT, MICROSOFT'S ENTIRE LIABILITY REGARDING SUPPORT SERVICES SHALL BE GOVERNED BY THE TERMS OF THAT AGREEMENT. BECAUSE SOME STATES AND JURISDICTIONS DO NOT ALLOW THE EXCLUSION OR LIMITATION OF LIABILITY, THE ABOVE LIMITATION MAY NOT APPLY TO YOU.

MISCELLANEOUS

This EULA is governed by the laws of the State of Washington USA, except and only to the extent that applicable law mandates governing law of a different jurisdiction.

Should you have any questions concerning this EULA, or if you desire to contact Microsoft for any reason, please contact the Microsoft subsidiary serving your country, or write: Microsoft Sales Information Center/One Microsoft Way/Redmond, WA 98052-6399.

Gear Up for Success

Register Today!

Return this
Microsoft® Mastering:
Microsoft Visual Basic® 6.0 Fundamentals

registration card today to receive advance notice about
the latest developer training titles and courseware!

For information about Mastering Series products and training, visit our Web site at
http://msdn.microsoft.com/mastering

Microsoft®
Mastering Series
Developer Training

OWNER REGISTRATION CARD   0-7356-0898-9

Microsoft® Mastering:
Microsoft Visual Basic® 6.0 Fundamentals

FIRST NAME   MIDDLE INITIAL   LAST NAME

INSTITUTION OR COMPANY NAME   TITLE

MAILING ADDRESS   SUITE/APARTMENT/MAILSTOP #

ADDRESS LINE 2

CITY   STATE/PROVINCE   ZIP/POSTAL CODE

E-MAIL ADDRESS (INTERNET STANDARD, E.G. JOHNSMITH@BUSINESS.COM)   (AREA CODE) PHONE NUMBER

U.S. and Canada addresses only. Fill in information above and mail postage-free.
Please mail only the bottom half of this page.

start faster
go
farther

For information about Microsoft Press® products, visit our Web site at

mspress.microsoft.com

Microsoft Press